Mac OS® X UNIX®
TOOLBOX

Mac OS® X UNIX®
TOOLBOX

1000+ Commands for Mac OS® X Power Users

Thomas Myer
Christopher Negus
François Caen

WILEY

Wiley Publishing, Inc.

Mac OS® X UNIX® Toolbox: 1000+ Commands for Mac OS® X Power Users

Published by
Wiley Publishing, Inc.
10475 Crosspoint Boulevard
Indianapolis, IN 46256
www.wiley.com

ISBN: 978-0-470-47836-3

Manufactured in the United States of America

10 9 8 7 6 5 4 3 2 1

Library of Congress Cataloging-in-Publication Data

Myer, Thomas.
  Mac OS X UNIX toolbox : 1000+ commands for Mac OS X power users / Thomas Myer, Christopher Negus, François. Caen.
    p. cm.
  Includes index.
  ISBN 978-0-470-47836-3 (pbk.)

 1. Mac OS. 2. UNIX (Computer file) 3. Macintosh (Computer)--Programming. I. Negus, Chris, 1957- II. Caen, François. III. Title.
  QA76.76.O63M926 2009
  005.4'46--dc22
                                2009001890

To Hope, for loving me anyway.

— Thomas Myer

About the Authors

Thomas Myer currently resides in Austin, Texas, where he runs Triple Dog Dare Media, a consulting group that builds CodeIgniter applications, writes technical documentation and copy, and works as a systems analyst for hire. He is the author of *Lead Generation on the Web, No Nonsense XML Web Development with PHP, Professional CodeIgniter,* and *From Geek to Peak: Your First 365 Days as a Technical Consultant,* as well as dozens of articles on technology and business. If you have any feedback on this book, or wish to discuss anything related to Web development, writing, or marketing, contact him via his website at www.tripledogs.com.

Christopher Negus is the author of the *Fedora* and *Red Hat Linux Bibles,* as well as *BSD UNIX Toolbox.* Chris served for eight years on development teams for the UNIX operating system at AT&T, where UNIX was created and developed.

François Caen, through his company Turbosphere LLC, hosts and manages business application infrastructures, 95 percent of which run on Linus systems.

Credits

Acquisitions Editor
Jenny Watson

Development Editor
William Bridges

Technical Editor
Brian Joseph

Production Editor
Daniel Scribner

Copy Editor
Luann Rouff

Editorial Manager
Mary Beth Wakefield

Production Manager
Tim Tate

Vice President and Executive Group Publisher
Richard Swadley

Vice President and Executive Publisher
Barry Pruett

Associate Publisher
Jim Minatel

Project Coordinator, Cover
Lynsey Stanford

Compositor
Jeff Lytle, Happenstance Type-O-Rama

Proofreader
Publication Services, Inc.

Indexer
Melanie Belkin

Acknowledgments

I would like to acknowledge all the work done by the developers, project managers, analysts, and others on the Mac OS X team. They've created something wonderful in this stable, secure, and speedy little OS. I've had a great deal of fun and joy working with it, which is more than most people can say when it comes to computing.

Special thanks to Jenny Watson for being such a joy to work with. Even more thanks to Bill Bridges, who took my calls, answered my questions, and kept things moving forward even when it looked like we were going to become permanently stuck in the weeds.

I wouldn't have been able to work on this book if it weren't for my ever-loving and ever-patient wife, Hope. Your name says it all—you fill my life with hope and joy and love and…well, everything. Thanks for being such a champ.

—Thomas Myer

Contents at a Glance

Contents

Contents

Contents

Contents

Introduction

Mac OS X UNIX Toolbox is loosely based on the BSD UNIX Toolbox written by Chris Negus and François Caen. When I was asked by Wiley to extend what they had done into the world of Mac OS X, I heartily agreed to do so, partly because the original was such an excellent resource.

From the very beginning, I decided to keep to the spirit and structure of the original title as much as I could. Thankfully, about 90 percent of what you experience UNIX-wise on Mac OS X is the same as on BSD or Linux environments, so I was able, for the most part, to abide by this agreement. In some cases, though, I had to nip and tuck a few sections; in others, I had to add a bit back in.

At the end of the day, what you hold is a handbook with more than 1,000 specific command lines to help you become a Mac OS X power user. Whether you are a systems administrator or desktop user, the book will show you commands to create file systems, troubleshoot networks, lock down security, and dig out almost anything you care to know about your Mac OS X system.

Of course, Mac OS X being what it is, not everything in this book is about the command line (although most of it is). In some cases, I show you not only how to do things on the venerated command line, but also how to take advantage of the Mac OS X GUI. Either way, you learn how to leverage UNIX to do your job.

Who Should Read This Book

This book is for anyone who wants to access the power of a Mac OS X system as a systems administrator or user. You may be a free and open-source software (FOSS) enthusiast, a UNIX professional, or possibly a computer professional who is increasingly finding the Windows systems in your data center supplanted by BSD, Linux, and Mac OS X systems.

The bottom line is that you want to find quick and efficient ways of getting Mac OS X systems working at peak performance. These may be a few desktop systems at work, a file and print server at your school, or a home web server that you're setting up mostly for fun.

In the best case, you should already have some experience with BSD, Linux, or other UNIX-like systems. However, if you are a computer professional with skills managing other types of operating systems, such as Windows, you should be able to leverage your knowledge and use the specific commands covered in the book.

What This Book Covers

I assume that you're new to Mac OS X, but that you're coming to that platform from some other UNIX platform, such as Linux or BSD. In other words, I assume that you know something about the command line, but don't yet know the Mac OS X Way. I will show you that way, pointing out how to get to the shell, how to run commands, and how things (most of which you may take for granted) have changed from one flavor of UNIX (i.e., the one you're used to) to Mac OS X's flavor of UNIX. The book will then supplement that knowledge with information you need to do the following activities:

❑ **Get software**—Mac OS X can be extended using various package managers. Using these package managers, you can install both binary packages and source code. I will introduce you to Fink, which you'll use to find, download, install, and manage software from the command line.

❑ **Access applications**—Find what's available from the Mac OS X distribution.

❑ **Use the shell**—Find neat techniques and tips for using the shell.

❑ **Play with GUI tools**—Use the command-line options to run products such as iTunes, TextEdit, and Safari.

❑ **Work with files**—Use, manipulate, convert, and secure a wide range of file types in Mac OS X.

❑ **Administer file systems**—Access, format, partition, and monitor your file storage hardware (hard disks, CD/DVD drives, floppy disks, USB flash drives, and so on). Then create, format, and check the file systems that exist on those hardware devices.

❑ **Back up and restore data**—Use simple commands to gather, archive, and compress your files into efficient backup archives. Then store those archives locally or on remote computers.

❑ **Work with processes**—List running processes in a variety of ways, such as by CPU use, processor use, or process ID. Then change running processes to have them run in the background or foreground. Send signals to processes to have them reread configuration files, stop and resume processing, or stop completely (abort).

❑ **Manage the system**—Run commands to check system resources, such as memory usage, run levels, and more.

❑ **Monitor networks**—Bring wired and wireless network connections up and down. Check routing, DNS, and host information. Keep an eye on network traffic.

❑ **Get network resources**—Connect to UNIX and Windows remote file systems using FTP, NFS, and Samba facilities.

❑ **Do remote administration**—Access and administer other computers using remote login (ssh, telnet, and so on) and screen. Learn about remote administration interfaces, such as SWAT and CUPS.

❑ **Lock down security**—Set up firewalls and system logging to secure your Mac OS X systems.

❑ **Get reference information**—Use the appendixes at the end of this book to get more information about the shell (such as metacharacters and shell variables) and personal configuration files.

If we've done it right, it will be easier to use this book than to Google for the command lines or GUI tools you need.

After you've mastered many of the features described in this book, you'll have gained the following advantages:

❑ **Hundreds of commands**—By compressing a lot of information into a small space, you will have access to hundreds of useful commands, in over 1,000 command lines, in a handy form to carry with you.

❑ **Transferable knowledge**—Most of the same commands and options you use in Mac OS X systems will work exactly the same way on other UNIX-like systems. Different UNIX systems, however, offer different graphical administration tools; and even within a particular distribution, graphical tools change more often than commands do.

❑ **Quick problem solving**—By the time others have started up a desktop and launched a graphical administration tool, you will have already run a half dozen commands and solved the problem.

❑ **Enduring value**—Many of the commands described in this book were used in early UNIX systems, so you are gaining tools that reflect the experience of thousands of computer experts for more than 30 years.

Because the full documentation for commands used in Mac OS X systems consists of thousands of man pages, info text, and help messages, you will surely want to reach beyond the pages of this book from time to time. Luckily, Mac OS X and other UNIX systems include helpful information installed on the system itself. Chapter 1 contains descriptions of how to access this information, which is probably already installed, or can be easily installed, on your system.

How This Book Is Structured

This book is neither a pure reference book (with alphabetically listed components) nor a guide (with step-by-step procedures for doing tasks). Instead, the book is organized by topic, and includes the most useful commands and options you will likely work with.

Chapter 1 provides you with a basic understanding of what Mac OS X is and how it relates to the operating systems that are derived from BSD, such as FreeBSD, NetBSD, and OpenBSD. Then it describes some of the vast resources available to support your experience with this book, such as man pages, info material, and help text. Chapter 2 provides a quick overview of the Mac OS X environment and how you can set it up to get easy access to UNIX tools. It also includes a quick introduction to Fink, a package manager that will enable you to install additional tools mentioned in this book.

Chapters 3, 4, 5, and 6 describe commands that a regular user may find useful on Mac OS X systems. Chapter 3 describes tools for using the shell, Chapter 4 covers commands for working with files, and Chapter 5 describes how to manipulate text. Chapter 6 walks you through more advanced shell scripting and introduces AppleScripting.

Starting with Chapter 7, we get into topics relating to system administration. Creating and checking file systems is covered in Chapter 7, while commands for doing data backups are described in Chapter 8. Chapter 9 explains how to manipulate running processes, and Chapter 10 describes administrative tools for managing basic components, such as hardware modules, CPU use, and memory use.

Chapter 11 begins the chapters devoted to managing network resources by describing how to set up and work with network interfaces. Chapter 12 covers text-based commands for file transfer, file sharing, chats, and e-mail. Tools for doing remote system administration are included in Chapter 13.

Chapter 14 covers how to lock down security, using features such as firewalls and logging. Following that are six appendixes that provide additional reference information for text editing, shell features (metacharacters and variables), personal configuration files, AppleScript commands, a quick Perl primer, and some interesting packages available via Fink that you might want to explore.

What You Need to Use This Book

This is definitely not a book you curl up with on your next vacation. Nor is it meant to entertain you. Throughout, I fully expect you to be sitting in front of a Mac OS X system, scratching your head with one hand and holding this book in the other, looking for a solution.

In other words, the book is meant to be a companion as you work on a problem related to Mac OS X. You'll probably be working on a desktop system at home or work, but a fair number of you will be working on a file, web, or print server running Mac OS X.

All the commands in this book have been tested against a 64-bit x86 system running Mac OS X 10.5 (Leopard). Specifically, I'm running a MacBook Pro. My technical editor checked everything on a MacBook Pro (running Mac OS X 10.5) primarily, but he also used a MacBook (running Mac OS X 10.5) and (once) a PowerMac (running Mac OS X 10.4).

I assume that you're running Leopard, but don't despair if you're on Tiger, as most of what is covered here also pertains to that earlier release. In addition, please note that nearly every command available from the shell has been around for a long time (some dating back more than 30 years to the original UNIX days), and most will work exactly as described here on NetBSD, OpenBSD, and other derivative systems, regardless of CPU architecture.

Furthermore, many of the commands described in this book will also work on other UNIX and Linux systems. Because this book focuses on Mac OS X, descriptions will differ from other UNIX-like systems most prominently in the areas of packaging, installation, and GUI administration tools.

Conventions

To help you get the most from the text and keep track of what's happening, we've used a number of conventions throughout the book. In particular, we have created styles for showing commands that allow us to fit as many command lines as possible in the book.

With command examples, computer output (shell prompts and messages) is shown in regular monospace font, computer input (the stuff you type) is shown in bold monospace font, and a short description (if included) appears in italics. Here is an example:

```
$ ls *jpg          List all JPEG files in the current directory
hat.jpg
dog.jpg
...
```

To save space, output is sometimes truncated (or skipped altogether). Three dots (...) are sometimes used to indicate that additional output was cut. If a command is particularly long, backslashes will appear at the end of each line to indicate that input is continuing to the next line, as shown here:

```
# oggenc NewSong.wav -o NewSong.ogg \
    -a Bernstein -G Classical         \
    -d 06/15/1972 -t "Simple Song"   \
    -l "Bernsteins Mass"              \
    -c info="From Kennedy Center"
```

In the preceding example, you can type the backslashes to have all that information included in the single command; or you can simply put all the information on a single line (excluding the backslashes). Note that command prompts are shown in one of two ways:

```
$          Indicates a regular user prompt
#          Indicates the root prompt
```

As noted, when a dollar sign prompt ($) appears, any user can run the command. With a pound sign prompt (#), you probably need to be the root user in order for the command to work.

Notes and warnings appear as follows:

Warnings and notes are offset and placed in italic like this.

As for styles in the text:

❑ We *highlight* new terms and important words with italic when we introduce them.

❑ We show keyboard strokes like this: ⌘N or Ctrl+N.

❑ We show filenames, URLs, and code within the text like so: `persistence.properties`.

One final technique used in this book is to highlight text that describes what an upcoming command is meant to do. For example, we may say something like "use the following command to **display the contents of a file**." We've styled descriptions in this way to provide you with quick visual cues, so you can easily scan the page for that command you just knew had to be there.

1

Starting with UNIX on Mac OS X

Are you an old hand at the Mac? Do you use the underlying UNIX just once in a while? Many times a day? Never heard of it? Regardless of your skill level, a book that presents efficient ways to use, check, fix, secure, and enhance UNIX on Mac OS X can be an invaluable resource.

Mac OS X UNIX Toolbox is that resource.

Mac OS X UNIX Toolbox is aimed primarily at Mac OS X power users and systems administrators. To give you what you need, we tell you how to quickly locate and get software, monitor the health and security of your systems, and access network resources. In short, we cut to the most efficient ways of using UNIX systems.

IN THIS CHAPTER

Finding Mac OS X resources

Quick and powerful commands

Handy references to many useful utilities

Working as Mac OS X gurus do

Our goal with *Mac OS X UNIX Toolbox* is to pack a lot of useful information for using UNIX tools and systems into a small package that you can carry around with you. To that end, we describe the following:

❑ **Commands**—Tons of command-line examples to use BSD systems in helpful and clever ways

❑ **GUI tools**—Quick pointers to graphical administration tools to configure your system

❑ **Software packages**—Short procedures to find and download tons of applications

❑ **Online resources**—Listings of the best locations to find BSD forums, mailing lists, IRC channels, and other online resources

❑ **Local documentation**—Tools for gathering more information from man pages, doc directories, help commands, and other resources on your BSD system

Because you're not a beginner with Mac OS X, you won't see a lot of screenshots of windows, icons, and menus. What you will see, however, is the quickest path to getting the information you need in order to use UNIX on Mac OS X to its fullest extent.

If this sounds useful to you, please read on.

About FreeBSD, NetBSD, and OpenBSD

Mac OS X is a modern operating system that combines the power of a UNIX-based operating system and the simplicity and elegance of the Macintosh UI. Its open-source core, called Darwin, is a direct descendant of various BSD projects. It is based in part on BSD 4.4 Lite, but many libraries and utilities are from FreeBSD and NetBSD. Because of this history, it's useful to delve into the history of BSD.

In the early 1970s, AT&T released the UNIX source code to several colleges and universities, allowing them to begin changing, adapting, and improving that code as they pleased. That decision has led to the development of every major free and open-source software operating system today, not the least of which are the systems based on the Berkeley Software Distribution (BSD).

The twisty history of BSD is easy to Google, if you care to learn the details. For our purposes, here are the highlights:

❑ BSD began as a set of software add-ons to AT&T's Sixth Edition UNIX.

❑ Over the years, BSD developers split off on their own development path, rewriting software with the intention of replacing all AT&T copyrighted code.

❑ In the early 1990s, AT&T's UNIX System Laboratories sued BSD developers (Berkeley Software Design, Inc.) for copyright infringement.

❑ Although the lawsuit was eventually settled (with only a few files needing to be changed from the BSD code), the Linux operating system was able to become a leader of open-source software development while questions surrounding how free BSD was were being threshed out.

❑ In 1995, the final version of BSD from Berkeley was released under the name 4.4BSD-Lite, release 2. Today's BSD operating systems, including FreeBSD, NetBSD, and OpenBSD, are all based to some extent on 4.4BSD-Lite.

Operating systems derived from BSD have a well-earned reputation for stability and security. BSD was developed at a time when computing resources (disk space, network bandwidth, and memory) were meager by today's standards, so BSD systems were operated by efficient commands, instead of the bloated applications and dumbed-down graphical interfaces often seen today.

Because of the nature of BSD systems, people running those systems required a high level of expertise. Even when simplified graphical user interfaces based on the X Window System began to appear, to effectively operate a BSD system you still needed to know about such things as kernels, device drivers, modules, and daemons. Because security came before ease of use, a BSD expert would need to know how to deal with the fact that many features you might want are not installed or are turned off by default.

If you are someone who has used Linux before, transitioning to a BSD system shouldn't be too hard. However, BSD systems tend to behave a bit more like older UNIX systems than they do like Linux. Many interfaces are text-based, offering a lot of power if you know what you are doing. Despite that fact, however, all the major desktop components that, for example, you get with the GNOME desktop environment are available with BSD systems, so you don't have to live on the command line.

Here is a list of popular BSD-based operating systems still being developed today:

❑ **FreeBSD** (www.freebsd.org) is the most popular of the BSD operating system distributions. It can be operated as a server, workstation, or desktop system, but has also been used in network appliances and special-purpose embedded systems. It has a reputation for maximum performance.

❑ **NetBSD** (www.netbsd.org) has a reputation for being very portable, with versions of NetBSD running as an embedded system on a variety of hardware. NetBSD can run on anything from 32-bit and 64-bit PCs to personal digital assistants (PDAs) to VAX minicomputers.

❑ **OpenBSD** (www.netbsd.org) is a popular system for network servers, although it can operate as a workstation or network appliance as well. The goal of OpenBSD is to attain maximum security. Unlike FreeBSD and NetBSD, which are covered under the BSD license, OpenBSD is covered primarily under the more permissive Internet Systems Consortium (ISC) license.

❑ **DragonFly BSD** (www.dragonflybsd.org) was originally based on FreeBSD. Its goal was to develop technologies different from FreeBSD in such areas as symmetric multiprocessing and concurrency. Therefore, the focus has been on expanding features in the kernel.

Other free (as in no cost, as well as freedom to do what you like with the code) operating systems based on BSD include Darwin (on which Mac OS X is based) and the desktop-oriented systems PC-BSD and DesktopBSD. FreeSBIE is a live CD BSD system. Proprietary operating systems that have been derived from BSD include the following:

❑ **Mac OS X** (www.apple.com/macosx) is produced by Apple, Inc., and is focused on providing an easy-to-use graphical interface to sell with its line of computers. There is also a Mac OS X Server product available. Although Mac OS X was originally based on Darwin, it is considered a closed-source operating system with open-source components.

❑ **SunOS** (www.sun.com) was developed by Sun Microsystems and was very popular as a professional workstation system. Sun stopped development of SunOS in favor of Solaris. However, because Solaris represented a merging of SunOS and UNIX System V, many BSD features made their way into Solaris

You can find a longer list of BSD distributions at the DistroWatch site (`http://distrowatch.com/search.php?category=BSD`). Besides offering descriptions of those BSD distributions, you can also find links to where you can purchase or download the software.

Finding Mac OS X Resources

The best place to find Mac OS X resources is at `www.apple.com/macosx/`. There you'll find guided tours, documentation, and links to the Developer Connection (`developer.apple.com`).

Apple's Developer Connection is an invaluable resource for anyone contemplating more advanced development work, either in Mac OS X or the iPhone. Membership in the Developer Connection program gives you access to pre-release software and technical support, as well as a complete set of resources for developing tools.

Although much of the information provided in the Developer Connection area is not specific to UNIX (as it involves programming in Carbon or Objective-C), having access to the information and community of developers is a good thing overall.

Focusing on Mac OS X Commands

Many important tasks on Mac OS X can be done from both the graphical interface and the command line. However, the command line has always been, and still remains, the interface of choice for UNIX power users.

Graphical user interfaces (GUIs) are meant to be intuitive. With some computer experience, you can probably figure out, for example, how to add a user, change the time and date, and configure a sound card from a GUI. For these cases, we'll mention which graphical tool you could use for the job. For the following cases, however, you will probably need to rely on the command line:

❑ **Almost anytime something goes wrong**—Ask a question at an online forum to solve some UNIX problem you are having and the help you get will almost always come in the form of commands to run. In addition, command-line tools typically offer much more feedback if there is a problem configuring a device or accessing files and directories.

❑ **Remote systems administration**—If you are administering a remote server, you may not have graphical tools available. Although remote GUI access (using X applications or VNC) and web-based administration tools may be available, they usually run more slowly than what you can do from the command line.

❑ **Features not supported by GUI**—GUI administration tools tend to present the most basic ways of performing a task. More complex operations often require options that are only available from the command line.

The bottom line is that in order to unlock the full power of your Mac OS X system, you must be able to use shell commands. Thousands of commands are available to monitor and manage every aspect of your system.

Whether you are a UNIX guru or a novice, however, one challenge looms large: How do you remember the most critical commands and options you need, when a command shell might only show you this:

```
$
```

Mac OS X UNIX Toolbox is not just another command reference or rehash of man pages. Instead, this book presents commands on Mac OS X according to how you actually use them. In other words, instead of listing commands alphabetically, we group together commands for working with file systems, connecting to networks, and managing processes, so you can access commands by what you want to do, not only by how they are named.

Likewise, we won't just give you a listing of every option available for every command. Instead, we provide working examples of the most important and useful options to use with each command. From there, we'll describe quick ways to find more options, if you need them, from man pages, the info facility, and help options.

Finding Commands

All the commands described in this book should be installed when you are ready to run them. However, note that this book is based on the latest release of Mac OS X (version 10.5, called Leopard), so if you are running Tiger (10.4) you may not have something installed.

You might type a command and see a message similar to the following:

```
mycommand: command not found
```

This might happen for the following reasons:

❑ You mistyped the command name.

❑ The command is not in your PATH.

❑ You may need to be the root user for the command to be in your PATH.

❑ The command is not installed on your computer.

Table 1-1 shows some commands you can run to look for a command you want to use.

Table 1-1: Finding Commands

Command and Sample Output	Description
`$ type mount` `mount is /sbin/mount`	Show the first mount command in PATH.

`$ whereis mount`
`mount: /sbin/mount`
`/usr/share/man/man8/mount.8.gz`
	Show binary and man page for mount.

`$ locate xrdb.1.gz` `/usr/local/man/man1/xrdb.1.gz`	Find xrdb.1.gz anywhere in the file system.
`$ which umount` `/sbin/umount`	Find the umount command anywhere in your PATH or aliases.

`$ pkg_info -W convert`
`/usr/local/bin/convert`
`was installed by package`
`ImageMagick-6.3.6.9`
	Find which package the convert command is from

If you suspect that the command you want is not installed, the best remedy is probably to upgrade to the latest version of Mac OS X.

Command Reference Information in UNIX

Original BSD, Linux, and UNIX documentation was all done on manual pages, generally referred to as *man pages*. A slightly more sophisticated documentation effort appeared a bit later with the *info* facility. Within each command itself, help messages are almost always available.

This reference information is component oriented—in other words, there are separate man pages for nearly every command, file format, system call, device, and other component of a BSD system. Documentation more closely aligned to whole software packages is typically stored in a subdirectory of the `/usr/local/share/doc` directory.

All three reference features—man pages, info documents, and help messages—are available in BSD systems.

Using help Messages

The -h or --help options are often used to display help messages for a command. The following example illustrates how to display help for the man command:

```
$ man --help
man, version 1.6c
```

```
usage: man [-adfhktwW] [section] [-M path] [-P pager] [-S list]
[-m system] [-p string] name …

   a : find all matching entries
   c : do not use cat file
   d : print gobs of debugging information
   D : as for -d, but also display the pages
   f : same as whatis(1)
   h : print this help message
   k : same as apropos(1)
   K : search for a string in all pages
   t : use troff to format pages for printing
   w : print location of man page(s) that would be displayed
       (if no name given: print directories that would be searched)
   W : as for -w, but display filenames only

   C file    : use `file' as configuration file
   M path    : set search path for manual pages to `path'
   P pager   : use program `pager' to display pages
   S list    : colon separated section list
   m system  : search for alternate system's man pages
   p string  : string tells which preprocessors to run
                   e - [n]eqn(1)   p - pic(1)    t - tbl(1)
                   g - grap(1)     r - refer(1)  v - vgrind(1)

 …
```

The preceding output shows how the man command line is used and lists available options.

Using man Pages

Suppose you want to **find man pages for commands related to a certain word**. Use the apropos command to search the man page database. This shows man pages that have crontab in the man page NAME line:

```
$ apropos crontab
crontab(1)    -  maintain crontab files for individual users (V3)
crontab(5)    -  tables for driving cron
```

The apropos output here shows each man page NAME line that contains crontab. The number shows the man page section in which the man page appears. (We discuss sections shortly.)

The whatis command is a way to show NAME lines alone for commands that contain the word you enter:

```
$ whatis cat
cat        (1)  - concatenate files and print on the standard output
```

The easiest way to **display the man page for a term** is with the man command and the command name, as shown in the following example:

```
$ man find
FIND(1)        FreeBSD General Commands Manual              FIND(1)
NAME
       find -- walk a file hierarchy
SYNOPSIS
       find [-H | -L | -P] [-EXdsx] [-f pathname] [pathname ...] expression
...
```

The preceding command displays the first man page found for the find command. As shown in the earlier example, some terms have multiple man pages. For example, there is a man page for the crontab command and one for the crontab files. Man pages are organized into sections, as shown in Table 1-2.

Table 1-2: man Page Sections

Section	Description
1	General user commands
2	System calls
3	Programming routines/library functions
4	Devices
5	Configuration files and file formats
6	Games
7	Miscellaneous
8	Administrative commands and daemons
9	Kernel Interface

The following code shows some other examples of useful options with the man command.

```
$ man -a mount          Shows all man pages related to component
$ man 5 crontab         Shows section 5 man page for component
$ man mount -P more     Use more, not less to page through
$ man -f mount          Same as the whatis command
$ man -k mount          Same as the apropos command
```

Man pages are also available on the Internet. Here are some useful sites for finding BSD man pages:

```
www.freebsd.org/cgi/man.cgi
www.openbsd.org/cgi-bin/man.cgi
http://netbsd.gw.com/cgi-bin/man-cgi?++NetBSD-current
```

Using info Documents

In some cases, developers have put more complete descriptions of commands, file formats, devices, or other BSD components in the info database. You can enter the info database by simply typing the `info` command or by opening a particular component:

```
$ info ls
```

The previous command shows information on the `ls` command. Use up, down, left, and right arrows and Page Up and Page Down to move around the screen. The Home and End keys go to the beginning and end of a node, respectively. When you are displaying the info screen, you can get around using the keystrokes shown in Table 1-3.

Table 1-3: Moving Through the Info Screen

Keystroke	Movement
?	Display the basic commands to use in info windows.
L	Go back to the previous node you were viewing.
n, p, u	Go to the node that is next, previous, or up.
Tab	Go to the next hyperlink in this node.
Enter	Go to the hyperlink under the cursor.
R	Follow a cross-reference.
Q	Quit and exit from info.

Software packages that have particularly extensive text available in the info database include gimp, festival, libc, automake, zsh, sed, tar, and bash. Files used by the info database are stored in the `/usr/share/info` directory.

Summary

Although you certainly can read this book from cover to cover if you like, it is designed to be used as a reference to the hundreds of features in Mac OS X systems that are most useful to power users and systems administrators. Because information is organized by topic, instead of alphabetically, you don't have to know the commands in advance to find what you need to get the job done.

Most of the features described in this book will work equally well on Mac OS X as well as FreeBSD, NetBSD, OpenBSD, and other BSD systems. In fact, many of the commands described here are in such widespread use that you could use them exactly as described here on most Linux and UNIX systems as well.

However, there are some differences when it comes to working on Mac OS X, and the next chapter provides a brief introduction for anyone new to the world of Mac OS X UNIX.

2

New to Mac OS X?

If you're like most UNIX geeks, you probably want to find the command line on your new MacBook Pro or iMac or Mac server and start figuring things out. Although there's nothing wrong with that approach, it might be good to slow down a bit and figure out the differences between the flavor of BSD UNIX on Mac OS X and other flavors of UNIX you've used in the past.

For most of you, there won't be much of a difference. For some, there will be one or two things that have changed that you'll absolutely love. For others, there will be a whole bunch of things that will take getting used to—but it is hoped that you'll learn to love the changes.

IN THIS CHAPTER

Getting to Know UNIX on Mac OS X

Finding Terminal

The folder structure

Your home directory

Spotlight

Getting and using Fink

Mounting and unmounting

Learning to love launchd

The goal of this chapter is very simple: to provide you with a Cook's tour of UNIX on Mac OS X. By the end of the chapter, you should be familiar with your environment, and we'll take some time along the way to make some customizations and additions that will make you more productive.

What Is Mac OS X UNIX?

Mac OS X 10.5 (Leopard) is marketed as an "Open Brand UNIX 03 Registered Product, conforming to the SUSv3 and POSIX 1003.1 specification for the C API, Shell Utilities, and Threads." What this means in layman's terms is that Leopard can compile and run all existing UNIX code.

Furthermore, Leopard supports both 64- and 32-bit applications on the same platform. All major graphical libraries (Cocoa, X11, and OpenGL) are available. Leopard is also multicore optimized, thereby enabling vastly improved scheduling, memory management, and processor affinity algorithms.

In short, you've got full support for UNIX on Mac OS X. It isn't some kind of add-on or afterthought. The guts, a collection of open-source technologies called Darwin, form the foundation of the UNIX experience on Mac OS X. By itself, Darwin is not Mac OS X, because it lacks some of the proprietary pieces that make the Mac OS X experience different from other UNIX variants (such as the Aqua interface, Carbon, Cocoa, OpenGL, Quartz, as well as QuickTime, the iLife suite, Safari, and the XCode development environment, to name a few).

The Mac OS X kernel is called xnu, which consists of a Mach-based core, an object-oriented runtime environment, and a BSD-based operating system. Mach provides critical low-level services, most of which are transparent to applications and users. For example, it handles hardware abstraction, processor management, preemptive multi-tasking, virtual memory management, kernel debugging, console I/O, and more.

We won't discuss the BSD side of the equation here, as the rest of the book is largely devoted to many of the commands and structures inherent in that operating system. For now, suffice it to say that there are enough similarities to bring most knowledgeable users quite a bit of comfort. The rest of this chapter covers some of the differences.

Finding Terminal and Utilities

In Chapter 3, you'll be working with Terminal, which is the utility you use to get to a command prompt. Right now, though, you'll notice that there's no intuitive way to find Terminal. There's no shortcut on your desktop, no icon on your Dock, or anything that points the way to a Terminal prompt. We're going to correct that right now.

Open a Finder window and double-click on the Macintosh HD item in the left navigation pane, as shown in Figure 2-1.

Next, double-click the Applications folder on the right. Scroll down to the Utilities folder under Applications and double-click that to open the screen shown in Figure 2-2.

Finally, double-click the Terminal application icon shown in Figure 2-2 to open the Terminal application window, shown in Figure 2-3.

The Terminal application window is now in your Dock, but who wants to repeat a long series of steps each time, especially when you consider that you'll likely be using Terminal a lot as a UNIX geek?

Not to worry, it's very simple to add Terminal to the Dock. Simply control-click (or right-click if you have a multi-button mouse) the Terminal icon and select Keep in Dock from the contextual menu, as shown in Figure 2-4. This will keep Terminal at your fingertips.

Here's another handy trick: Add the entire Utilities folder to your Dock as a stack of items. Simply drag the Utilities folder from Finder to the right-hand side of your Dock and drop it on the Dock. You can then click the stack icon to reveal shortcuts for every item in the Utilities folder (see Figure 2-5).

Figure 2-1: To find and use Terminal, first click on Macintosh HD

Name	Date Modified	Size	Kind
▶ Applications	Nov 12, 2008, 11:31 AM	--	Folder
▶ Developer	Jul 3, 2008, 10:32 PM	--	Folder
gpg.docs.english.pkg	Apr 13, 2006, 12:15 PM	Zero KB	Install...ckage
▶ Library	Jun 25, 2008, 4:51 PM	--	Folder
Macintosh HD/Users...older/318/mtrace.txt	Oct 16, 2007, 4:11 PM	24 KB	Plain text
MAU 1.1.2 Update Log	Oct 29, 2007, 5:28 PM	16 KB	Simpl...ument
▶ Previous Systems	Feb 13, 2008, 8:27 PM	--	Folder
sblibng.log	Oct 5, 2007, 11:19 PM	4 KB	Log File
▶ sw	Jun 26, 2008, 3:50 PM	--	Folder
▶ System	Oct 4, 2008, 9:59 AM	--	Folder
User Guides And Information	Jun 4, 2007, 5:35 PM	4 KB	Alias
▶ Users	Feb 12, 2008, 1:07 PM	--	Folder

Figure 2-2: Select the Terminal utility

Name	Date Modified	Size	Kind
▶ Adobe Utilities	Jul 15, 2007, 10:22 AM	--	Folder
AirPort Utility	Aug 25, 2008, 6:55 PM	41 MB	Application
Audio MIDI Setup	Sep 23, 2007, 11:53 PM	13.4 MB	Application
Bluetooth File Exchange	Jun 24, 2008, 7:54 PM	1.6 MB	Application
Boot Camp Assistant	Feb 12, 2008, 1:35 PM	12.4 MB	Application
Built-In Keyboard Firmware Update	Feb 26, 2008, 2:33 PM	1.9 MB	Application
ColorSync Utility	Feb 12, 2008, 1:35 PM	11.4 MB	Application
Console	Jul 27, 2007, 7:30 PM	10.6 MB	Application
DigitalColor Meter	Sep 24, 2007, 12:43 AM	924 KB	Application
Directory	Oct 4, 2008, 9:58 AM	58.2 MB	Application
Directory Utility	Oct 4, 2008, 9:58 AM	58.8 MB	Application
Disk Utility	Oct 4, 2008, 9:58 AM	32.7 MB	Application
Grab	Sep 23, 2007, 11:50 PM	1.1 MB	Application
Grapher	Jun 19, 2007, 5:19 PM	76.2 MB	Application
▶ Java	Oct 4, 2008, 9:58 AM	--	Folder
Keychain Access	Jul 12, 2008, 1:26 PM	16.3 MB	Application
MacBook Pro EFI Firmware Update	May 4, 2008, 6:15 PM	5.1 MB	Application
Migration Assistant	Nov 3, 2008, 1:31 PM	12.2 MB	Application
Network Utility	Jun 24, 2008, 7:54 PM	2.4 MB	Application
ODBC Administrator	Jul 5, 2007, 2:20 PM	16.2 MB	Application
Podcast Capture	Jun 24, 2008, 7:54 PM	18.4 MB	Application
RAID Utility	Jun 24, 2008, 7:54 PM	4 MB	Application
Remote Install Mac OS X	Nov 3, 2008, 1:31 PM	1.8 MB	Application
System Profiler	Sep 24, 2007, 12:34 AM	9.2 MB	Application
Terminal	Feb 12, 2008, 1:35 PM	40.5 MB	Application
VoiceOver Utility	Jun 24, 2008, 7:54 PM	2 MB	Application
X11	Oct 4, 2008, 9:58 AM	904 KB	Application

13

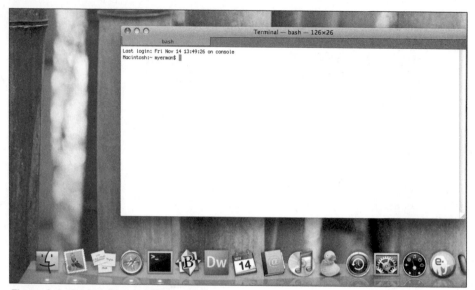

Figure 2-3: Terminal application window

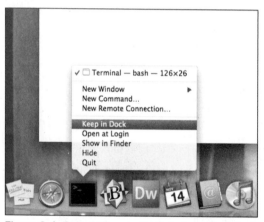

Figure 2-4: Select Keep in Dock to keep Terminal readily available

You can change the way this stack is displayed by control- or right-clicking on the stack and changing the view option to Fan, Grid, or List. The example in Figure 2-5 is of a grid, but a list can be a lot more compact, as pictured in Figure 2-6.

Figure 2-5: Clicking the Stack icon shows all your shortcuts

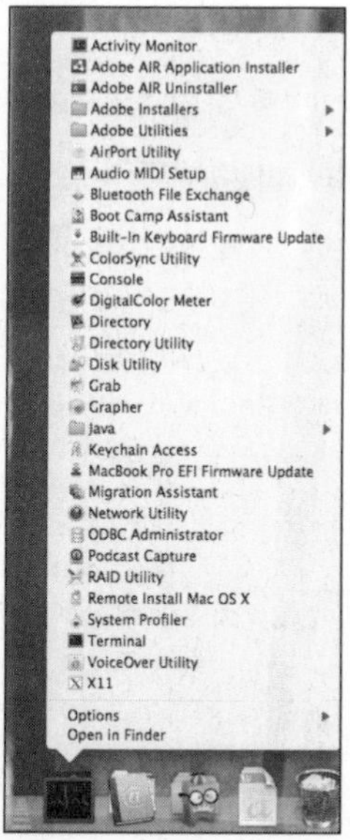

Figure 2-6: A list shows shortcuts
more compactly

Directory Structure

Now that you've got Terminal set up on the Dock and your Utilities folder in a stack, let's have a quick look at the directory structure. In Terminal, type the following command:

```
ls -a /
```

You'll see a whole bunch of familiar folders (such as /etc and /bin) but a lot of other stuff that doesn't seem to make much sense (such as /.Spotlight-V100 and /.Trashes).

Table 2-1 lists the major folders you'll see off the root folder. One thing to notice right away is that the file system is case neutral, which can throw some UNIX pros off at first. For example, each of the following commands results in the same output:

```
ls /etc
ls /Etc
ls /eTc
```

Table 2-1: Mac OS X Root Directory

File or Folder	Description
/.DS_Store	Contains Finder settings for the current directory. This folder is generated for any directory viewed in Finder.
/.Spotlight-V100	Contains Spotlight-specific metadata
/.Trashes	Contains files that have been dragged to the Trash
/.com.apple.timemachine.supported	Indicates that a drive can be used by Time Machine as a backup target
/.fseventsd	Used by the FSEvents API
/.hotfiles.btree	A B-Tree index that provides fast access to frequently used files
/Applications	Holds all Mac OS X applications
/bin	Contains essential system binaries
/Desktop DB	Contains housekeeping information used by Finder
/Desktop DF	See /Desktop DB
/dev	Contains device-specific files

Table 2-1: Mac OS X Root Directory *(continued)*

File or Folder	Description
/Developer	Contains Apple's XCode tools and documentation (but only if you've installed them)
/etc	Contains system configuration files. This is a symbolic link to /private/etc.
/home	Used by the automounter for NFS-mounted home directories
/Installer Log File	Used by some third-party installers
/Library	Contains support files for locally installed applications
/lost+found	Stores orphaned files discovered by fsck
/mach_kernel	Contains the Darwin kernel
/mach_kernel.ctfsys	Contains an alternate copy of the kernel (used by dtrace)
/net	Used by the automounter for NFS-mounted directories
/Network	Contains network-mounted Application, Library, and User folders
/opt	Contains the MacPorts installation (if installed)
/private	Contains the tmp, var, etc, and cores directories
/sbin	Contains executables for system administration and configuration
/sw	Contains the Fink installation (if installed)
/System	Contains various folders, the most important of which is Library, which holds support files for the system and system applications
/tmp	Holds temporary files. A symbolic link to /private/tmp.
/User Guides and Information	An alias to /Library/Documentation/User Guides and Information

Continued

Table 2-1: Mac OS X Root Directory *(continued)*

File or Folder	Description
/Users	Contains home directories for users on the system (root user's home is /var/root)
/usr	Contains BSD UNIX applications and support files
/var	Contains frequently modified files, such as log files. Symbolic link to /private/var.
/Volumes	Contains all visible mounted file systems, including removable media and mounted disk images

Your Home Directory

All users get their own home directory in the /Users directory. If your username were tsmith, then your home directory would be /Users/tsmith. You can also use the shorthand version of that path with the tilde (~). Just about any use of the tilde is allowed, such as the following:

```
cd ~
cd ~/documents
cp /tmp/*.doc ~/documents
```

You'll learn more about all of this in Chapters 3 through 5, but for now, it's important to know what's in your home directory, as Mac OS X creates a standard series of files and folders in your home directory. Table 2-2 provides a summary of these files and folders.

Table 2-2: Files and Folders in Your Home Directory

File or Folder	Description
Desktop	All files and folders that are currently on your desktop
Documents	This is the default location for documents you're working on in Pages, Keynote, Numbers, and many other applications. Most users create hierarchical subfolders for projects and other tasks.
Downloads	This is the default location for web downloads when using Safari.
Library	This is the local user's listing of support files for applications. This is also where mail downloads and addresses in Address Book are stored. This differs from the global support files found in /Library.
Movies	Default location for movies saved by iMovie

Table 2-2: Files and Folders in Your Home Directory *(continued)*

File or Folder	Description
Music	Default location for music and media files used by iTunes
Pictures	Default location for photos and other image files in iPhoto
Public	The folder that is shared when you turn on File Sharing
Sites	The folder that is used by the Apache web server when you turn on Web Sharing

It's a good idea to store your files in the right places, but you're free to create any structures you want (to a certain extent) inside your home directory. For example, if you create a lot of workflows, you might want to create a Workflows directory. You can also create your own Applications folder and keep user-specific applications there.

Also included in your home directory are numerous "dot files," such as .profile and others. These are examined in the next few chapters, as we look at BASH (Bourne Again Shell) and other shells.

Spotlight

Spotlight is Mac OS X's search engine. To use it, simply press ⌘-space (the space bar) or click the magnifying glass icon on the upper-right corner of your screen. Type in a search term, and Mac OS X searches through applications, audio files, iCal events, bookmarks, images, presentations, mail messages, PDFs, word processing documents, postscript files, vCard files, HTML documents, and much more to provide you with a list of results that match the initial query. Figure 2-7 shows what appears in Spotlight.

If you need a more detailed Spotlight search window with advanced toggles (such as searching by Kind of file, Location, Date, Name, Contents, and so on), press Option-⌘-space.

As a UNIX power user, you can appreciate the advanced metadata-based search functionality that Spotlight provides, although you may never use it, because you might feel more comfortable with the more traditional locate and find commands.

You can also run Spotlight searches from the command line using mdfind, like so:

```
mdfind mac os x
/Users/myerman/Desktop/mac_os_x_toolbox/478363c03.doc
/Users/myerman/Desktop/478363c02_new.doc
/Users/myerman/Documents/Microsoft User Data/Word Work File A_94721220
/Users/myerman/Desktop/mac_os_x_toolbox/478363c02.doc
/Users/myerman/Library/Caches/Metadata/Safari/History/http:%2F%2Fwww.google.com%
2Fsearch?hl=en&client=safari&rls=en-us&q=mac+os+x+sites+folder&btnG=Search&aq=f&
oq=.webhistory
...
```

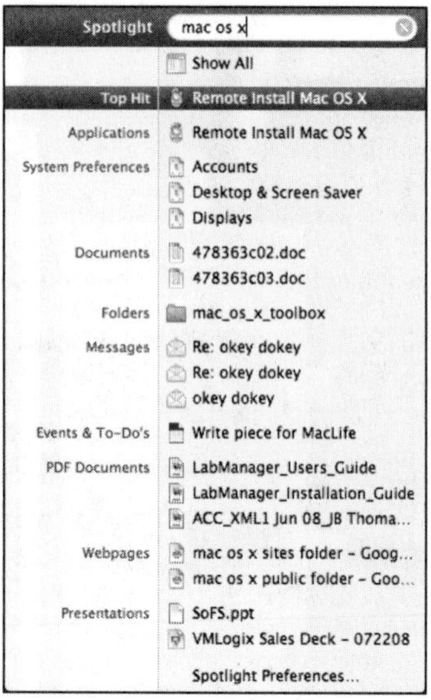

Figure 2-7: Spotlight is the Mac OS X's search engine

You'll find that Spotlight command-line searches are a great alternative to find or locate. However, it's worth knowing how Mac OS X stores all the metadata for a particular file. The mdls utility can give you insight into the attributes stored by Spotlight for a file:

```
mdls ~/desktop/mac_os_x_toolbox*
kMDItemContentCreationDate      = 2008-11-02 12:10:22 -0600
kMDItemContentModificationDate = 2008-11-13 16:43:09 -0600
kMDItemContentType              = "public.folder"
kMDItemContentTypeTree          = (
    "public.folder",
    "public.directory",
    "public.item"
)
kMDItemDisplayName              = "mac_os_x_toolbox"
kMDItemFSContentChangeDate      = 2008-11-13 16:43:09 -0600
kMDItemFSCreationDate           = 2008-11-02 12:10:22 -0600
kMDItemFSCreatorCode            = ""
kMDItemFSFinderFlags            = 0
kMDItemFSHasCustomIcon          = 0
kMDItemFSInvisible              = 0
kMDItemFSIsExtensionHidden      = 0
kMDItemFSIsStationery           = 0
kMDItemFSLabel                  = 0
kMDItemFSName                   = "mac_os_x_toolbox"
kMDItemFSNodeCount              = 24
kMDItemFSOwnerGroupID           = 501
```

```
kMDItemFSOwnerUserID        = 501
kMDItemFSSize               = (null)
kMDItemFSTypeCode           = ""
kMDItemKind                 = "Folder"
kMDItemLastUsedDate         = 2008-11-14 14:40:07 -0600
kMDItemUsedDates            = (
    2008-11-02 00:00:00 -0500,
    2008-11-03 00:00:00 -0600,
    2008-11-08 00:00:00 -0600,
    2008-11-10 00:00:00 -0600,
    2008-11-12 00:00:00 -0600,
    2008-11-13 00:00:00 -0600,
    2008-11-14 00:00:00 -0600
)
```

All this information is just a sampling of the kinds of queries you can run. For example, to run the previous search on "mac os x" but limit the result set to folders, use the following:

```
mdfind "kMDItemKind == 'Folder'" 'mac os x'
/Users/myerman/Desktop/mac_os_x_toolbox/art
/Applications
/Applications/Utilities
/Users/myerman/Desktop
/Users/myerman/Desktop/mac_os_x_toolbox
/Users/myerman/Library/Caches/TemporaryItems
...
```

Getting and Using Fink

Fink is an open-source project available for download at fink.sourceforge.net. It's an indispensable tool that no UNIX geek on Mac OS X should be without. It enables you to install tools, utilities, and other goodies that have been ported from BSD or Linux to the Mac OS X environment.

When you download Fink, double-click the DMG file and follow the prompts provided by the installation wizard, shown in Figure 2-8.

During the installation process, Fink will ask you if it's okay to add a line to your .profile file. You indeed want this to happen, so click Yes (see Figure 2-9).

Once Fink is installed, you can access its features from Terminal by typing the following:

```
fink -h
```

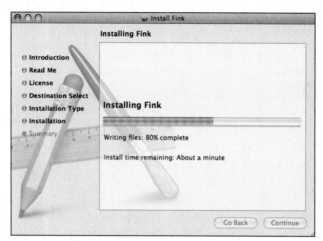

Figure 2-8: The Fink installation wizard

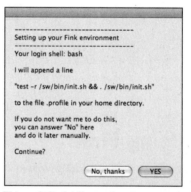

Figure 2-9: Adding a line to your .profile file

This will display help text that looks like the following:

```
Fink 0.27.13
Usage: fink [options] command [package…]
       fink install pkg1 [pkg2 …]

Common commands:
    install     - install/update the named packages
    remove      - remove the named packages
    purge       - same as remove but also removes all configuration files
    update      - update the named packages
    selfupdate  - upgrade fink to the lastest release
    update-all  - update all installed packages
    configure   - rerun the configuration process
```

```
list            - list available packages, optionally filtering by name, see 'fink
list --help' for more options
  apropos       - list packages matching a search keyword
  describe      - display a detailed description of the named packages
  index         - force rebuild of package cache
  validate      - performs various checks on .info and .deb files
  scanpackages  - rescans the list of binary packages on the system
  cleanup       - reclaims disk space used by temporary or obsolete files
  show-deps     - list run-time and compile-time package dependencies

Common options:
  -h, --help             - Display this help text.
  -q, --quiet            - causes fink to be less verbose, opposite of --verbose
  -V, --version          - display version information
  -v, --verbose          - causes fink to be more verbose, opposite of --quiet
  -y, --yes              - assume default answer for all interactive questions
  -b, --use-binary-dist  - download pre-compiled packages from the binary
distribution if available
  --no-use-binary-dist   - Opposite of use-binary-dist

See the fink(8) manual page for a complete list of commands and options.
Visit http://www.finkproject.org for further information.
```

The most important commands you'll use are fink list and fink install. The former tells you what packages are available for installation, and the latter enables you to install that package. During the course of this book, you will likely need to install various packages (such as wget), so now is a good time to get set up with Fink.

Mounting and Unmounting Drives

One of the nice things about Mac OS X is that it automounts drives. For example, attach a USB thumb drive to your iMac or MacBook Pro. Within seconds, you'll see a drive icon appear on your desktop, as shown in Figure 2-10.

Figure 2-10: The Drive icon appears on your desktop

Now go to Terminal and run an `ls` command on `/Volumes`:

```
ls /Volumes
Macintosh HD    TDDMTHUMB
```

As you can see, it's already been mounted! No need to manually mount the new drive. Now run `df -h`:

```
df -h
Filesystem      Size    Used    Avail   Capacity    Mounted on
/dev/disk0s2    149Gi   86Gi    62Gi    59%         /
devfs           107Ki   107Ki   0Bi     100%        /dev
fdesc           1.0Ki   1.0Ki   0Bi     100%        /dev
map -hosts      0Bi     0Bi     0Bi     100%        /net
map auto_home   0Bi     0Bi     0Bi     100%        /home
/dev/disk1s1    974Mi   578Mi   396Mi   60%         /Volumes/TDDMTHUMB
```

To unmount the drive, simply right-click the drive's icon on the desktop and select the Eject option. You can also click the Eject icon next to the item's name in the Finder window (see Figure 2-11). You'll learn how to unmount a drive via the command line in Chapter 12.

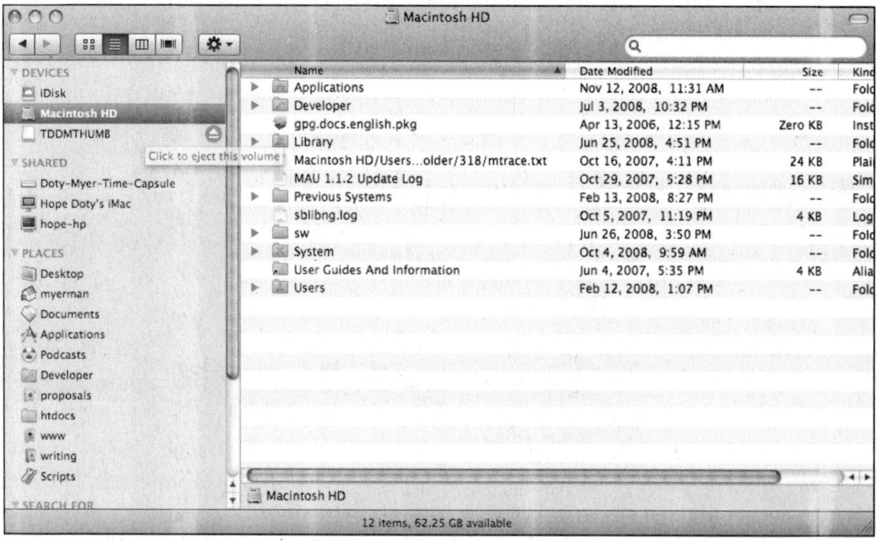

Figure 2-11: To unmount a drive, click the Eject icon

Learning to Love Launchd

Starting with Mac OS X 10.4 (Tiger), Apple introduced a new system startup program called launchd. The launchd daemon takes over many tasks from cron, xinetd, mach_init, and init, all of which have traditionally handled system initialization, called scripts, run startup items, and prepped the system for the user.

All of these systems still exist on Mac OS X, but launchd has superseded them in many instances. The launchd daemon isn't just a cosmetic change, however. First, it gives you a unified way to automatically launch programs (you no longer have to look at init and other places, not to mention maintain separate config files). Second, it provides a big performance boost to the system. Finally, it provides a more secure way of handling new processes.

For example, when a nonroot user launches a program, the launchd daemon handling the jobs runs with nonroot user privileges, offering an extra layer of security. From a performance perspective, this new launchd daemon only uses system resources when it is started, and can be independently shut down and restarted as needed.

What does this all mean to you? You may need to stop and think a bit before going with instinctual responses to certain tasks. For example, there's no need to write a script that monitors a folder—launchd already does that automatically. Nor is there any need to cause a system reboot to launch a new job, as launchctl (the launchd job controller) enables you to keep the user in his or her workflow.

You'll learn more about launchd in Chapter 9. For now, know that it's there and that it may represent a new way of working for you.

Summary

In this chapter, you learned a few things about Mac OS X and how it differs with the brand of UNIX that you may be familiar with. Regardless of whether you come from another BSD flavor, UNIX, System V, or some other variety of UNIX, you'll find that most things are still the same in Mac OS X.

By the end of this chapter, you should have easy access to Terminal in your Dock, your Utilities folder should be in a handy stack, and you should be familiar with the folder structure and your home directory. You've also downloaded Fink to get access to additional utilities and tools as needed, and it is hoped that you're feeling better about automounting and launchd.

It's now time to become more familiar with Terminal and the shell.

3

Using the Shell

The use of a shell command interpreter (usually just called a shell) dates back to the early days of the first UNIX systems. Besides their obvious use of running commands, shells have many built-in features such as environment variables, aliases, and a variety of functions for programming.

There are several different shells to choose from on Mac OS X systems. In the past, tcsh was used as the default shell. More recently, the Bourne Again Shell (bash) has been the default.

This chapter offers information that will help you use most UNIX shells, in general, and the bash shell, in particular.

Terminal Windows and Shell Access

The most common way to access a shell from a Mac OS X graphical interface is using a Terminal window. To open a Terminal window from Mac OS X, open the Applications folder and select Utilities ⇨ Terminal. This opens a Terminal window, displaying a bash shell prompt. Figure 3-1 shows an example of a Terminal window.

The commands shown in Figure 3-1 illustrate that the *current shell* is the bash shell (/bin/bash); the *current user* is the desktop user who launched the window (myerman), and the *current directory* is that user's home directory (/Users/myerman). The username (myerman) and the shell (bash) appear in the title bar.

The Terminal window not only enables you to access a shell; it also has controls for managing your shells. For example, click Shell ⇨ New Tab ⇨ Basic to open another shell on a different tab, click Shell ⇨ New

Window ⇨ Basic to **open a new Terminal window,** or select Shell ⇨ Set Title to **set a new title in** the title bar.

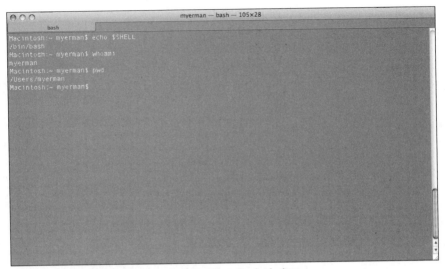

Figure 3-1: Type shell commands into a Terminal window

You can also use keyboard shortcuts to work with a Terminal window. Open a **shell on a new tab** by typing ⌘T, **open a new Terminal window** with ⌘N, **close a tab** with ⌘W, and **close a Terminal window** with ⌘Q. ⌘Q will also quit Terminal if you only have one window or tab open. Highlight text and copy it with ⌘C, and then **paste it in the same or different window** with ⌘V.

Other keyboard shortcuts for controlling Terminal windows include typing ⌘+ to **make the text larger** or ⌘- (that's ⌘ and a minus sign) to **make the text smaller.** Type Ctrl+D **to log out of a current application or exit a process.**

The Terminal window also supports user-specific settings (select Terminal ⇨ Preferences). Some profile settings are cosmetic (i.e., use bold fonts, cursor blinks, terminal bell, colors, anti-alias text, and fonts). Other settings are functional. For example, by default, the Terminal in 10.4 saves 10,000 scrollback lines, but is unlimited in 10.5. Some people like to customize how much memory is consumed by this process; others just leave it alone.

Using the Shell

After you open a shell from the Terminal window, the shell environment is set up based on the user who started the shell. Each user's default shell is assigned based on the user's entry in the /etc/passwd file. By default, the user's shell is set to bash (/ bin/bash). Examples in this section use the bash shell.

Bash shell settings for all users' shells are located in /etc/profile. User-specific shell settings are determined by commands executed from several dot files in the user's home directory (if they exist): .bash_profile, .bash_login, and .profile. When a shell is closed, any commands in the user's ~/.bash_logout file are executed. Changing settings in these files permanently changes the user's shell settings but does not affect shells that are already running. (Other shells use different configuration files.)

There are a variety of ways in which you can list and change your shell environment. One of the main ways is to change which user you are—in particular, to become the super user (see the section "Acquiring Super User Power" later in this chapter).

Using bash History

The Bourne Again Shell (bash) is used by many UNIX-like systems. Built into bash, as with other shells, is a history feature that enables you to review, change, and reuse commands that you have run in the past.

When bash starts, it reads the ~/.bash_history file and loads it into memory. This file is set by the value of $HISTFILE. During a bash session, commands are added to history in memory. When bash exits, history in memory is written back to the .bash_history file. The **number of commands held in history during a bash session** is set by $HISTSIZE, while the **number of commands actually stored in the history file** is set by $HISTFILESIZE:

```
$ echo $HISTFILE $HISTSIZE $HISTFILESIZE
/home/fcaen/.bash_history 500 500
```

To **list the entire history**, type **history**. To **list a previous number of history commands**, follow history with a number. The following example lists the previous five commands in your history:

```
$ history 5
975  mkdir extras
976  mv *doc extras/
977  ls -CF
978  vi house.txt
979  history
```

To **move among the commands** in your history, use the up arrow and down arrow. When a command is displayed, you can use the keyboard to **edit the current command** like any other command: left arrow, right arrow, Delete, Backspace, and so on. Here are some other ways to recall and run commands from your bash history:

```
$ !!                      Run the previous command
$ !997                    Run command number 997 from history
ls -CF
$ !997 *doc               Append *doc to command 997 from history
```

29

```
ls -CF *doc
$ !?CF?                  Run previous command line containing the CF string
ls -CF *doc
$ !ls                    Run the previous ls command
ls -CF *doc
$ !ls:s/CF/l             Run previous ls command, replacing CF with l
ls -l *doc
```

Another way to **edit the command history** is using the `fc` command. With `fc`, you open the chosen command from history using the vi editor. The edited command runs when you exit the editor. Change to a different editor by setting the `FCEDIT` variable (for example, `FCEDIT=gedit`) or on the `fc` command line. For example:

```
$ fc 978                          Edit command number 978, then run it
$ fc                              Edit the previous command, then run it
$ fc -e /usr/local/bin/nano 989   Use nano to edit command 989
```

(Use `pkg_add -r` to install the text editor you want, such as nano, if it is not already installed. Chapter 5 describes several text editors and the packages they are in.)

Use Ctrl+R to **search for a string in history**. For example, typing Ctrl+R followed by the string `ss` resulted in the following:

```
# <Ctrl+r>
(reverse-i-search)`ss': sudo /usr/bin/less /var/log/messages
```

Press Ctrl+R repeatedly to **search backward through your history list** for other occurrences of the `ss` string.

> **NOTE** *By default,* bash *command history editing uses emacs-style commands. If you prefer the vi editor, you can use vi-style editing of your history by using the* set *command to set your editor to vi. To do that, type the following:*
>
> `set -o vi.`

Using Command-Line Completion

You can use the Tab key to complete different types of information on the command line. Here are some examples where you type a partial name, followed by the Tab key, to **have bash try to complete the information you want** on your command line:

```
$ tracer<Tab>           Command completion: Completes to traceroute command
$ cd /Users/my<Tab>     File completion: Completes to /Users/myerman directory
$ cd ~myer<Tab>         User homedir completion: Completes to /Users/myerman
$ echo $PA<Tab>         Env variable completion: Completes to $PATH
$ ping @<Tab>           Host completion: Show hosts from /etc/hosts
@davinci.example.com    @ritchie.example.com   @thompson.example.com
@localhost              @zooey
```

Redirecting stdin and stdout

Like most UNIX systems, Mac OS X supports stdin, stdout, and stderror. Standard input (stdin) is usually a keyboard accepting interactive commands from a user, but it can also be a file full of commands or a separate process. Standard output (stdout) is usually the screen, but stdout can be redirected to a file of some sort. This is pretty useful if you're expecting a great deal of data from your initial command, or if the process creating the data is running constantly. Standard error (stderror) consists of messages that can be separated from the rest of the output.

Let's run a simple example to illustrate the three states. Typing a command in a shell makes it run interactively—what is termed *standard input* in the UNIX world. The resulting process has two output streams: stdout for normal command output and stderr for error output. In the following example, when /tmpp isn't found, an error message goes to stderr but output from listing /tmp (which is found) goes to stdout:

```
$ ls /tmp /tmpp
ls: /tmpp: No such file or directory
/tmp/:
gconfd-fcaen  keyring-b41WuB  keyring-ItEWbz  mapping-fcaen  orbit-fcaen
```

By default, all output is directed to the screen. Use the greater-than sign (>) to **direct output to a file**. More specifically, you can direct the standard output stream (using >) or the standard error stream (using 2>) to a file.

In the following example, stdout is redirected to the file output.txt, while stderr is still directed to the screen:

```
$ ls /tmp /tmmp > output.txt
ls: /tmpp: No such file or directory
```

In the next example, stderr (stream 2) is directed to errors.txt, while stdout goes to the screen:

```
$ ls /tmp /tmmp 2> errors.txt
/tmp/:
gconfd-fcaen  keyring-b41WuB  keyring-ItEWbz  mapping-fcaen  orbit-fcaen
```

In this example, the first two examples are combined:

```
$ ls /tmp /tmmp 2> errors.txt > output.txt
```

Finally, both streams are directed to the everything.txt file:

```
$ ls /tmp /tmmp > everything.txt 2>&1
```

To append to a file instead of overwriting it, use two greater-than signs:

```
$ ls /tmp >> output.txt
```

If you don't ever want to see an output stream, you can simply **direct the output stream to a special bit bucket file** (/dev/null):

```
# ls /tmp 2> /dev/null
```

> **TIP**   *Another time you may want to redirect stderr is when you run jobs with crontab. You could redirect stderr to a mail message that goes to the crontab's owner. That way, any error messages can be sent to the person running the job.*

Just as you can direct standard output from a command, you can also **direct standard input to a command**. For example, the following command e-mails the /etc/hosts file to the user named marlowe on the local system:

```
$ mail marlowe < /etc/hosts
```

Using pipes, you can **redirect output from one process to another process,** rather than just files. Here is an example where the output of the ls command is piped to the sort command to have the output sorted:

```
# ls /tmp | sort
```

In the next example, a **pipe and redirection are combined** (the stdout of the ls command is sorted and stderr is dumped to the bit bucket):

```
# ls /tmp/ /tmmp 2> /dev/null | sort
```

Pipes can be used for a ton of things:

```
# ls -la | grep -I bash | wc -1
# ps aux | grep firefox
# ps aux | less
# whereis -m pkg_add | awk '{print $2}'
```

The first command line in the preceding code lists all files in a directory, grabs those files that have bash in them (regardless of case), and does a count of how many lines are left (effectively counting files with bash in the name). The second command line displays Firefox processes taken from the long process list (assuming the Firefox web browser is running). The third command line enables you to page through the process list. The last line displays the word *pkg_add:* followed by the path to the pkg_add man page, and then displays only the path to the man page (the second element on the line).

Using backticks, you can **execute one section of a command line first and feed the output of that command to the rest of the command line.** Here is an example:

```
# ls -l `which traceroute`
-r-sr-xr-x  1 root  wheel  19836 Jan 15 18:33 /usr/sbin/traceroute
```

The preceding command line finds the full path to traceroute and does a long list (ls -l) of that command.

A more advanced and powerful way to **take the output of one command and pass it as param-eters to another** is with the `xargs` command. For example, after installing the cdrtools package, I ran the following command:

```
# find /usr/local/bin | grep iso | xargs ls
/usr/local/bin/growisofs       /usr/local/bin/isodump
/usr/local/bin/iso-info        /usr/local/bin/isoinfo
/usr/local/bin/iso-read        /usr/local/bin/isovfy
/usr/local/bin/isodebug        /usr/local/bin/mkisofs
```

To display the command `xargs` is going to run, use the `-t` option as follows:

```
# cd /usr/local/bin
# echo iso* | xargs -t ls
ls iso-info iso-read isodebug isodump isoinfo isovfy
iso-info        isodebug        isoinfo
iso-read        isodump         isovfy
```

In the preceding example, the entire output of `echo` is passed to `pkg_info`. Using the `-t` option to `xargs`, a verbose output of the command line appears before the command is executed. Now have `xargs` pass each output string from `ls` as input to individual `rpm` commands. Use the `-I` option to define `{}` as the placeholder for the string:

```
# ls /usr/local/bin/mk* | xargs -t -I {} pkg_info -W {}
pkg_info -W /usr/local/bin/mkbundle
/usr/local/bin/mkbundle was installed by package mono-1.2.5.1
pkg_info -W /usr/local/bin/mkisofs
/usr/local/bin/mkisofs was installed by package cdrtools-2.01_6
```

As you can see from the output, separate `pkg_info` commands are run for each option passed by `ls`.

Using Aliases

Use the `alias` command to **set and list aliases**. By default, no aliases are set in a user's `~/.bashrc` file. Here's how to **list the aliases that are currently set** for that shell:

```
# alias
h           (history 25)
j           (jobs -l)
la          (ls -a)
lf          (ls -FA)
ll          (ls -lA)
```

Aliases can also be set simply as a way of adding options to the default behavior of a command (such as `alias ls="ls -lah"`, so that file listings always show all files and display byte sizes in human-friendly terms). To **define other aliases for the bash shell**, use the alias command, followed by the alias name and command to run. For example:

```
$ alias fi="find . | grep $*"
```

Using the alias just shown, typing `fi string` causes the current directory and its subdirectories to be searched for any filenames containing the string you entered. You can **add an alias to your .bashrc file** as follows:

```
# alias la='ls -la' >> ~/.bashrc
```

Remove an alias from the current bash session using the `unalias` command:

```
# unalias la          Unalias the previously aliased la command
# unalias -a          Unalias all aliased commands
```

Tailing Files

To watch the contents of a plain text file grow over time, you can use the `tail` command. For example, you can watch as messages are added to the `/var/log/install.log` file as follows:

```
# tail -f /var/log/install.log
```

Press Ctrl+C to exit the `tail` command.

Acquiring Super User Power

When you open a shell, you are able to run commands and access files and directories based on your user/group ID and the permissions set for those components. Many system features are restricted to the *root user*, also referred to as the *super user*.

On Mac OS X, the root user is disabled by default. If you need to do something as root, use the `sudo` command.

The `sudo` command provides very granular delegation of power to users other than the root user. When you have multiple users, the `sudo` facility is a great tool for granting specific escalated privileges and logging everything the users do with those privileges. Unless otherwise specified, `sudo` runs as root.

Simply add the `sudo` command in front of the command you wish to run:

```
$ sudo /usr/bin/less /var/log/apache2/error_log
Password:
```

After users type their own password, they can page through the `/var/log/apache2/error_log` file. A timestamp is set at that time as well. For the next five minutes (by default), that user can type the preceding command line and it will work without issuing the password prompt.

Using Environment Variables

Small chunks of information that are useful to your shell environment are stored in what are referred to as *environment variables*. By convention, environment variable names are all uppercase (although that convention is not enforced). If you use the bash shell, some environment variables might be set for you from various bash start scripts: /etc/profile and ~/.bash_profile (if it exists).

To **display all the environment variables**, in alphabetical order, that are already set for your shell, type the following:

```
$ set | less
Apple_PubSub_Socket_Render=/tmp/launch-HxsiSD/Render
BASH=/bin/bash
BASH_ARGC=()
BASH_ARGV=()
BASH_LINENO=()
BASH_SOURCE=()
BASH_VERSINFO=([0]="3" [1]="2" [2]="17" [3]="1" [4]="release" [5]="i386-apple-darwin9.0")
BASH_VERSION='3.2.17(1)-release'
COLUMNS=153
COMMAND_MODE=unix2003
...
```

The output just shown contains only a few examples of the environment variables you will see. You can also **set, or reset, any variables yourself.** For example, to assign the value 123 to the variable ABC (and then display the contents of ABC), type the following:

```
$ ABC=123
$ echo $ABC
123
```

The variable ABC exists only in the shell in which it was created. If you launch a command from that shell (ls, cat, firefox, and so on), that new process will not see the variable. Start a new bash process and test this:

```
$ bash
$ echo $ABC

$
```

You can **make variables part of the environment and inheritable by children processes** by exporting them:

```
$ export ABC=123
$ c
$ echo $ABC
123
```

You can also concatenate a string to an existing variable:

```
# export PATH=$PATH:/home/fcaen
```

To list your bash's environment variables use the following:

```
# env
```

When you are ready to create your own environment variables, avoid using names that are already commonly used by the system for environment variables. See Appendix B for a list of shell environment variables.

Creating Simple Shell Scripts

Shell scripts are good for automating repetitive shell tasks. Bash and other shells include the basic constructs found in various programming languages, such as loops, tests, case statements, and so on. The main difference is that there is only one type of variable: strings.

Later, in Chapter 6, you'll learn a lot more about working with shell scripting, but for now here's a brief set of examples to get your feet wet.

Editing and Running a Script

Shell scripts are simple text files. You can create them using your favorite text editor (such as vi). In order to run, the shell script file must be executable. For example, if you created a shell script with a filename of myscript.sh, you could make it executable as follows:

```
$ chmod u+x myscript.sh
```

Alternately, instead of making it executable, you could precede the script with the bash command to run it (bash myscript.sh). Note that the first line of your bash scripts should always be the following:

```
#!/bin/bash
```

As with any command, besides being executable the shell script you create must also either be in your PATH or be identified by its full or relative path when you run it. In other words, if you just try to run your script, you may get the following result:

```
$ myscript.sh
bash: myscript.sh: command not found
```

In this example, the directory containing `myscript.sh` is not included in your PATH. To correct this problem, you can edit your PATH, copy the script to a directory in your PATH, or enter the full or relative path to your script as shown here:

```
$ mkdir ~/bin ; cp myscript.sh ~/bin/ ; PATH=$PATH:~/bin
$ cp myscript.sh /usr/local/bin
$ ./myscript.sh
$ /tmp/myscript.sh
```

Avoid putting a dot (.) into the PATH to indicate that commands can be run from the current directory. This is a technique that could result in commands that have the same filename as important, well-known commands (such as `ls` or `cat`). The proper file could end up being overridden if a command of the same name exists in the current directory.

Adding Content to Your Script

Although a shell script can be a simple sequence of commands, shell scripts can also be used as you would any programming language. For example, a script can produce different results based on giving it different input. This section describes how to use compound commands, such as `if/then` statements, `case` statements, and `for/while` loops in your shell scripts.

The following example code assigns the string abc to the variable MYSTRING. It then tests the input to determine whether it equals abc and acts based on the outcome of the test. The test is the section that takes place between the brackets ([ ]):

```
MYSTRING=abc
if [ $MYSTRING = abc ] ; then
echo "The variable is abc"
fi
```

To **negate the test**, use ! = instead of =, as shown in the following:

```
if [ $MYSTRING != abc ] ; then
echo "$MYSTRING is not abc";
fi
```

The following are examples of **testing for numbers**:

```
MYNUMBER=1
if [ $MYNUMBER -eq 1 ] ; then echo "MYNUMBER equals 1"; fi
if [ $MYNUMBER -lt 2 ] ; then echo "MYNUMBER <2"; fi
if [ $MYNUMBER -le 1 ] ; then echo "MYNUMBER <=1"; fi
if [ $MYNUMBER -gt 0 ] ; then echo "MYNUMBER >0"; fi
if [ $MYNUMBER -ge 1 ] ; then echo "MYNUMBER >=1"; fi
```

Let's look at some **tests on filenames**. In this example, you can check whether a file exists (-e), whether it's a regular file (-f), or whether it is a directory (-d). These checks are done with if/then statements. If there is no match, then the else statement is used to produce the result:

```
filename="$HOME"
if [ -e $filename ] ; then echo "$filename exists"; fi
if [ -f "$filename" ] ; then
    echo "$filename is a regular file"
elif [ -d "$filename" ] ; then
    echo "$filename is a directory"
else
    echo "I have no idea what $filename is"
fi
```

Table 3-1 shows examples of tests you can perform on files, strings, and variables.

Table 3-1: Operators for Test Expressions

Operator	Test being performed
-a *file*	Check that the file exists (same as –e)
-b *file*	Check whether file is a special block device
-c *file*	Check whether file is a character special (such as serial device)
-d *file*	Check whether file is a directory
-e *file*	Check whether file exists (same as –a)
-f *file*	Check whether file exists and is a regular file (for example, not a directory, socket, pipe, link, or device file)
-g *file*	Check whether file has the set-group-id bit set
-h *file*	Check whether file is a symbolic link (same as –L)
-k *file*	Check whether file has the sticky bit set
-L *file*	Check whether file is a symbolic link (same as –h)
-n *string*	Check whether the string length is greater than 0 bytes
-O *file*	Check whether you own the file
-p *file*	Check whether the file is a named pipe
-r *file*	Check whether the file is readable by you
-s *file*	Check whether the file exists and is it larger than 0 bytes

Table 3-1: Operators for Test Expressions *(continued)*

Operator	Test being performed
`-S file`	Check whether the file exists and is a socket
`-t fd`	Check whether the file descriptor is connected to a terminal
`-u file`	Check whether the file has the set-user-id bit set
`-w file`	Check whether the file is writable by you
`-x file`	Check whether the file is executable by you
`-z string`	Check whether the length of the string is 0 (zero) bytes
`expr1 -a expr2`	Check whether both the first and the second expressions are true
`expr1 -o expr2`	Check whether either of the two expressions is true
`file1 -nt file2`	Check whether the first file is newer than the second file (using the modification timestamp)
`file1 -ot file2`	Check whether the first file is older than the second file (using the modification timestamp)
`file1 -ef file2`	Check whether the two files are associated by a link (a hard link or a symbolic link)
`var1 = var2`	Check whether the first variable is equal to the second variable
`var1 -eq var2`	Check whether the first variable is equal to the second variable
`var1 -ge var2`	Check whether the first variable is greater than or equal to the second variable
`var1 -gt var2`	Check whether the first variable is greater than the second variable
`var1 -le var2`	Check whether the first variable is less than or equal to the second variable
`var1 -lt var2`	Check whether the first variable is less than the second variable
`var1 != var2` `var1 -ne var2`	Check whether the first variable is not equal to the second variable

Another frequently used construct is the `case` command. Using the `case` statement, you can test for different cases and take an action based on the result. Similar to a switch statement in programming languages, case statements can take the place of several nested if statements:

```
case "$VAR" in
   string1)
       { action1 };;
   string2)
       { action2 };;
   *)
       { default action } ;;
esac
```

You can find examples of case usage in the system start-up scripts found in the /etc/rc.d/ directory. Each initscript takes actions based on what parameter was passed to it, and the selection is done via a large case construct.

The bash shell also offers **standard loop constructs,** illustrated by a few examples that follow. In the first example, all the values of the NUMBER variable (0 through 9) appear on the for line:

```
for NUMBER in 0 1 2 3 4 5 6 7 8 9
do
    echo The number is $NUMBER
done
```

In the following examples, the output from the ls command (a list of files) provides the variables on which the for statement acts:

```
for FILE in `/bin/ls`; do echo $FILE; done
```

Instead of feeding the whole list of values to a for statement, you can increment a value and **continue through a while loop until a condition is met.** In the following example, VAR begins as 0, and the while loop continues to increment until the value of VAR becomes 3:

```
VAR=0
while [ $VAR -lt 3 ]; do
    echo $VAR
    VAR=$[$VAR+1]
Done
```

Another way to get the same result as the while statement just shown is to use the until statement, as shown in the following example:

```
VAR=0
until [ $VAR -eq 3 ]; do echo $VAR; VAR=$[$VAR+1]; done
```

If you are just starting with shell programming, refer to the *Bash Guide for Beginners* (`http://tldp.org/LDP/Bash-Beginners-Guide/html/index.html`). You can use that guide, along with reference material such as the `bash` man page, to step through many examples of shell scripting techniques. If you use the C shell (`csh`), see *Introduction to the C Shell* (`http://docs.freebsd.org/44doc/usd/04.csh/paper.html`) for further information.

Summary

Despite the powerful Mac OS X interface, the shell is still the preferred interface for UNIX power users. The `bash` shell is used by default for all users. It includes many helpful features for recalling commands (history), completing commands, assigning aliases, and redirecting output from and input to commands. You can make powerful commands of your own using simple shell scripting techniques.

4

Working with Files

Everything in the Mac OS X file system can be viewed as a file. This includes data files, directories, devices, named pipes, links, and other types of files. Associated with each file is a set of information that determines who can access the file and how they can access it. This chapter covers many commands for exploring and working with files.

IN THIS CHAPTER

Setting permissions

Traversing the file system

Creating and copying files

Using hard/symbolic links

Changing file attributes

Searching for files

Listing and verifying files

Understanding File Types

Directories and regular files are the file types you will use most often, by far. However, you'll encounter several other types of files as you use Mac OS X. From the command line, there are many ways you can create, find, and list different types of files.

Files that provide access to the hardware components on your computer are referred to as *device files*. There are character and block devices. You can use *hard links* and *soft links* to make the same file accessible from different locations. Regular users will also use, though less directly, *named pipes* and *sockets*, which provide access points for processes to communicate with each other.

Using Regular Files

Regular files consist of data files (documents, music, images, archives, and so on) and commands (binaries and scripts). You can determine the type of a file using the file command. In the following example, you change to the directory containing Safari configuration files and use file to view some of the file types in that directory:

```
$ cd ~/library/safari
$ file *
Bookmarks.plist:    Apple binary property list
```

```
Downloads.plist:    XML 1.0 document text
Form Values:        data
History.plist:      Apple binary property list
HistoryIndex.sk:    data
LastSession.plist:  Apple binary property list
WebpageIcons.db:    SQLite database (Version 3)
   …
```

The `file` command that was run shows document and image files of different formats, related to Safari. It can look inside the files and determine whether a file contains text with HTML markup (used in web pages), plain text, or an image.

Regular files can be created by any application that can save its data. If you just want to **create some blank files to start with**, there are many ways to do that. Here are two examples:

```
$ touch /tmp/newfile.txt              Create a blank file
$ cat /dev/null > /tmp/newfile2.txt   Create an empty file
```

Doing **a long list on a file is another way to determine its file type**. For example:

```
$ ls -l /tmp/newfile2.txt       List a file to see its type
-rw-rw-r-- 1 chris chris 0 Sep 5 14:19 newfile2
```

A dash in the first character of the 10-character permission information (`-rw-rw-r--`) indicates that the item is a regular file. (Permissions are explained in the section "Setting File/Directory Permissions" later in this chapter.) Commands are also regular files but are usually saved as executables. Here are some examples:

```
$ ls -l /usr/bin/apropos
-r-xr-xr-x 1 root wheel 2248 Jan 12 2007 /usr/bin/apropos
$ file /usr/bin/apropos
/usr/bin/apropos: Bourne shell script text executable
$ file /bin/ls

/bin/ls: Mach-O universal binary with 2 architectures
/bin/ls (for architecture i386):       Mach-O executable i386
/bin/ls (for architecture ppc7400):    Mach-O executable ppc
```

This shows that the `apropos` command is executable by the x settings for owner, group, and others. By running `file` on `apropos`, you can see that it is a shell script. That's opposed to a binary executable, such as the `ls` command indicated earlier.

Using Directories

A *directory* is a container for files and subdirectories. Directories are set up in a hierarchy from the root (/) down to multiple subdirectories, each separated by a slash (/). Directories are called *folders* when you access them in Finder.

To create new directories for storing your data, you can use the `mkdir` command. Here are examples of using `mkdir` to **create directories in different ways**:

```
$ mkdir /tmp/new          Create "new" directory in /tmp
$ mkdir -p /tmp/a/b/c/new  Create parent directories as needed for "new"
$ mkdir -m 700 /tmp/new2   Create new2 with drwx——— permissions
```

The first `mkdir` command simply adds the `new` directory to the existing `/tmp` directory. The second example creates directories as needed (subdirectories a, b, and c) to create the resulting `new` directory. The last command adds the -m option to set directory permissions as well.

You can **identify the file as a directory** because the first character in the 10-character permission string for a directory is a `d`:

```
$ file /tmp/new
/tmp/new: directory
$ ls -ld /tmp/new
drwxr-xr-x  2 chris chris 4096 Sep  5 14:53  /tmp/new
```

Note also that the execute bits (x) must be on if you want people to be able to `cd` to that directory.

Using Symbolic and Hard Links

Instead of copying files and directories to different parts of the file system, links can be set up to access that same file from multiple locations. Mac OS X supports both *soft links* (usually called *symbolic links*) and *hard links*.

When you try to open a *symbolic link* that points to a file or change to one that points to a directory, the command you run acts on the file or directory that is the target of that link. The target has its own set of permissions and ownership that you cannot see from the symbolic link. The symbolic link can exist on a different disk partition than the target. In fact, the symbolic link can exist even if the target doesn't.

> **NOTE** *When you use commands such as* tar *to back up files that include symbolic links, there are ways of choosing whether or not the actual file the symbolic link points to is archived. If you do back up the actual file, restoring the file can cause the link to be overwritten (which may not be what you want). See the* tar *man page for details on different ways to back up symbolic links.*

A hard link can be used only on files, not directories, and is basically a way of giving multiple names to the same physical file. Every physical file has at least one hard link, which is commonly thought of as the file itself. Any additional names (hard links) that point to that single physical file must be on the same partition as the original target file (in fact, one way to tell that files are hard links is that they all have the same inode number).

Changing permission, ownership, date/timestamps, or content of any hard link to a file results in all the others being changed as well. However, deleting one link will not remove the file; it will continue to exist until the last link (or, technically, the last inode) to the file is deleted.

Here are some examples of using the ln command to **create hard and symbolic links:**

```
$ touch myfile
$ ln myfile myfile-hardlink
$ ln -s myfile myfile-symlink
$ ls -li myfile*
292007 -rw-rw-r--  3 francois francois 0 Mar 25 00:07 myfile
292007 -rw-rw-r--  3 francois francois 0 Mar 25 00:07 myfile-hardlink
292008 lrwxr-xr-x  2 francois francois 6 Mar 25 00:09 myfile-symlink -> myfile
```

Note that after creating the hard and symbolic link files, you use the ls -li command to list the results. The -li option shows the inodes associated with each file. You can see that myfile and myfile-hardlink both have the inode number of 292007 (signifying the exact same file on the hard disk). The myfile-symlink symbolic link has a different inode number; and although the hard link simply appears as a file (-), the symbolic link is identified as a link (1) with wide-open permissions. You won't know if you can access the file the symbolic link points to until you try it or list the link target.

Using Device Files

When applications need to communicate with your computer's hardware, they direct data to *device files*. By convention, device files are stored in the /dev directory. Historically, devices were generally divided into block devices (such as storage media) and character devices (such as serial ports and terminal devices). Mac OS X, however, uses only character devices to communicate with the hardware.

Here are **examples of device files:**

```
$ ls -l /dev/*          List devices
crw-r----- 1 root  operator  0,  94 Jan 29 19:12 acd0    CD drive
crw-r----- 1 root  operator  0,  85 Jan 29 19:12 ad0     Hard Drive
crw--w---- 1 chris tty       0, 100 Jan 31 06:07 ttyp0   Remote login terminal
crw------- 1 chris tty       0,  60 Jan 30 07:18 ttyv0   First virtual terminal
crw------- 1 root  wheel     0,  61 Jan 29 19:12 ttyv1   Second virtual terminal
```

Using Named Pipes and Sockets

When you want to allow one process to send information to another process, you can simply pipe (|) the output from one to the input of the other. However, to provide a presence in the file system from which a process can communicate with other processes, you can create *named pipes* or *sockets*. Named pipes are typically used for interprocess communication on the local system, whereas sockets can be used for processes to communicate over a network.

Named pipes and sockets are often set up by applications in the /tmp directory. Here are some **examples of named pipes and sockets:**

```
$ ls -l /tmp/.TV-chris/tvtimefifo-local /tmp/.X11-unix/X0
prw-------  1 chris chris 0 Sep 26  2007 /tmp/.TV-chris/tvtimefifo-local
srwx------  1 chris wheel 0 Sep  4 01:30 /tmp/fam-chris/fam-
```

The first listing is a named pipe set up by a TV card player (note the p at the beginning indicating a named pipe). The second listing is a socket set up for interprocess communications.

To **create your own named pipe,** use the mkfifo command as follows:

```
$ mkfifo mypipe
$ ls -l mypipe
prw-r--r--  1 chris chris 0 Sep 26 00:57 mypipe
```

To find where named pipes and sockets exist on your system, you can use the -type option to the find command, as described later in this chapter.

Setting File and Directory Permissions

You can restrict the ability to access files, run commands, and change to a directory with permission settings for user, group, and other users. When you have a long list (ls -l) of files and directories, the beginning 10 characters shown indicate what the item is (file, directory, character device, and so on), along with whether or not the item can be read, written, or executed. Figure 4-1 illustrates the meaning of those 10 characters.

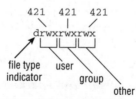

Figure 4-1: Read, write, and
execute permissions are set for files and directories

To follow along with the examples in this section, create a directory called /tmp/test and a file called /tmp/test/hello.txt. Then do a long listing of those two items, as follows:

```
$ mkdir /tmp/test
$ echo "some text" > /tmp/test/hello.txt
$ ls -ld /tmp/test/ /tmp/test/hello.txt
drwxrwxr-x  2 francois wheel 4096 Mar 21 13:11 /tmp/test
-rw-r--r--  2 francois wheel   10 Mar 21 13:11 /tmp/test/hello.txt
```

After creating the directory and file, the first character of the long listing shows /tmp/test as a directory (d) and hello.txt as a file (-). Other types of files that would appear as the first character include character devices (c), block devices (b) or symbolic links (1), named pipes (p), and sockets (s).

The next nine characters represent the permissions set on the file and directory. The first rwx indicates that the owner (francois) has read, write, and execute permissions on the directory. Likewise, the group wheel has the same permission (rwx). All other users have only read and execute permission (r-x); the dash indicates the missing write permission. For the hello.txt file, the user and group have read permission (r--) and others have read permission (r--).

When you set out to change permissions, each permission can be represented by an octal number (where read is 4, write is 2, and execute is 1) or a letter (rwx). Generally speaking, read permission lets you view the contents of the directory, write lets you change (add or modify) the contents of the directory, and execute lets you change to (in other words, access) the directory.

If you don't like the permissions currently set on the files or directories you own, you can change those permissions using the chmod command.

Changing Permissions with chmod

The chmod command enables you to change the access permissions of files and directories. Table 4-1 shows several chmod command lines and how they change access to the directory or file.

Table 4-1: Changing Directory and File Access Permission

chmod Command (Octal or Letters)	Original Permission	New Permission	Description
chmod 0700	any	drwx------	The directory's owner can read or write files in that directory, as well as change to it. All other users (except root) have no access.

Table 4-1: Changing Directory and File Access Permission *(continued)*

chmod Command (Octal or Letters)	Original Permission	New Permission	Description
chmod 0711	any	drwx--x--x	Same as 0700 for owner. All others can change to the directory, but not view or change files in the directory. This can be useful for server hardening, whereby you prevent someone from listing directory contents but allow access to a file in the directory if someone already knows it's there.
chmod go+r	drwx------	drwxr--r--	Adding read permission to a directory may not give desired results. Without execute on, others can't view the contents of any files in that directory.
chmod 0777			
chmod a=rwx	any	drwxrwxrwx	All permissions are wide open. Anyone anywhere in the world can read, write, or execute this file. Obviously, this isn't secure at all.
chmod 0000			
chmod a-rwx	any	d---------	All permissions are closed. This is good to protect a directory from errant changes, but backup programs that run as non-root may fail to back up the directory's contents.

Continued

Table 4-1: Changing Directory and File Access Permission *(continued)*

chmod Command (Octal or Letters)	Original Permission	New Permission	Description
chmod 666	any	-rw-rw-rw-	Open read/write permissions completely on a file
chmod go-rw	-rw-rw-rw-	-rw-------	Don't let anyone except owner view, change, or delete the file.
chmod 644	any	-rw-r--r--	Only the owner can change or delete the file, but all can view it.

The first 0 in the mode line can usually be dropped (e.g., you can use 777 instead of 0777). That placeholder has special meaning. It is an octal digit that can be used on commands (executables) to indicate that the command can either run as a set-UID program (4), run as a set-GID program (2), or become a *sticky* program (1). With set-UID and set-GID, the command runs with the assigned user or group permissions (instead of running with the permissions of the user or group that launched the command).

> **WARNING!** SUID *should not be used on shell scripts. A shell script that is owned by the root user is vulnerable to being exploited, which may result in an attacker gaining access to a shell with root user permissions.*

Having the sticky bit on for a directory prevents users from removing or renaming files from that directory that they don't own (/tmp is an example). Given the right permission settings, however, users can change the contents of files they don't own in a sticky bit directory. The final permission character is t instead of x on a sticky directory. A command with the sticky bit turned on used to cause the command to stay in memory, even while not being used. This is an old UNIX feature that is not supported in most modern BSD, UNIX, and Linux systems.

The -R option is a handy feature of the chmod command. With -R, you can **recursively change permissions of all files and directories starting from a point in the file system.** Here are some examples:

```
# chmod -R 700 /tmp/test     Open permission only to owner below /tmp/test
# chmod -R 000 /tmp/test     Close all permissions below /tmp/test
# chmod -R a+rwx /tmp/test    Open all permissions to all below /tmp/test
```

Note that the -R option is inclusive of the directory you indicate. The preceding permissions, for example, would change for the /tmp/test directory itself, and not just for the files and directories below that directory.

Setting the umask

Permissions given to a file or directory are assigned originally at the time that item
is created. How those permissions are set is based on the user's current *umask* value.
Using the umask command, you can **set the permissions given to files and directories** when
you create them:

```
$ umask 0066    Make directories drwx-x-x and files -rw----
$ umask 0077    Make directories drwx---- and files -rw----
$ umask 0022    Make directories drwxr-xr-x and files -rw-r-r-
$ umask 0777    Make directories d------ and files ------
```

Changing Ownership

When you create a file or directory, your user account is assigned to that file or directory. So is your primary group. As root user, you can **change the ownership (user) and group
assigned to a file to a different user or group** using the chown and chgrp commands, respectively. Here are some examples:

```
# chown chris test/         Change owner to chris
# chown chris:market test/   Change owner to chris and group to market
# chgrp market test/         Change group to market
# chown -R chris test/       Change all files below test/ to owner chris
```

The recursive option to chown (-R) just shown is useful if you need to change the ownership of an entire directory structure. As with chmod, using chown recursively changes
permissions for the directory named, along with its contents. For example, you might
use chown recursively when a person leaves a company or stops using your web service.
You can use chown -R to reassign their entire /Users directory to a different user.

Traversing the File System

Basic commands for changing directories (cd), checking the current directory (pwd),
and listing directory content (ls) are well known even to casual shell users, so this
section focuses on some less-common options to those commands, as well as other
lesser-known features for moving around the file system. Here are some quick examples of cd for **moving around the file system:**

```
$ cd                  Change to your home directory
$ cd $HOME            Change to your home directory
$ cd ~                Change to your home directory
$ cd ~francois        Change to francois' home directory
$ cd -                Change to previous working directory
$ cd $OLDPWD          Change to previous working directory (bash shell)
$ cd ~/web            Change to web in your home directory (if it exists)
$ cd ..               Change to parent of current directory
$ cd /usr/bin         Change to usr/bin from root directory
$ cd usr/bin          Change to usr/bin beneath current directory
```

If you want to **find out what your current directory is,** use pwd (print working directory):

```
$ pwd
/Users/myerman
```

Creating *symbolic links* is a way to access a file from other parts of the file system (see the section "Using Symbolic and Hard Links" earlier in this chapter for more information on symbolic and hard links). However, symbolic links can cause some confusion about how parent directories are viewed. The following commands **create a symbolic link** to the /tmp directory from your home directory and indicate how to tell where you are related to a linked directory:

```
$ cd $HOME
$ ln -s /tmp tmp-link
$ ls -l tmp-link
lrwxrwxrwx 1 myerman myerman 13 Mar 24 12:41 tmp-link -> /tmp
$ cd tmp-link/
$ pwd
/Users/myerman/tmp-link
$ pwd -P                  Show the permanent location
/tmp
$ pwd -L                  Show the link location
/Users/myerman/tmp-link
$ cd -L ..                Go to the parent of the link location
$ pwd
/Users/myerman
$ cd tmp-link
$ cd -P ..                Go to the parent of the permanent location
$ pwd
/
```

Using the -P and -L options to pwd and cd, you can **work with symbolically linked directories in their permanent or link locations,** respectively. For example, cd -L .. takes you up one level to your home directory, whereas cd -P .. takes you up one level above the permanent directory (/). Likewise, the -P and -L options to pwd show permanent and link locations, respectively.

If you use the csh or bash shells, they can remember a list of working directories for you. Such a list can be useful if you want to return to previously visited directories. That list is organized in the form of a stack. Use pushd and popd to **add and remove directories:**

```
$ pwd
/Users/myerman
$ pushd /usr/share/man/
/usr/share/man ~
$ pushd /var/log/
/var/log /usr/share/man ~
$ dirs
/var/log /usr/share/man ~
```

```
$ dirs -v
 0  /var/log
 1  /usr/share/man
 2  ~
$ popd
/usr/share/man ~
$ pwd
/usr/share/man
$ popd
~
$ pwd
/Users/myerman
```

The dirs, pushd, and popd commands can also be used to manipulate the order of directories on the stack. For example, pushd -0 pushes the last directory on the stack to the top of the stack (making it the current directory). The pushd -2 command pushes the third directory from the bottom of the stack to the top.

Copying Files

Provided you have write permission to the target directory, copying files and directories can be done with some fairly simple commands. The standard cp command will copy a file to a new name or the same name in a new directory, with a new timestamp associated with the new file. Other options to cp enable you to retain date/timestamps, copy recursively, and prompt before overwriting. Here are some examples:

```
# cd ; mkdir public_html ; touch index.html
# cp -i index.html public_html/        Copy with new time stamp
# cp -il index.html public_html/        Create hard link instead of copy
# cp -Rv public_html/ /mnt/usb/        Copy all files recursively (with verbose)
```

The preceding examples show ways of copying files related to a personal web server. In the first cp example just shown, if an index.html file exists in public_html, you are prompted before overwriting it with the new file. In the next example, the index .html file is hard-linked to a file of the same name in the public_html directory. In that case, because both hard links point to the same file, editing the file from either location will change the contents of the file in both locations. (The link can be done only if public_html/ and your home directory are in the same file system.)

The cp -Rv command copies all files below the public_html/ directory, updating ownership and permission settings to match those of the user running the command. It also uses current date/timestamps. If, for example, /mnt/usb represented a USB flash drive, that command would be a way to copy the contents of your personal web server to that drive.

The dd command is another way to **copy data**. This command is very powerful because on Mac OS X, everything is a file, including hardware peripherals. Here is an example:

```
$ dd if=/dev/zero of=/tmp/mynullfile count=1
1+0 records in
1+0 records out
512 bytes transferred in 0.000253 secs (2022113 bytes/sec)
```

/dev/zero is a special file that generates null characters. In the example just shown, the dd command takes /dev/zero as the input file and outputs to /tmp/mynullfile. The count is the number of blocks. By default, a block is 512 bytes. The result is a 512-byte long file full of null characters. You could use less or vi to view the contents of the file, but a better tool to view the file would be the od (Octal Dump) command:

```
$ od -vt x1 /tmp/mynullfile        View an octal dump of a file
```

Here's another example of the dd command. This sets the block size to 2 bytes and copies 10 blocks (20 bytes):

```
$ dd if=/dev/zero of=/tmp/mynullfile count=10 bs=2
10+0 records in
10+0 records out
20 bytes transferred in 0.000367 secs (54507 bytes/sec)
```

> **WARNING!** *The following dd commands overwrite the contents of your disk partitions. To be on the safe side, examples show data being written to USB drives. That enables you to use something such as a USB memory stick, which we presume can be overwritten without harming the contents of your hard drives. Don't try these commands if you have any confusion about the devices you are using.*

The following command line **clones the first partition of the second IDE drive** to the first USB drive. This can be useful for backing up a small partition to a USB memory stick. Note that the following command will overwrite the contents of your USB drive:

```
# dd if=/dev/ad1s1 of=/dev/da0s1
```

The next example **makes a compressed backup** of the first partition of the primary master IDE drive. Typically, the partition should be unmounted before a backup such as this:

```
# umount /dev/da0s1
# dd if=/dev/da0s1 | gzip > bootpart.gz
```

The following command copies a boot image (diskboot.img) to your USB flash drive (assuming the drive appears as /dev/da0):

```
# dd if=diskboot.img of=/dev/da0
```

This example copies the master boot record (MBR) from the second IDE hard drive to a file named mymbrfile:

```
# dd if=/dev/ad1s1 of=mymbrfile bs=512 count=1
```

If you add the dd_rescue program to your BSD system (pkg_add -r dd_rescue), you can create an ISO image with a command similar to dd but it has many options and much more verbose feedback:

```
# dd_rescue /dev/acd0 myimage.iso
dd_rescue: (info): ipos:      139264.0k, opos:      139264.0k, xferd:
139264.0k8.0k
                   errs:            0, errxfer:       0.0k, succxfer:
139264.0k
          +curr.rate:    6702kB/s, avg.rate: 8312kB/s, avg.load: 16.6%
```

Searching for Files

Your Mac OS X system can be configured to keep a database of all the files in the file system (with a few exceptions defined in /etc/locate.rc) by periodically running the /usr/libexec/locate.updatedb script. The locate command enables you to search that database. The results come back instantly because the database is searched and not the actual file system. Before locate was available, most Mac OS X users ran the find command to find files using the command-line utility. Both locate and find are covered here.

Generating the locate Database

You can generate the locate database by running the following script:

```
$ /usr/libexec/locate.updatedb
```

Note that by running this script as a regular user, the database will include only files that are accessible to all users, as well as that user in particular. You can run this script with sudo to gather all files on your computer, but that could pose a security risk by allowing nonroot users to see files you might otherwise want hidden from their sites.

After you run the locate.updatedb script, the /var/db/locate.database is created. You could add that script to a cron job to run periodically. You are now ready to use the locate command to search for files.

Finding Files with locate

Because the database contains the name of every node in the file system, and not just commands, you can use `locate` to **find commands, devices, man pages, data files, or anything else identified by a name** in the file system. Here is an example:

```
$ locate apache
...
 /Applications/MAMP/Library/bin/apachectl
...
```

The preceding example found the apachectl binary. `locate` is case sensitive unless you use the `-i` option, as shown here:

```
$ locate -i ImageMagick-6
/usr/local/share/ImageMagick-6.3.6
/usr/local/share/ImageMagick-6.3.6/ChangeLog
...
```

Here are some examples using `locate` with regular expressions and output limits:

```
$ locate *python*vim          Locate files with python and vim in the name
...
/usr/share/vim/vim70/autoload/pythoncomplete.vim
/usr/share/vim/vim70/ftplugin/python.vim
/usr/share/vim/vim70/indent/python.vim
/usr/share/vim/vim70/syntax/python.vim
/usr/share/vim/vim72/autoload/pythoncomplete.vim
/usr/share/vim/vim72/ftplugin/python.vim
/usr/share/vim/vim72/indent/python.vim
/usr/share/vim/vim72/syntax/python.vim
$ locate -l 5 python          Limit number of files found to five
/Applications/MAMP/Library/lib/python2.3
/Applications/MAMP/Library/lib/python2.3/site-packages
/Applications/MAMP/Library/lib/python2.3/site-packages/drv_libxml2.py
/Applications/MAMP/Library/lib/python2.3/site-packages/libxml2.py
/Applications/MAMP/Library/lib/python2.3/site-packages/libxml2mod.la

locate: [show only 5 lines]
```

You can find information about the location and size of the `locate` database as follows:

```
$ locate -S
Database: /var/db/locate.database
Compression: Front: 21.64%, Bigram: 61.00%, Total: 15.57%
Filenames: 276585, Characters: 13071602, Database size: 2035326
Bigram characters: 793708, Integers: 9379, 8-Bit characters: 0
```

To **update the `locate` database immediately,** run the `locate.updatedb` command again manually:

```
$ /usr/libexec/locate.updatedb
```

Locating Files with find

Before the days of `locate`, the way to find files was with the `find` command. Although `locate` will come up with a file faster, `find` has many other powerful options for finding files based on attributes other than the name.

> **NOTE** *Searching the entire file system can take a long time to complete. Before searching the whole file system, consider searching a subset of the file system or excluding certain directories or remotely mounted file systems.*

This example searches the root file system (/) recursively for files named `wlan`:

```
$ find / -name "wlan_wep.ko" -print
find: /tmp/fam-root: Permission denied
find: /usr/local/etc/samba: Permission denied
/usr/share/man/man4/wlan_wep.4.gz
/usr/share/man/cat4/wlan_wep.4.gz
/boot/kernel/wlan_wep.ko
```

Running `find` as a normal user can result in long lists of `Permission denied` as `find` tries to enter a directory to which you do not have permissions. You can **filter out the inaccessible directories:**

```
$ find / -name wlan_wep.ko 2>&1 | grep -v "Permission denied"
```

Or, you can **send all errors to the /dev/null bit bucket:**

```
$ find / -name wlan_wep.ko 2> /dev/null
```

Because searches with `find` are case sensitive and must match the name exactly (e100 won't match e100.ko), you can **use regular expressions to make your searches more inclusive.** Here's an example:

```
$ find / -name 'wlan_wep*' 2> /dev/null
/boot/kernel/wlan_wep.ko
/boot/GENERIC/wlan_wep.ko
/usr/share/man/man4/wlan_wep.4.gz
...
```

You can also **find files based on timestamps.** The following command line finds files in /usr/bin/ that have been accessed in the past two minutes:

```
$ find /usr/bin/ -amin -2
```

```
/usr/bin/
/usr/bin/find
```

This finds files that have not been accessed in /Users/myerman for over 60 days:

```
$ find /Users/myerman/ -atime +60
```

Use the -type d option to find directories. The following command line finds all directories under /etc and redirects stderr to the bit bucket (/dev/null):

```
$ find /etc -type d -print 2> /dev/null
```

The following command line finds files in ~ with permissions that match 777:

```
$ find ~ -perm 777
~/documents/file1.doc
~/documents/file2.doc
...
```

The exec option to find is very powerful, as it lets you act on the files found with the find
command. The following command finds all the files in /var owned by the user marlowe (which must be a valid user) and executes the ls -l command on each one:

```
$ find /var -user marlowe -exec ls -l {} \;
```

An alternative to the find command's exec option is xargs:

```
$ find /var -user marlowe | xargs ls -l
```

There are big differences in how the two commands just shown operate, leading to
very different performance. The find -exec command spawns the command ls for
each result it finds. The xargs command works more efficiently by passing many
results as input to a single ls command.

To negate a search criterion, place an exclamation point (!) before that criterion. The next
example finds all the files that are not owned by the group root and are regular files,
and then does an ls -l on each:

```
$ find / ! -group wheel -type f  2> /dev/null | xargs ls -l
```

The next example finds the files in /sbin that are regular files and are not executable
by others, and then feeds them to an ls -l command:

```
$ find /sbin/ -type f ! -perm o+x  | xargs ls -l
```

Finding files by size is a great way to determine what is filling up your hard disks. The following command line finds all files that are greater than 10MB (+10M), lists those files from largest to smallest (ls -lS), and directs that list to a file (/tmp/bigfiles.txt):

```
$ find / -xdev -size +10M  | xargs ls -lS > /tmp/bigfiles.txt
```

In this example, the -xdev option prevents any mounted file systems, besides the root file system, from being searched. This is a good way to keep the find command from searching special file systems (such as the /proc file system, if that is mounted) and any remotely mounted file systems, as well as other locally mounted file systems.

Using Other Commands to Find Files

Other commands for finding files include the whereis and which commands. Here is an example of the whereis command:

```
$ whereis man
man: /usr/bin/man /usr/share/man/man1/man1.gz
```

The whereis command is useful because it not only finds commands, but also **finds man pages and configuration files associated with a command.** From the example of whereis for the word man, you can see the man executable, its configuration file, and the location of man pages for the man command.

The which command, shown in the following example, is useful when you're looking for the actual location of an executable file in your PATH:

```
$ which bash
/bin/bash
```

Finding Out More About Files

Now that you know how to find files, you can get more information about those files. Using less common options to the ls command enables you to list information about a file that you won't see when you run ls without options. Commands such as file help you identify a file's type. With md5sum and sha1sum, you can verify the validity of a file.

Listing Files

Although you are probably quite familiar with the ls command, you may not be familiar with many of the useful options for ls that can help you find out a lot about the files on your system. Here are some examples of **using ls to display long lists** (-1) of files and directories:

```
$ ls -1      Files and directories in current directory
$ ls -la     Includes files/directories beginning with dot (.)
$ ls -lt     Orders files by time recently changed
$ ls -lS     Orders files by size (largest first)
$ ls -li     Lists the inode associated with each file
$ ls -ln     List numeric user/group IDs, instead of names
$ ls -lh     List file sizes in human-readable form (K, M, etc.)
$ ls -lR     List files recursively, from current and subdirectories
```

When you list files, there are also ways to **have different types of files appear differently** in the listing:

```
$ ls -F                Add a character to indicate file type
BSD6.2@    BSD7/   memo.txt   pipefile|   script.sh*  xpid.socket=
$ ls -G                Show file types as different colors
$ ls -C                Show files listing in columns
```

In the -F example, the output shows several different file types. The BSD6.2@ indicates a symbolic link to a directory, FC8/ is a regular directory, memo.txt is a regular file (no extra character), pipefile| is a named pipe (created with mkfifo), script .sh* is an executable file, and xpid.socket= is a socket. The last two examples display different file types in different colors and list output in columns, respectively.

Verifying Files

When files such as software packages and CD or DVD images are shared over the Internet, often a sha1sum or md5sum file is published with it. Those files contain checksums that can be used to ensure that the file you downloaded is exactly the one that the repository published.

The following are examples of downloading an ISO image file, and then using the md5 and sha256 commands to **verify checksums of the file:**

```
$ wget -c ftp://ftp.freebsd.org/pub/FreeBSD/releases/i386/ISO-IMAGES/6.3/6.3-
RELEASE-i386-disc1.iso
$ md5 6.3-RELEASE-i386-disc1.iso
MD5 (6.3-RELEASE-i386-disc1.iso) =
    cdb0dfa4b2db3e4c9cc19138f4fb2ada
$ sha256 6.3-RELEASE-i386-disc1.iso
SHA156 (6.3-RELEASE-i386-disc1.iso) =
    15081a56d184a18c7cc3a5c3cd0d7d5b7d9304c9cc1d5fc40d875b0fd3047721
```

Which command you choose depends on whether the provider of the file you are checking distributed md5sum or sha1sum information. FreeBSD offers both md5 and sha1 files. For example, here is what the CHECKSUM.MD5 file for the FreeBSD 6.3 distribution looks like:

```
MD5 (6.3-RELEASE-i386-bootonly.iso) = ab1db0ae643e8c12ddbe855f533b8fae
MD5 (6.3-RELEASE-i386-disc1.iso) = cdb0dfa4b2db3e4c9cc19138f4fb2ada
MD5 (6.3-RELEASE-i386-disc2.iso) = e73a3d9cf5f3bfbf07384ef0a93ae5d5
MD5 (6.3-RELEASE-i386-disc3.iso) = 123840107a5578ce22875c440d41f453
MD5 (6.3-RELEASE-i386-docs.iso) = 17aa87ccfb01f4453d8ce078874029ab
```

With all the ISO files listed in this CHECKSUM.MD5 file contained in the current directory, you can verify them all at once using the -c option and the Linux-compatible md5sum command. Here is an example:

```
$ /usr/compat/linux/usr/bin/md5sum -c CHECKSUM.MD5
6.3-RELEASE-i386-bootonly.iso: OK
6.3-RELEASE-i386-disc1.iso: OK
6.3-RELEASE-i386-disc2.iso: OK
6.3-RELEASE-i386-disc3.iso: OK
6.3-RELEASE-i386-docs.iso: OK
```

To verify only one of the files listed in the checksum file, you could do something like the following:

```
$ grep bootonly CHECKSUM.MD5 | /usr/compat/linux/usr/bin/md5sum -c
6.3-RELEASE-i386-bootonly.iso: OK
```

If you had a SHA1SUM file instead of an MD5SUM file to check against, you could use the sha1sum command in the same way. By combining the find command described earlier in this chapter with the m5 command, you can verify any part of your file system. For example, here's how to create an MD5 checksum for every file in the /etc directory so they can be checked later to see if any have changed:

```
# find /etc -type f -exec md5 {} \; 2>/dev/null > /tmp/md5.list
```

The result of the previous command line is a /tmp/md5.list file that contains a 128-bit checksum for every file in the /etc directory. Later, you could type the following command to see if any of those files have changed:

```
# cd /etc
# /usr/compat/linux/usr/bin/md5sum -c /tmp/md5.list | grep -v 'OK'
./hosts.allow: FAILED
md5sum: WARNING: 1 of 1668 computed checksums did NOT match
```

As shown in the output, only one file changed (hosts.allow), so the next step is to check the changed file and see if the changes to that file were intentional.

Summary

Dozens of commands are available for exploring and working with files in Mac OS X. Commands such as chmod can change the permissions associated with a file.

To move around the file system, people use the cd command most often. However, to move repeatedly among the same directories, you can use the pushd and popd commands to work with a stack of directories.

Copying files is done with the cp command, but the dd command can be used to copy files (such as disk images) from a device (such as a CD-ROM drive). For creating directories, you can use the mkdir command.

Instead of keeping multiple copies of a file around on the file system, you can use symbolic links and hard links to have multiple filenames point to the same file or directory. Symbolic links can be anywhere in the file system, whereas hard links must exist on the same partition as the original file.

To search for files, Mac OS X offers the locate and find commands. To verify the integrity of files you download from the Internet, you can use the md5, sha256, md5sum, and sha1sum commands.

5

Manipulating Text

With only a shell available on the first UNIX systems (on which BSD systems were based), using those systems meant dealing primarily with commands and plain text files. Documents, program code, configuration files, e-mail, and almost anything you created or configured was represented by text files. To work with those files, developers created many text manipulation tools.

Despite having graphical tools for working with text, most seasoned UNIX users find command-line tools to be more efficient and convenient. Text editors such as Vi (Vim), Emacs, Nano, and Pico are available with most BSD distributions, including Mac OS X. Commands such as grep, sed, and awk can be used to find, and possibly change, pieces of information within text files.

This chapter explains how to use many popular commands for working with text files on Mac OS X. It also explores some of the less common uses of text manipulation commands that you might find interesting.

Matching Text with Regular Expressions

Many of the tools for working with text enable you to use *regular expressions*, sometimes referred to as *regex* or RegEx, to identify the text you are looking for based on some pattern. You can use these strings to find text within a text editor, or use them with search commands to scan multiple files for the strings of text you want.

A RegEx search pattern can include a specific string of text (as in a word such as *UNIX*) or a location (such as the end of a line or the beginning of a word). It can also be specific (find just the word *hello*) or more inclusive (find any word beginning with *h* and ending with *o*).

Appendix C includes reference information for shell metacharacters that can be used in conjunction with regular expressions to do the exact kinds of matches you are looking for. This section shows examples of using regular expressions with several different tools you encounter throughout this chapter.

Table 5-1 shows some examples using basic regular expressions to match text strings.

Table 5-1: Matching Using Regular Expressions

Expression	Matches
a*	a, ab, abc, aecjejich
^a	Any "a" appearing at the beginning of a line
*a$	Any "a" appearing at the end of a line
a.c	Three-character strings that begin with "a" and end with "c"
[bcf]at	bat, cat, or fat
[a-d]at	aat, bat, cat, dat, but not Aat, Bat, and so on
[A-D]at	Aat, Bat, Cat, Dat, but not aat, bat, and so on
1[3-5]7	137, 147, and 157
\tHello	A tab character preceding the word Hello
\.[tT][xX][Tt]	.txt, .TXT, .TxT or other case combinations

Many examples of regular expressions are used in examples throughout this chapter. Keep in mind that not every command that incorporates RegEx uses its features the same way.

Editing Text Files

There are many text editors in the BSD/UNIX world. The most common editor is Vi, which can be found on virtually any UNIX system available today. That is why knowing how to at least make minor file edits in Vi is a critical skill for any BSD administrator. One day, if you find yourself in a minimalist, foreign BSD, Linux, or other UNIX environment, trying to bring a server back online, Vi is the tool that will almost always be there.

On Mac OS X, an improved version of Vi is available called Vim (it's already installed). Vim (Vi IMproved) will provide the most up-to-date, feature-rich, and user-friendly Vi editor. For more details about using Vi and Vim, refer to Appendix A.

Traditionally, the other popular UNIX text editor has been Emacs and its more graphical variant, XEmacs. Emacs is a powerful multi-function tool that can also act as a mail/news reader or shell and perform other functions. Emacs is also known for its very complex series of keyboard shortcuts that require three arms to execute properly.

In the mid-1990s, Emacs was ahead of Vi in terms of features. Now that Vim is widely available, both can provide all the text-editing features you'll ever need. If you are not already familiar with either Vi or Emacs, we recommend you start by learning Vi.

Many other command-line and GUI text editors are available for BSD systems. Text-based editors that you may find to be simpler than Vi and Emacs include Pico and Nano. Start any of those editors by typing its command name, optionally followed by the filename you want to edit. The following sections offer some quick descriptions of how to use each of those editors.

Using the Pico and Nano Editors

Pico is a popular, very small text editor, distributed as part of the Pine e-mail client. Although Pico is free, it is not truly open source. However, it is available on Mac OS X. As an alternative to Pico, you can use an open-source clone of Pico called Nano (Nano's *ano*ther editor). This section describes the Nano editor.

Nano (represented by the nano command) is a compact text editor that runs from the shell, but is screen oriented (owing to the fact that it is based on the curses library). Nano is popular with those who formerly used the Pine e-mail client because Nano's editing features are the same as those used by Pine's Pico editor. On the rare occasion that you don't have the Vi editor available, Nano may be available.

Unlike Vi, instead of having command and typing modes, you can just begin typing. To **open a text file for editing**, just type **nano** and the filename or use some of the following options:

```
$ nano memo.txt        Open memo.txt for editing
$ nano -B memo.txt     When saving, backup previous to ~.filename
$ nano -m memo.txt     Turn on mouse to move cursor (if supported)
$ nano +83 memo.txt    Begin editing on line 83
```

To **add text**, just begin typing. Use arrow keys to move the cursor left, right, up, or down. Use the Delete key to delete text under the cursor, or the Backspace to erase text to the left of the cursor. Press Enter to add a line break. Press Ctrl+G to read help text. Table 5-2 shows the control codes for Nano that are described on the help screen.

Table 5-2: Control Keys for Editing with Nano

Control Code	Function Key	Description
Ctrl+G	F1	Show help text. (Press Ctrl+X to exit help.)
Ctrl+X	F2	Exit Nano (or close current file buffer).
Ctrl+O	F3	Save the current file.
Ctrl+J	F4	Justify current text in the current paragraph.
Ctrl+R	F5	Insert a file into the current file.
Ctrl+W	F6	Search for text.
Ctrl+Y	F7	Go to the previous screen.
Ctrl+V	F8	Go to the next screen.
Ctrl+K	F9	Cut (and store) the current line or marked text.
Ctrl+U	F10	Uncut (paste) the previously cut line into the file.
Ctrl+C	F11	Display current cursor position.
Ctrl+T	F12	Start spell checking.
Ctrl+_		Go to selected line and column numbers.
Ctrl+\		Search and replace text.
Ctrl+6		Mark text, starting at the cursor (Ctrl+6 to unset mark).
Ctrl+F		Go forward one character.
Ctrl+B		Go back one character.
Ctrl+Space		Go forward one word.
Alt+Space		Go backward one word.
Ctrl+P		Go to the previous line.
Ctrl+N		Go to the next line.
Ctrl+A		Go to the beginning of the current line.
Ctrl+E		Go to the end of the current line.
Alt+9		Go to the beginning of the current paragraph.
Alt+0		Go to the end of the current paragraph.

Table 5-2: Control Keys for Editing with Nano *(continued)*

Control Code	Function Key	Description
Alt+\		Go to the first line of the file.
Alt+/		Go to the last line of the file.
Alt+]		Go to the bracket matching the current bracket.
Alt+=		Scroll down one line.
Alt+-		Scroll down up line.

Listing, Sorting, and Changing Text

Instead of just editing a single text file, you can use a variety of commands to display, search, and manipulate the contents of one or more text files at a time.

Listing Text Files

The most basic method to display the content of a text file is with the cat command. The cat command con*cat*enates (in other words, outputs as a string of characters) the contents of a text file to your display (by default). You can then use different shell metacharacters to **direct the contents of that file in different ways**. For example:

```
$ cat myfile.txt              Send entire file to the screen
$ cat myfile.txt > copy.txt   Direct file contents to another file
$ cat myfile.txt >> myotherfile.txt  Append file contents to another file
$ cat -s myfile.txt           Discard multiple consecutive blank lines
$ cat -n myfile.txt           Show line numbers with output
$ cat -b myfile.txt           Show line numbers only on non-blank lines
```

However, if your block of text is more than a few lines long, using cat by itself becomes impractical. That's when you need better tools to look at the beginning or the end, or page through the entire text.

To **view the top of a file**, use head:

```
$ head myfile.txt
$ cat myfile.txt | head
```

Both these command lines use the head command to output the top 10 lines of the file. You can specify the line count as a parameter to display any number of lines from the beginning of a file. For example:

```
$ head -n 50 myfile.txt       Show the first 50 lines of a file
$ ps auwx | head -n 15        Show the first 15 lines of ps output
```

This can also be done using this outdated (but shorter) syntax:

```
$ head -50 myfile.txt
$ ps auwx | head -15
```

You can use the `tail` command in a similar way to **view the end of a file or command output**:

```
$ tail -n 15 myfile.txt          Display the last 15 lines in a file
$ tail -15 myfile.txt            Display the last 15 lines in a file
$ ps auwx | tail -n 15           Display the last 15 lines of ps output
```

The `tail` command can also be used to **continuously watch the end of a file** as the file is written to by another program. This is very useful for reading live log files when troubleshooting apache, sendmail, or many other system services:

```
# tail -f /var/log/messages      Watch system messages live
# tail -f /var/log/maillog       Watch mail server messages live
# tail -f /var/log/auth.log      Watch login attempt messages live
```

Paging Through Text

When you have a large chunk of text and need to get to more than just its beginning or end, you need a tool to **page through the text**. The original UNIX system pager was the more command:

```
$ ps aux | more        Page through the output of ps (press spacebar)
$ more myfile.txt       Page through the contents of a file
```

However, `more` has some limitations. For example, in the first line of the preceding example, with `ps`, `more` could not scroll up. The `less` command was created as a more powerful and user-friendly `more`. (The common saying when `less` was introduced was "What is less? `less` is more!" We recommend you no longer use `more`; use `less` instead.

> **NOTE** *The* `less` *command has another benefit worth noting. Unlike text editors such as Vi, it does not read the entire file when it starts. This results in faster start-up times when viewing large files.*

The `less` command can be used with the same syntax as `more` in the preceding examples:

```
$ ps aux | less          Page through the output of ps
$ cat myfile.txt | less   Page through the contents of a file
$ less myfile.txt         Page through a text file
```

The `less` command enables you to **navigate** using the up and down arrow keys, PageUp, PageDown, and the spacebar. If you are using `less` on a file (not standard input), press v to open the current file in Vi. As in Vi, G takes you to the end of the file. F takes you to the end of the file and then scrolls the file as new input is added, similar to a `tail -f`.

As in Vi, while viewing a file with less, you can **search for a string** by pressing / (forward slash) followed by the string and Enter. To search for further occurrences, press / and Enter repeatedly. To search backwards, press ? followed by the search string and Enter.

To **scroll forward and back** while using less, use the f and b keys, respectively. For example, 10f scrolls forward ten lines, and 15b scrolls back 15 lines. Type **d** to scroll down half a screen, and **u** to scroll up half a screen.

Paginating Text Files with pr

The pr command provides a quick way to format a bunch of text into a form where it can be printed. This can be particularly useful if you want to print the results of some commands without having to open a word processor or text editor. With pr, you can **format text into pages with header information** such as date, time, filename, and page number. Here is an example:

```
$ ls ~/documents | sort | pr -4 | less     Paginate ports directory in 4 cols
```

In this example, the ls command lists the contents of the ~/documents directory and pipes that list to the sort command, to be sorted alphabetically. Next, that list is piped to the pr command, which converts the single-column list into four columns (-4) and paginates it. Finally, the less command enables you to page through the text.

Instead of paging through the output, you can **send the output to a file or a printer.** Here are some examples of that:

```
$ ls ~/documents | sort | pr -4 | less > pkg.txt    Send pr output to a file
$ ls ~/documents | sort | pr -4 | less | lpr        Send pr output to printer
```

Other **text manipulation** you can do with the pr command includes double-spacing the text (-d), or offsetting the text a certain number of spaces from the left margin (for example, -o 5 to indent five spaces from the left).

Searching for Text with grep

The grep command comes in handy when you need to **perform more advanced string searches in a file.** In fact, the phrase *to grep* has actually entered the computer jargon as a verb, just as *to Google* has entered the popular language. Here are examples of the grep command:

```
$ grep myerman myfile.txt            Show lines containing myerman
# grep -i ftp /etc/services          Show lines containing FTP
$ ps aux | grep init                 Show init lines from ps output
```

```
$ ps aux | grep "\[*\]"          Show bracketed commands
$ dmesg | grep "[ ]ata\|^ata"    Show ata kernel device information
```

In addition to being examples of the grep command, these command lines have some particular uses. By searching /etc/services for ftp, you can see port numbers associated with FTP services. Displaying bracketed commands that are output from the ps command is a way to see commands for which ps cannot display options. The last command checks the kernel buffer ring for any ATA device information, such as hard disks and CD-ROM drives.

The grep command can also **recursively search a few or a great many files at the same time.** The following command recursively searches (-R) files in the /usr/local/etc and /etc directories for the string ftp (-i for any case):

```
$ grep -Ri ftp /usr/local/etc /etc | less
```

Add line numbers (-n) to your grep command to **find the exact lines** where the search terms occur:

```
$ grep -Rin ftp /etc /usr/local/etc | less
```

To colorize the searched term in the search results, add the --color option:

```
# grep --color -Rin ftp /etc/services | less
```

By default, in a multi-file search, the filename is displayed for each search result. Use the -h option to **disable the display of filenames.** This example searches for the string relay in the files dmesg.today, dmesg.yesterday, and so on:

```
# grep -h acpi /var/log/dmesg*
```

If you want to **ignore case** when you search messages, use the -i option:

```
# grep -i audio /var/log/messages    Search file for audio (any case)
```

To **display only the name of the file** that includes the search term, add the -l option:

```
$ grep -Ril FTP /etc
```

To **display all lines that do not match the string,** add the -v option:

```
# grep -v "#" /etc/ttys | less  Show lines that don't contain comments
```

> **NOTE** *When piping the output of* ps *into* grep, *here's a trick to prevent the* grep *process from appearing in the* grep *results:*
>
> ```
> # ps aux | grep -v "grep"
> ```

Checking Word Counts with wc

There are times when you need to know the number of lines that match a search string. The wc command can be used to **count the lines** that it receives. For example, the following command lists how many times a specific IP address appears in log files:

```
$ grep 192.198.1.1 /var/log/* | wc -l
```

The wc command has other uses as well. By default, wc **prints the number of lines, words, and bytes in a file**:

```
$ wc ~/documents/project1/README    List counts for a single file
    385    3006   19945  ~/documents/project1/README
$ wc ~/documents/project2/*          List single counts/totals for many files
    385    3006   19945  ~/documents/project2/README
    118     813    5364  ~/documents/project2/coderules.doc
    ...
   6658   52200  339141  total
```

Sorting Output with sort

It can also be useful to **sort the content of a file or the output of a command**. This can be helpful in bringing order to disorderly output. The following examples list the names of all files in the ~/documents directory and sort the results in alphanumeric order (forward and reverse):

```
$ ls ~/documents | sort       Sort in alphanumeric order
$ ls ~/documents | sort -r    Sort in reverse alphanumeric order
```

The following command **sorts processes based on descending memory usage** (fourth field of ps output). The -k option specifies the key field to use for sorting. 4,4 indicates that the fourth field, and only the fourth field, is a key field.

```
$ ps aux | sort -r -k 4,4
```

Finding Text in Binaries with Strings

Sometimes you need to read the ASCII text that is inside a binary file. Occasionally, you can learn a lot about an executable that way. For those occurrences, use strings to **extract all the human-readable ASCII text**. Here are some examples:

```
$ strings /bin/ls | grep -i libc   Find occurrences of libc in ls
$ cat /bin/ls | strings             List all ASCII text in ls
$ strings /bin/ls                   List all ASCII text in ls
```

Replacing Text with sed

Finding text within a file is sometimes the first step toward replacing text. Editing streams of text is done using the sed command. The sed command is actually a full-blown scripting language. For the examples in this chapter, we cover basic text replacement with the sed command.

If you are familiar with text replacement commands in Vi, sed has some similarities. In the following example, you would **replace only the first occurrence per line** of *marlowe* with *kafka*. Here, sed takes its input from a pipe, while sending its output to stdout (your screen). The original file itself is not changed:

```
$ cat myfile.txt | sed s/marlowe/kafka/
```

Adding a g to the end of the substitution line, as in the following command, causes every occurrence of *marlowe* to be changed to *kafka*. In addition, in the following example, input is directed from the file myfile.txt, and output is directed to mynew-file.txt:

```
$ sed s/marlowe/kafka/g < myfile.txt > mynewfile.txt
```

The next example replaces the first occurrences of myname on each line in the /etc/hosts file with yourname. The output is directed to the /tmp/hosts file:

```
$ sed 's/myname/yourname/' < /etc/hosts > /tmp/hosts
```

Although the forward slash is the sed command's default delimiter, you can **change the delimiter** to any other character of your choice. Changing the delimiter can make your life easier when the string contains slashes. For example, the previous command line containing a path could be replaced with either of the following commands:

```
$ sed 's-/nsswitch.conf-/nsswitch.conf and stuff-' < /etc/hosts | grep nss
$ sed 's!/termios.h!/termios.h and stuff!' < /etc/gettytab | grep termios
```

In the first line shown, a dash (-) is used as the delimiter. In the second case, the exclamation point (!) is the delimiter.

The sed command can **run multiple substitutions at once**, by preceding each one with -e. Here, in the text streaming from myfile.txt, all occurrences of *marlowe* are changed to *MARLOWE,* and all occurrences of *kafka* are changed to *KAFKA*:

```
$ sed -e s/marlowe/MARLOWE/g -e s/kafka/KAFKA/g < myfile.txt
```

You can use sed to **add newline characters to a stream of text**. The following example is done from the bash shell. Where Enter appears, press the Enter key. The > on the second line is generated by bash, not typed in:

```
$ echo aaabccc | sed 's/b/\Enter
> /'
aaa
ccc
```

The trick just shown does not work on the left side of the sed substitution command. When you need to substitute newline characters, it's easier to use the tr command.

Translating or Removing Characters with tr

The tr command is an easy way to do simple character translations on-the-fly. In the following example, newlines are replaced with spaces, so all the files listed from the current directory are outputted on one line:

```
$ ls | tr '\n' ' '          Replace newline characters with spaces
```

The tr command can be used to replace one character with another, but it does not work with strings as sed does. The following command replaces all instances of the lowercase letter f with a capital F:

```
$ tr f F < myfile.txt       Replace every f in the file with F
```

You can also use the tr command to simply delete characters. Here are two examples:

```
$ ls | tr -d '\n'           Delete new lines (resulting in one line)
$ tr -d f < myfile.txt      Delete every letter f from the file
```

The tr command can do some nifty tricks when you specify ranges of characters to work on. Here's an example of changing lowercase letters to uppercase letters:

```
$ echo chris | tr a-z A-Z     Translate chris into CHRIS
CHRIS
```

The same result can be obtained with the following syntax:

```
$ echo chris | tr '[:lower:]' '[:upper:]'     Translate chris into CHRIS
```

Checking Differences Between Two Files with diff

When you have two versions of a file, it can be useful to know the differences between the two files. For example, when changing a configuration file, people often leave a copy of the original configuration file. When that occurs, you can use the diff command to discover which lines differ between your new configuration and the original configuration, in order to see what you have done. For example:

```
$ cp ~/documents/file1.txt ~/documents/file1.bak
Make some changes to the file1.txt file
$ diff ~/documents/file1.txt ~/documents/file1.bak
```

You can change the output of diff to what is known as *unified format*. Unified format can be easier to read by human beings. It adds three lines of context before and after each block of changed lines that it reports and then uses + and - to show the difference between the files. The following set of commands creates a file (f1.txt) containing a sequence of numbers (1–7), creates a file (f2.txt) with one of those numbers changed (using sed), and compares the two files using the diff command:

```
$ for NUM in 1 2 3 4 5 6 7; do echo $NUM >> f1.txt; done
$ cat f1.txt                    Display contents of f1.txt
1
2
3
4
5
6
7
$ sed s/4/FOUR/ < f1.txt > f2.txt    Change 4 to FOUR and send to f2.txt
$ diff f1.txt f2.txt
4c4                             Shows line 4 was changed in file
< 4
---
> FOUR
$ diff -u f1.txt f2.txt             Display unified output of diff
--- f1.txt 2007-09-07 18:26:06.000000000 -0500
+++ f2.txt 2007-09-07 18:26:39.000000000 -0500
@@ -1,7 +1,7 @@
1
2
3
-4
+FOUR
5
6
7
```

The diff -u output adds information such as modification dates and times to the regular diff output. The sdiff command can be used to give you yet another view. The sdiff command can **merge the output of two files** interactively, as shown in the following output:

```
$ sdiff f1.txt f2.txt
1                                          1
2                                          2
3                                          3
4                                        | FOUR
5                                          5
6                                          6
7                                          7
```

Another variation on the diff theme is vimdiff, which opens the two files side by side in Vim and outlines the differences in color.

The output of `diff -u` can be fed into the `patch` command. The `patch` command takes an old file and a diff file as input and **outputs a patched file**. Using the previous example, use the `diff` command between the two files to generate a patch and then apply the patch to the first file:

```
$ diff -u f1.txt f2.txt > patchfile.txt
$ patch f1.txt < patchfile.txt
Hmm...  Looks like a unified diff to me...
The text leading up to this was:
  ...
$ cat f1.txt
1
2
3
FOUR
5
6
7
```

That is how many OSS developers (including kernel developers) distribute their code patches. The `patch` and `diff` can also be run on entire directory trees. However, that usage is outside the scope of this book.

Using awk and cut to Process Columns

Another massive text processing tool is the `awk` command. The `awk` command is a full-blown programming language. Although there is much more you can do with the `awk` command, the following examples show you a few tricks related to **extracting columns of text**:

```
$ ps aux | awk '{print $1,$11}'              Show columns 1, 11 of ps
$ ps aux | awk '/myerman/ {print $11}'       Show myerman's processes
$ ps aux | grep myerman | awk '{print $11}'  Same as above
```

The first example displays the contents of the first column (user name) and eleventh column (command name) from currently running processes outputted from the ps command (`ps aux`). The next two commands produce the same output, with one using the `awk` command and the other using the `grep` command to find all processes owned by the user named `myerman`. In each case, when processes owned by myerman are found, column 11 (command name) is displayed for each of those processes.

By default, the `awk` command assumes that the delimiter between columns is spaces. You can **specify a different delimiter** with the `-F` option as follows:

```
$ awk -F: '{print $1,$5}' /etc/passwd   Use colon delimiter to print cols
```

You can get similar results with the cut command. As with the previous awk example, you specify a colon (:) as the column delimiter to process information from the /etc/passwd file:

```
$ cut -d: -f1,5 /etc/passwd          Use colon delimiter to print cols
```

The cut command can also be used with ranges of fields. The following command prints columns 1 through 5 of the /etc/passwd file:

```
$ cut -d: -f1-5 /etc/passwd          Show columns 1 through 5
```

Instead of using a dash (-) to indicate a range of numbers, you can use it to print all columns from a particular column number and above. The following command displays all columns from column 5 and above from the /etc/passwd file:

```
$ cut -d: -f5- /etc/passwd           Show columns 5 and later
```

We prefer to use the awk command when columns are separated by a varying number of spaces, such as the output of the ps command. We prefer the cut command when dealing with files delimited by commas (,) or colons (:), such as the /etc/passwd file.

Summary

BSD and UNIX systems traditionally use plain text files for system configuration, documentation, output from commands, and many forms of stored information. As a result, many commands have been created to search, edit, and otherwise manipulate plain text files. Even with today's powerful and elegant Mac OS X GUI, the ability to manipulate plain text files is critical to becoming a power UNIX user.

This chapter explores some of the most popular commands for working with plain text files in UNIX systems. These commands include text editors (such as Vi, Nano, and Pico), as well as commands that can edit streaming data (such as sed and awk commands). There are also commands for sorting text (sort), counting text (wc), and translating characters in text (tr).

6

Advanced Scripting

In the past three chapters, you've learned how to work with Terminal, use basic shell commands, organize some commands into simple scripts, work with files, and manipulate text.

IN THIS CHAPTER

Advanced Shell Scripting

AppleScripting: Working with the open command

In this chapter, you're going to learn how to create some more advanced shell scripts. You'll also learn the basics of AppleScripting. Finally, you'll be introduced to the open command, a powerful tool that enables you to open files, Finder windows, and applications such as iTunes and Word straight from the command line. The goal of this chapter is to make you more proficient in automating certain administrative functions. Think of this chapter as a summary of what you've already learned, and a necessary step toward success in more advanced topics, which we'll cover from this chapter through Chapter 14.

Shell Scripting on Mac OS X

You got a taste in Chapter 3 of what shell scripts are about. At its most basic, a shell script is nothing more than a series of commands that have been saved into an executable file.

For example, if you are monitoring the server load on a particular machine, you might use the uptime command, like so:

```
uptime
14:28  up 2 days, 40 mins, 2 users, load averages: 0.08 0.51 0.45
```

The response is fairly expected—current time, how long the machine has been up, how many users are connected to it, and load averages over the past 1, 5, and 15 minutes.

What if this output is too much for your purposes? What if all you wanted was the current time and the one-minute load average? That's easily remedied by piping the output of uptime to the `cut` command, and extracting what you need, like so:

```
uptime | cut -d' ' -f1,12
14:33 0.03
```

So far, nothing too strenuous has happened, and in fact you could probably just keep this as a one-line history item that you could recall repeatedly. In fact, running `history` gives us its position:

```
history
534  uptime | cut -d' ' -f1,12
```

Running !534 from the command line would give us another reading:

```
!534
uptime | cut -d' ' -f1,12
14:36 0.38
```

Let's add a bit more complexity to the equation. What if we needed to know something else about the state of our system? What if this were a web server, and we needed to know, for example, how many Apache processes were running, as well as the number of MySQL processes, and maybe the size of the Apache error log?

Well, now we're going far beyond simple command lines and piping—we need to start thinking about creating a shell script that will help us gather this information.

Creating a Basic Shell Script

When you create a shell script in an editor such as Vi or Nano, the first line of the script should call the interpreter—in this case, the BASH shell. It's called the hash-bang line (or she-bang line, if you prefer), and it points the way to the interpreter that will actually make the script run:

```
#!/bin/bash
```

The rest of the script is made up of instructions. These instructions can be an orderly set of shell commands or they can be wrapped in conditional logic or loops. For example, we can simply echo our previous command by inserting it whole cloth into our script:

```
#!/bin/bash
uptime | cut -d' ' -f1,12
```

Saving this file as `getinfo.sh`, making it executable (chmod +x getinfo.sh), and then running it will give us the expected results:

```
14:53 0.03
```

So far, nothing to write home about, but we've now saved something valuable from the vicissitudes of history, quite literally. But what if we wanted to make this output a little more user friendly? We could add some labels by using the echo command. The -n command-line flag enables us to add a label without a new line, thereby putting the label and the data on the same line:

```
#!/bin/bash
echo -n "Time and server load: "
uptime | cut -d' ' -f1,12
```

Running the script again, we get the following:

```
Time and server load: 15:04 0.11
```

We can repeat the same process when trying to get the number of Apache processes. We merely pipe the output of ps, grep the lines containing httpd, ignore our grep command, and then count the results with wc:

```
#!/bin/bash
echo -n "Time and server load: "
uptime | cut -d' ' -f1,12
echo -n "Apache: "
ps aux | grep httpd | grep -v grep | wc -l
```

Here's what we get when we run the command:

```
Time and server load: 15:07 0.19
Apache:      12
```

Next, we add a similar line to count mysqld processes:

```
#!/bin/bash
echo -n "Time and server load: "
uptime | cut -d' ' -f1,12
echo -n "Apache: "
ps aux | grep httpd | grep -v grep | wc -l
echo -n "MySQL: "
ps aux | grep mysqld | grep -v grep | wc -l
```

Here's the result:

```
Time and server load: 15:10 0.04
Apache:      12
MySQL:        2
```

Getting the size of the Apache error log is fairly simple, as all you need to know is its location. Once you have that, you can use wc to get a line count. For the purposes of this example, all log files (Apache, PHP, and MySQL) are stored in one place, thanks to MAMP (a Mac-based Apache/MySQL/PHP stack similar to LAMP for Linux), so we can actually grab all log files and add them to our report:

```
#!/bin/bash
echo -n "Time and server load: "
uptime | cut -d' ' -f1,12
echo -n "Apache: "
ps aux | grep httpd | grep -v grep | wc -l
echo -n "MySQL: "
ps aux | grep mysqld | grep -v grep | wc -l
echo "Log files:"
wc -l /Applications/MAMP/logs/*log
```

Notice that there is a new line inserted after the "Log files:" line, giving us the following:

```
Time and server load: 15:16 0.71
Apache:       12
MySQL:        2
Log files:
   2180 /Applications/MAMP/logs/apache_error_log
      7 /Applications/MAMP/logs/mysql_error_log
   2635 /Applications/MAMP/logs/php_error.log
   4822 total
```

Adding Command-Line Arguments

We now have something that starts being useful for the administrator trying to glean what is happening. He or she can interactively run this command from a Terminal window to see what's happening at any given moment.

An administrator can also just as easily run this script using cron or launchd, and append the results to a log file that can then be perused later. Each entry would be a small snapshot of the server at a given time.

However, we still haven't even scratched the surface of what shell scripting offers us. For example, the cut command pulls out the first and twelfth columns, giving us the current time and the one-minute server load. What if we wanted the current time and the fifteen-minute server load?

We could create a second copy of our script and run that, but that seems like a waste. Why not allow for some command-line arguments? Let's allow the user to run the script with one argument—either a 1, a 5, or a 15, to indicate which server load read-out the user wants.

To allow that, we need to tell our shell script that it should allow arguments from the user to affect the script. The easiest way to do that is to add the special variable $1 to your script. In shell parlance, $0 refers to the command or script being run, and $1 through $9 to the arguments passed to that script or command.

Therefore, for our purposes, adding $1 to the third line of our script should do the trick, right? Wrong. Remember, we want to allow users to give the script a 1, a 5, or a 15 because that's how administrators think of server-load readouts. They don't want to have to think about which column (based on a space-delimited report) these readouts translate to. We also need to guard against the possibility of zero arguments (or even a blank or nonsensical argument, like the word "foo") being passed to our script.

First, let's make sure that we have exactly one argument. We can do that by using the $# variable, which gives us a count of arguments on the command line. A simple test of this variable can boot the user out of the script if the test fails, or set the column number (the MYCOL variable below) to 12:

```
#!/bin/bash

if [ $# -eq "0" -o $# -gt "1" ]
then
   echo "Usage: $0 <argument>"
   echo "  where <argument> is 1, 5, or 15"
   exit
else
   MYCOL=12
fi

echo -n "Time and server load: "
uptime | cut -d' ' -f1,$MYCOL
echo -n "Apache: "
ps aux | grep httpd | grep -v grep | wc -l
echo -n "MySQL: "
ps aux | grep mysqld | grep -v grep | wc -l
echo "Log files:"
wc -l /Applications/MAMP/logs/*log
```

In the preceding example, I set MYCOL to 12 regardless—if there's one argument to the script, then 12 it is! That's obviously not right, so now that we've protected ourselves from too many (or too few) arguments, we can translate the user input into a column count for the cut command (excuse the excessive alliteration).

To achieve that goal, we can use a *case statement*. A case statement enables us to simplify a conditional statement without a bunch of nested "if" statements. Each statement is an expression that the case command tries to match. In our case, we're trying to match a 1, a 5, or a 15, and nothing else.

Here's a first attempt at translating each of those inputs to a column count:

```
#!/bin/bash

if [ $# -eq "0" -o $# -gt "1" ]
then
   echo "Usage: $0 <argument>"
   echo "  where <argument> is 1, 5, or 15"
```

```
      exit
  else
    case $1 in
    1)
    MYCOL=12
    ;;

    5)
    MYCOL=13
    ;;

    15)
    MYCOL=14
    ;;

    *)
    echo "Usage: $0 <argument>"
    echo "  where <argument> is 1, 5, or 15"
    exit

    esac
fi

echo -n "Time and server load: "
uptime | cut -d' ' -f1,$MYCOL
echo -n "Apache: "
ps aux | grep httpd | grep -v grep | wc -l
echo -n "MySQL: "
ps aux | grep mysqld | grep -v grep | wc -l
echo "Log files:"
wc -l /Applications/MAMP/logs/*log
```

Notice the use of the * special case at the end? This tells the case statement how to evaluate anything that isn't matched by the other expressions. Typing in an argument of Lincoln should give us the same error as typing in any number that isn't 1, 5, or 15.

What else could we do to make this script a little better? Well, for starters, we could simplify that usage error message and place it in a reusable variable, like so:

```
#!/bin/bash
ERROR_MSG="Usage: $0 [1|5|15]"
if [ $# -eq "0" -o $# -gt "1" ]
then
    echo $ERROR_MSG
    exit
else
    case $1 in
    1)
    MYCOL=12
    ;;

    5)
```

```
      MYCOL=13
      ;;

      15)
      MYCOL=14
      ;;

      *)
      echo $ERROR_MSG
      exit

      esac
fi
```

Things to Watch Out For

Before we move on, let's take a moment to note some peculiarities in shell scripting. For example, when closing out an if or case statement, did you notice the use of fi and esac? These mark the end of a conditional portion of your script.

Notice the brackets around the if test? There needs to be a space after the opening bracket ([) and before the closing bracket (]). The preceding test without spaces will cause a syntax error:

```
if [$# -eq "0" -o $# -gt "1"]   #error! does not compute!
```

Here's another spacing issue that will annoy beginning shell scripters. When you first set a variable's value, don't put any spaces between the variable name, the equal sign, and the value:

```
MYCOL = 14   #error! shell tries to find a command called MYCOL
MYCOL=14 #you're okay
```

Furthermore, when you're ready to use your new variable, remember to put a $ sign in front of the name:

```
echo $MYCOL #prints 14
```

Using the Script Command

Sometimes you want a transcript of what you've been working on, for either learning or auditing purposes. The script command enables you do this. Invoking the script command on the command line without any arguments will save all commands and outputs from those commands to a file called typescript.

Here's a transcript of a recent script session done for illustrative purposes. Notice that the date, uptime, and df commands are recorded, along with their output. Also notice that I pressed Ctrl-D to exit the transcript process.

```
Macintosh:desktop myerman$ script
Script started, output file is typescript
bash-3.2$ date
Mon Nov 17 13:42:39 CST 2008
bash-3.2$ uptime
13:42  up 2 days, 23:54, 2 users, load averages: 0.97 0.77 0.54
bash-3.2$ df -h
Filesystem     Size   Used  Avail Capacity  Mounted on
/dev/disk0s2   149Gi   88Gi   60Gi    60%   /
devfs          108Ki  108Ki   0Bi    100%   /dev
fdesc          1.0Ki  1.0Ki   0Bi    100%   /dev
map -hosts       0Bi    0Bi   0Bi    100%   /net
map auto_home    0Bi    0Bi   0Bi    100%   /home
bash-3.2$ exit

Script done, output file is typescript
```

Running a command like `cat typescript | less` will print out everything you've done.

AppleScripting

Although technically not a UNIX thing, AppleScripting is available on any Mac OS X machine, and it can be used to great effect by system administrators. AppleScript was designed to be a very English-like language for doing things on the Mac. Typical examples show you how to create dialog boxes for copying files, downloading URLs, or controlling iTunes or iChat.

You can create AppleScripts with any text editor, but most of the time, you use the Script Editor (found at `/Applications/AppleScript`). When you open the Script Editor (see Figure 6-1), you see a simple editor that allows you to enter commands, run them, and record them.

With the Script Editor open, let's create your first AppleScript, admittedly one of the most useless programs ever written, but you've got to start somewhere:

```
display dialog "I am a dialog box." --this is a comment
```

After you enter this line, click the Run button. As shown in Figure 6-2, the `display dialog` command opens a dialog box with the argument printed in it (in this case, "I am a dialog box"). Two dashes (--) are treated as the comment marker—the compiler ignores anything after that on a line.

Let's create something a bit more useful, something that can help us with administrative work. Let's say that we want to monitor a folder that contains certain files, such as files in the web server root. Again, we're going to use the MAMP example (/Applications/MAMP/).

First, right-click (or Control-click) on the Desktop and select More ⇨ Enable Folder Actions from the menu. Open a new Finder window and navigate to the / Applications/MAMP folder. Right-click (or Control-click) on the htdocs folder and choose More ⇨ Attach a Folder Action, as shown in Figure 6-3.

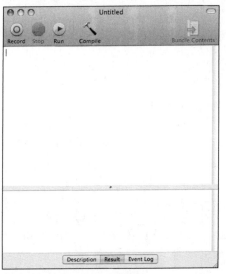

Figure 6-1: The Script Editor

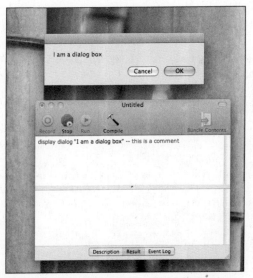

Figure 6-2: Your First Simple AppleScript

Figure 6-3: Attaching a folder action to the htdocs folder

Folder actions are basically AppleScripts that have been attached to a folder, and they can prove endlessly helpful in many contexts. Fortunately, Mac OS X ships with a list of sample scripts that you can use right away. These scripts are located in /Library/ Scripts/Folder Action Scripts. The one we're going to attach is the script called add – new item alert (see Figure 6-4).

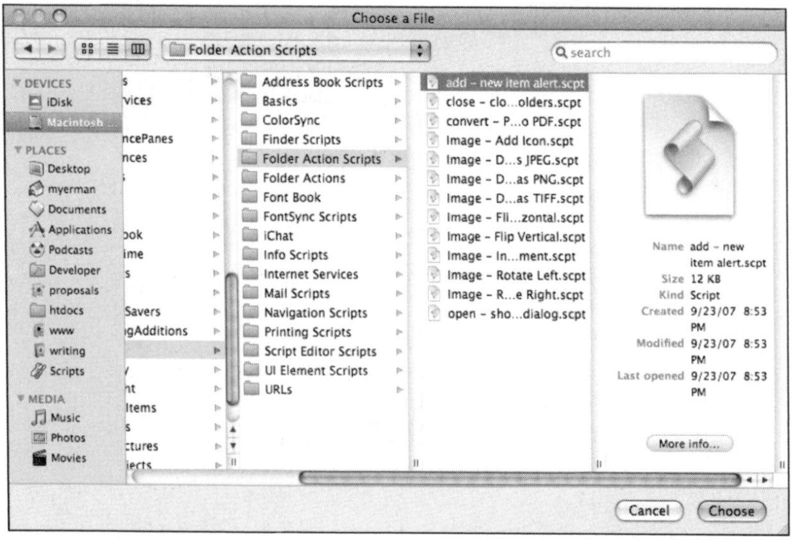

Figure 6-4: Attaching a script

Now, whenever a new file is added to that folder, we should get an alert. If you open a Terminal window and enter the following commands, you should see an Alert window pop up in a few seconds (as shown in Figure 6-5):

```
cd /Applications/MAMP/htdocs
touch test.html
```

There's a lot more to learn, of course, and there are various good AppleScript books out there.

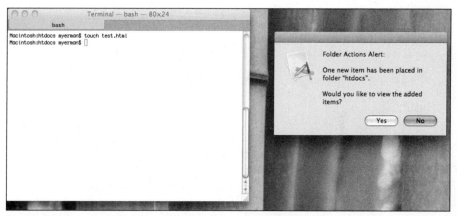

Figure 6-5: The Alert window in action

Working with the Open Command

Every Mac OS X user has used either an iLife or an iWork product at some point or another. If you're working with music, you reach for iTunes. If it's photos you need to manage, you reach for iPhoto. Chatting is handled by iChat. On the business side of the house, you've got Pages (word processor), Keynote (presentation software), and Numbers (spreadsheet).

All of these programs are normally initiated by clicking their icons on the Dock or in the Finder. However, you can open just about any directory, file, or application from the command line with the open command.

To open a Finder window containing your working directory, enter the following command in a Terminal window:

```
open ~
```

To open an application, just add the -a switch and its name. To open iTunes, enter the following command:

```
open -a iTunes
```

Using the open command on a file will open that file in its default editor. For example, the following command will open an HTML file in Safari:

```
open test.html
```

You can, of course, redirect the application with the -a switch. To open the same HTML file in BBEdit, simply edit the command:

```
open -a BBEdit test.html
```

Please remember that Mac OS X is case neutral, so adjusting the case of an application's name also works equally well:

```
open -a bbedit test.html
```

To force a file to be opened by TextEdit, use -e:

```
open -e test.html
```

You can open multiple files at once using wildcards (see Figure 6-6). The following example opens various .php files with TextEdit:

```
open -e *.php
```

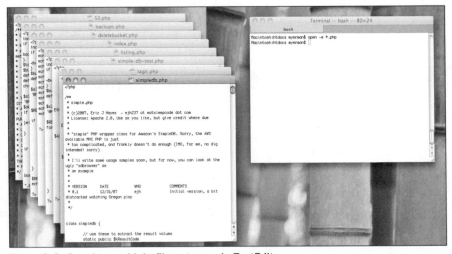

Figure 6-6: Opening multiple files at once in TextEdit

If you already have an application window open, use the -n switch to open a new application instance:

```
open -e -n test2.html
```

Using the open command with a URL will open a Safari window or tab:

```
open http://www.google.com
```

Finally, the -f flag enables you to pipe input to a text editor. This is potentially useful, as you could create a series of piped commands (or even standard input) and then have it all end up in a text editor.

For example, if you needed to get a sorted list of all CSS files in all subdirectories, and then pipe that list to a new TextEdit document, you could try this command:

```
ls -1 * | egrep "\.css$" | sort -u | open -f
```

The result is shown in Figure 6-7.

Figure 6-7: Sending piped Input to TextEdit with the open command

One final note before we leave this subject. Many applications like BBEdit contain advanced command-line tools that enable you to do even more work right on the command line.

For example, if you're a BBEdit user, open BBEdit and select BBEdit ⇨ Install Command Line Tools from the menu. This will install two new tools on your system: bbedit and bbdiff. The first enables you to open files directly in BBEdit from the command line; the second enables you to run a diff program in BBEdit.

The bbedit commands work on multiple files; you can even pipe in commands to get the output into BBEdit. Typing in the command

```
ls -la ~ | bbedit
```

results in a directory listing being sent to BBEdit (see Figure 6-8).

It's a good idea to examine the different tools you use frequently to see whether they offer additional command-line tools that you can take advantage of.

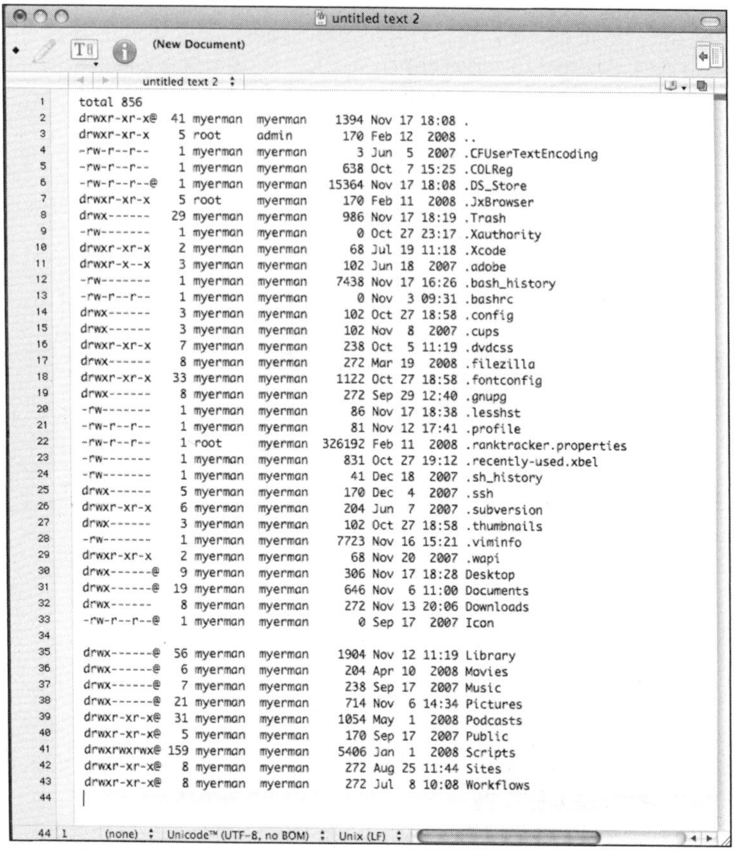

Figure 6-8: Sending output to BBEdit via command-line tools

Summary

In this chapter, you learned a little more about shell scripting and AppleScripting. You also learned how to perform more advanced tasks that involve Mac applications by working with the open command right on the command line. It is hoped that you have become more familiar with these powerful tools.

7

Administering File Systems

File systems provide the structures in which files, directories, devices, and other elements of the system are accessed from your Mac OS X system. Mac OS X supports many different file systems, including HFS+ (default), HFS, UFS, AFP, ISO 9660, FAT, UDF, NFS, SMBFS, NTFS (read only), FTP, and WebDAV.

HFS+ is the preferred file system on Mac OS X. It supports many advanced features, such as journaling, quotas, byte-range locking, Finder information in metadata, multiple encodings, hard and symbolic links, aliases, support for hiding file extensions on a per-file basis, and so on.

IN THIS CHAPTER

Understanding file system types

Partitioning disks

Mounting file systems

Unmounting file systems

Checking the systems

Checking disk space with du and df

Creating and managing disk partitions, and the file systems on partitions, are among the most critical jobs in administering a Mac OS X system. That's because if you mess up your file system, you might very well lose the critical data stored on your computer's hard disk or removable media.

This chapter contains commands for partitioning storage media, creating file systems, mounting and unmounting file systems, and checking file systems for errors and disk space.

Understanding File System Basics

If you're coming to Mac OS X from another BSD or Linux background, the first thing you need to know is that partitions on the Mac are called *volumes*. Each volume represents an addressable section of the hard disk that is assigned a specific function: a separate operating system (e.g., Linux or Windows XP), file storage, swap, and so on.

Typically, you probably won't need to change your default volume setup; but if you find yourself in a position where you need to support different operating systems or want a different file system setup, then you may need to repartition your system. We'll get to that later in this chapter.

NOTE *Partitioning your Mac OS X system will cause all data on it to be erased!*

Setting Up the Disk Initially

If you're used to working with other BSD flavors or Linux, you're probably accustomed to having to run an initial disk setup with a utility such as fdisk. It's highly unlikely that your iMac, MacBook Pro, or Mac Pro will need this step, as it ships with everything you need to get started, already set up.

Checking Your Disk Setup

You can check your disk setup anytime you want with the mount command. This command shows how the disk space is divided among several partitions that are then mounted in different places in the file system:

```
$ mount              Display mounted disk partitions
/dev/disk0s2 on / (hfs, local, journaled)
devfs on /dev (devfs, local)
fdesc on /dev (fdesc, union)
map -hosts on /net (autofs, automounted)
map auto_home on /home (autofs, automounted)
```

Next, to get a sense of how the disk space is distributed among the partitions on your hard disk, you can use the df command as follows:

```
$ df -h        Display disk space usage
Filesystem     Size   Used   Avail  Capacity  Mounted on
/dev/disk0s2   149Gi  88Gi   60Gi    60%      /
devfs          108Ki  108Ki  0Bi    100%      /dev
fdesc          1.0Ki  1.0Ki  0Bi    100%      /dev
map -hosts     0Bi    0Bi    0Bi    100%      /net
map auto_home  0Bi    0Bi    0Bi    100%      /home
```

This example assigned 150GB to the root partition /, which you would see as the Macintosh HD icon on your desktop. Right now, this particular system's root partition is 60 percent full, with 60GB free.

Understanding File System Types

To use Mac OS X, you can get by with very few different file system types. The Hierarchical File System Plus (HFS+) is used by default for most disk storage needs.

HFS+ is architecturally similar to HFS, with several important improvements:

❏ 32 bits used for allocation blocks (instead of 16). HFS divides the disk space on a partition into equally sized *allocation blocks*. Using 32 bits for identifying allocation blocks results in much less wasted space (and more files) than using 16 bits.

❏ Long filenames—up to 255 characters

❏ Unicode-based filename encoding

❏ Attributes for both files and directories can be extended in the future (as opposed to being limited to a fixed size)

❏ Largest file size is 2^{63} bytes

However, you might want to use other file system types with Mac OS X in some cases, including the following:

❏ **Other local operating systems:** If multiple operating systems (such as Windows, DOS, or Linux) are installed on your hard disk, you might want to access the data from the partitions containing those systems (even if only to read the data).

❏ **Other media:** You may have a CD, DVD, backup tape, or other media that contains data formatted in other file system types. Even in cases where Mac OS X can't create file systems of a certain type, it may be able to mount and use those file systems.

Most of the examples in this chapter use HFS+ file systems to illustrate how a file system is created and managed. However, Table 7-1 lists different file system types and describes when you might want to use them.

Table 7-1: File System Types Supported in Mac OS X

File System Type	Description
HFS+	Preferred file system used on Mac OS X. It supports journaling, quotas, byte-range locking, Finder information in metadata, multiple encodings, hard and symbolic links, aliases, hiding file extensions on a per-file basis, and more.
ufs	Default file system type used with FreeBSD and other BSD systems. Darwin's implementation of UFS is similar to that on *BSD, as was NEXTSTEP's, but they are not really compatible. Currently, only NetBSD supports it.
msdos	DOS file systems (FAT12, FAT16, and FAT32) are supported.
iso9660	System-independent file system type used on most data CDs
ntfs	Microsoft's New Technology File System (NTFS). Useful when file systems need to share files with most Windows systems (as with dual booting or removable drives). Read-only support.

Continued

Table 7-1: File System Types Supported in Mac OS X *(continued)*

File System Type	Description
udf	UDF (Universal Disk Format) is the file system used by DVD-ROM (including DVD-video and DVD-audio) discs, and by many CD-R/RW packet-writing programs.

Besides the file system types listed in Table 7-1, there are also what are referred to as *network shared file systems*. Locally, a network shared file system may be a ufs, ntfs, or other normal file system type. However, all or part of those file systems can be shared with network protocols such as Samba (smbfs file system type), NFS (nfs), and NetWare (nwfs).

For a good discussion of all this, please refer to www.kernelthread.com/mac/osx/arch_fs.html.

You can use procedures in the following sections to create, manage, mount, and otherwise use the file system types just described.

Creating and Managing File Systems

Mac OS X provides a default partitioning and file system scheme, but you can repartition your system easily enough. The following sections provide details about how to do that.

Partitioning Hard Disks

To repartition your system, boot from a Mac OS X install disc. Insert the install disc that came with your computer, and then restart the computer while holding the C key until the system restarts and you see the gray Apple icon.

To partition your hard disk, follow these steps:

1. From the Installer menu, select Open Disk Utility. In the window that opens, on the left, click the icon for the drive you would like to initialize or partition.

2. To the right, click the Partition tab.

3. In the pop-up menu under Volume Scheme:, choose the number of partitions you want to create during the initializing process.

4. After you have chosen the number of partitions you want, adjust their sizes by dragging the handles that represent the partition borders.

5. Click each of the partitions to adjust its properties. Under Volume Information, choose the format you'd like to use. The default option is Mac OS Extended (Journaled).

6. Click Partition.

7. After your drive is formatted and partitioned, continue with other installations from your install disc. You will need to re-install any operating systems that you want to work with (such as Mac OS X, Linux, etc.).

A Better Option: Nondestructive Partitioning

If, and only if, you've performed a recent backup (using either Time Machine or some other option), restart your Mac OS X system and then hold down the ⌘S key as it reboots.

This will start the Mac in a single-user mode that is very similar to a command shell on a Linux or other UNIX system. As soon as it comes up, type the following command to start essential services:

shell /etc/rc

Using the following command, retrieve information on the volumes that are currently on your system:

diskutil list

```
/dev/disk0
    #:                       TYPE NAME              SIZE        IDENTIFIER
    0:        GUID_partition_scheme               *149.1 Gi    disk0
    1:                        EFI                  200.0 Mi    disk0s1
    2:        Apple_HFS Macintosh HD              148.7 Gi    disk0s2
```

If you wanted to split the Macintosh HD volume into two partitions (one with about 120GB in it, and the other with the balance), you must first determine whether the disk can be resized using the following command:

diskutil resizeVolume disk0s2 limits

```
For device disk0s2 Macintosh HD:
    Current size:   159697911808 bytes
    Minimum size:   95972585472 bytes
    Maximum size:   159697911808 bytes
```

As you can see, the current size of the volume is 159GB. The smallest you can make it is 95GB, so our plan to split it at the 120GB barrier is just right. To actually resize the volume, use the following command (notice that we're creating a JHFS+ partition to install Mac OS 9 in):

diskutil resizeVolume disk0s2 120G JHFS+ Development 20G

Once this command is entered, various messages will flash on the screen indicating how much progress is being made toward the goal of repartitioning the drive. As soon as it's done, reboot in normal mode. You may need to tell Mac OS X which partition to boot to.

Mounting and Unmounting File Systems

Before you can use a regular file system, you need to attach it to a directory in your computer's file system tree by *mounting* it. Your root file system (/) and other file systems you use on an ongoing basis are typically automounted by Mac OS X. Sometimes, though, you need to manually mount file systems.

The mount command is used to view mounted file systems, as well as to mount any local (hard disk, USB drive, CD, DVD, etc.) or remote (NFS, Samba, etc.) file systems. Here are examples of the mount command for **listing mounted file systems**:

```
$ mount                       List mounted remote and local file systems
/dev/disk0s2 on / (hfs, local, journaled)
devfs on /dev (devfs, local)
fdesc on /dev (fdesc, union)
map -hosts on /net (autofs, automounted)
map auto_home on /home (autofs, automounted)
```

Use the -t option to **list only mounts of a specific file system type**:

```
$ mount -t hfs                 List mounted hfs file systems
/dev/disk0s2 on / (hfs, local, journaled)
```

Here is a simple mount command to **mount a local file system** (the /dev/ad0s4 device) on an existing directory named /mnt/music:

```
# mount /dev/ad0s4 /mnt/music       Mount a local file system
# mount -v /dev/ad0s4 /mnt/music/   Mount file system, more verbose
```

Use -t to **explicitly indicate the type of file system to mount**:

```
# mount -v -t ext2fs /dev/ad0s4 /mnt/music/  Mount an ext2 file system
/dev/ad0s4 on /mnt/music (ext2fs, local, fsid 5e00000008000000)
```

You can **specify mount options** by adding -o and a comma-separated list of options. By default, partitions are mounted with read/write access. You can explicitly specify to **mount a file system as read/write (rw) or read-only (ro)**:

```
# mount -v -t ext2fs -o rw /dev/ad0s4 /mnt/music  Mount read/write
/dev/ad0s4 on /mnt/music (ext2fs, local, fsid 5e00000008000000)
# mount -v -t ext2fs -o ro /dev/ad0s4 /mnt/music  Mount read-only
/dev/ad0s4 on /mnt/music (ext2fs, local, fsid 5e00000008000000)
```

A few other useful `mount` options you can use include the following:

❑ **noatime:** Does not update the access time on files. Good on file systems with a lot of I/O, such as mail spools and logs.

❑ **noexec:** Prevents execution of binaries located on this file system. Can be used to increase security—for example, for /tmp in environments with untrusted users.

To **unmount a file system,** use the `umount` command. You can `umount` the file system using the device name or the mount point, but you're better off `umounting` with the mount point in order to avoid mistyping the device name (many of which are very similar):

```
# umount -v /dev/ad0s4          Unmount by device name
/dev/sda1 umounted
# umount -v /mnt/music          Unmount by mount point
/tmp/diskboot.img umounted
```

If the device is busy, the unmount will fail. A common reason for an unmount to fail is that you have a shell open with the current directory of a directory inside the mount:

```
# umount -v /mnt/mymount/
umount: unmount of /mnt/music failed: Device busy
```

Checking File Systems

File systems are traditionally checked when the system first boots up. The `fsck` command, which actually depends on a set of file-system-specific `fsck` commands, can not only check for consistency problems in a file system, but also interactively repair those problems when necessary.

After file systems are mounted and users are allowed to access the system, `fsck` can be run again with the -B flag to do background checking. You can run `fsck` at any time to check, and possibly repair, a file system.

Instead of having `fsck` try to figure out the file system type you are checking, you can run the file-system-specific commands directly on your file systems. These commands include `fsck_ufs` and `fsck_msdosfs`.

The following example shows how to **check a UFS file system** by simply adding the device name of the disk partition you want to check to the `fsck_ufs` command:

```
# fsck_ufs /dev/ad0s4          Check UFS file system of inconsistencies
** /dev/ad0s4
** Last Mounted on /mnt/extra
** Phase 1 - Check Blocks and Sizes
** Phase 2 - Check Pathnames
** Phase 3 - Check Connectivity
```

```
** Phase 4 - Check Reference Counts
** Phase 5 - Check Cyl groups
377 files, 864 used, 373871 free (15 frags, 46732 blocks, 0.0% fragmentation)
```

The preceding example shows a file system check on slice four of IDE disk 1 (/dev/ad0s4). The slice is not currently mounted, so if fixes needed to be performed on the disk, they could be. Here are some other examples of options you can use when checking a file system with the fsck_ufs command:

```
# fsck_ufs -B /dev/ad0s1f        Run check in the background
# fsck_ufs -B -f ad0s1f       Force file system check, even if marked clean
** /usr/.snap/fsck_snapshot
** Last Mounted on /usr
** Phase 1 - Check Blocks and Sizes
** Phase 2 - Check Pathnames
** Phase 3 - Check Connectivity
** Phase 4 - Check Reference Counts
** Phase 5 - Check Cyl groups
198317 files, 1814392 used, 6730360 free (25136 frags, 838153 blocks, 0.3%
fragmentation)
# fsck_ufs -d /dev/ad0s1a      Print commands without executing (debug mode)
# fsck_ufs -y /dev/ad0s1c      Make fsck say yes to any questions (like repairs)
```

If you want to **check a DOS file system**, you can use the fsck_msdos command. In the following example, the second partition on a USB memory stick (/dev/da0s2) contains a DOS file system. You can create that DOS partition originally using the newfs_msdos command. (Memory sticks and SCSI drive device names begin with da, as opposed to IDE disks, which are named ad.)

```
# newfs_msdos /dev/md2a        Create DOS file system on USB device 1, slice 2
# fsck_msdosfs /dev/da0s2        Check DOS partition (on 2nd slice, 1st da device)
** /dev/da0s2 (NO WRITE)
** Phase 1 - Read and Compare FATs
** Phase 2 - Check Cluster Chains
** Phase 3 - Checking Directories
** Phase 4 - Checking for Lost Files
2712 files, 610448 free (38153 clusters)
MARK FILE SYSTEM CLEAN? no

***** FILE SYSTEM IS LEFT MARKED AS DIRTY *****
```

Note that the file system was listed as NO WRITE because it was currently mounted. Therefore, it could not be marked as clean. The file system can be marked as clean after unmounting the file system and running fsck_msdosfs again:

```
# umount /dev/da0s2
# fsck_msdosfs /dev/da0s2        Run check again after unmounting
** /dev/da0s2
** Phase 1 - Read and Compare FATs
** Phase 2 - Check Cluster Chains
** Phase 3 - Checking Directories
```

```
** Phase 4 - Checking for Lost Files
2712 files, 610448 free (38153 clusters)
```

If `fsck` encounters errors during the file system check (and you have not indicated -y to automatically respond yes and continue), you can **interactively say whether or not you want to fix the errors**. Here is an example:

```
# fsck_msdosfs /dev/da0s2          Check a file system that has errors
** /dev/da0s2
** Phase 1 - Read and Compare FATs
** Phase 2 - Check Cluster Chains
** Phase 3 - Checking Directories
/hello.txt starts with free cluster
Truncate? [yn] y
** Phase 4 - Checking for Lost Files
2713 files, 610448 free (38153 clusters)
MARK FILE SYSTEM CLEAN? [yn] y
MARKING FILE SYSTEM CLEAN

***** FILE SYSTEM WAS MODIFIED *****
```

In the preceding example, the file `hello.txt` was open in a text editor when the memory stick containing the file was unplugged. This subsequent file system check showed the error, which could be corrected by typing **y**.

Finding Out About File System Use

Running out of disk space can be an annoyance on your desktop system and potentially a disaster on your servers. To determine how much disk space is available and how much is currently in use, you can use the `df` command. To check how much space particular files and directories are consuming, use the `du` command.

The `df` command provides **utilization summaries of your mounted file systems**. Using the -h option, you can have the data (which is shown in bytes by default) converted to kilobytes (K), megabytes (M) and gigabytes (G), to make that output more human-readable:

```
$ df -h          Display space on file systems in human readable form
Filesystem     Size   Used   Avail Capacity  Mounted on
/dev/ad0s1a    496M    39M    417M      9%    /
devfs          1.0K   1.0K      0B    100%    /dev
/dev/ad0s1e    496M    32K    456M      0%    /tmp
/dev/ad0s1f     16G   3.5G     12G     23%    /usr
/dev/ad0s1d    1.2G    19M    1.1G      2%    /var
/dev/ad0s2     7.3G   593M    6.4G      8%    /mnt/debian
/dev/da0s1      48M   856K     45M      2%    /mnt/da0s1
```

Every file that is physically saved to a file system is represented by an inode. If your file system has many small files, it's possible that you might run out of inodes. To have the df command **check inode utilization**, use the -i option:

```
$ df -hi          Display how many inodes are available and used
Filesystem    Size   Used   Avail Capacity iused    ifree %iused  Mounted on
/dev/ad0s1a   496M    39M    417M      9%    1117    64673    2%   /
devfs         1.0K   1.0K      0B    100%       0        0  100%   /dev
/dev/ad0s1e   496M    34K    456M      0%      17    65773    0%   /tmp
/dev/ad0s1f    16G   3.5G     12G     23%  198316  2015570    9%   /usr
/dev/ad0s1d   1.2G    19M    1.1G      2%    2523   162339    2%   /var
```

If you have network mounts (such as Samba or NFS), these will also appear in your df output. To limit df output to local file systems, use the -l (as in local) option:

```
$ df -hl          Display disk space only for local file systems
```

To display output for a particular file system type, use the -T option:

```
$ df -ht ufs      Only display ufs file system types
Filesystem    Size   Used   Avail Capacity  Mounted on
/dev/ad0s1a   496M    39M    417M      9%   /
   ...
```

To check for disk space usage for particular files or directories in a file system, use the du command. The following command was run as the user named marlowe:

```
$ du -h /Users/         Show disk space usage for /home directory
du: /Users/kafka: Permission denied
4.0K    /Users/marlowe/Mail
52K     /Users/marlowe
64K     /Users/
```

The output shows that access to another home directory's disk use (in this case, /Users/kafka) was denied for security reasons. The next examples show how to avoid permission issues and get totals that are correct by using the root user account. This is clearly visible when we add -s to summarize:

```
$ du -sh /Users   Regular user is denied space totals to others' homes
du: /Users/kafka: Permission denied
du: /Users/horatio199: Permission denied
64K     /Users
# du -sh /Users   You can display summary disk use as root user
1.6G    /Users
```

You can specify multiple directories with the -c option and total them up:

```
# du -sch /Users /var   Show directory and total summaries
1.6G    /Users
111M    /var
1.7G    total
```

You can combine du with the find command to check disk space in all directories beneath a point in your directory structure. Use the following command to view the disk space used in directories beneath the /var file system:

```
# find /var -maxdepth 1 -type d -exec du -sh {} \;
 44M    /var
2.0K    /var/account
8.0K    /var/at
2.0K    /var/audit
...
438K    /var/log
 86K    /var/mail
4.0K    /var/msgs
 53K    /var/named
2.0K    /var/preserve
```

Summary

Creating and managing file systems is a critical part of Mac OS X system administration. Most BSD systems use the UNIX File System (UFS) as the primary file system type for storing data, but Mac OS X uses HFS+. Additionally, Mac OS X supports many other file systems, and can work with network file systems, such as NFS, nwfs, and smbfs.

8

Backups and Removable Media

Data backups in UNIX were traditionally done by running commands to
archive and compress the files to backup,
and then writing that backup archive to
tape. Options for archive tools, compression techniques, and backup media have
grown tremendously in recent years. Tape
archiving has, for many, been replaced by
techniques for backing up data over the
network, to other hard disks, or to CDs,
DVDs, or other low-cost removable media.

This chapter details some useful tools for
backing up and restoring your critical data.
The first part of the chapter details how
to use basic tools such as tar, gzip, and
rsync for backups.

IN THIS CHAPTER

**Creating backup archives
with tar**

**Compressing backups
with gzip and bzip2**

**Backing up over the
network with SSH**

**Doing network backups
with rsync**

**Working with Time
Machine**

Backing Up Data to Compressed Archives

If you are coming from a Windows background, you may be used to
tools such as WinZip and PKZIP, both of which archive and compress
groups of files in one application. BSD systems offer separate tools for
gathering groups of files into a single archive (such as tar) and compressing that archive for efficient storage (gzip, bzip2, and others).
However, you can also merge the two steps by using additional options
to the tar command.

Creating Backup Archives with tar

The tar command, which stands for *tape archiver*, dates back to early
UNIX systems. Although magnetic tape was the common medium that

tar wrote to originally, today tar is most often used to create an archive file that can be distributed using a variety of media.

That the tar command is rich in features is reflected in the dozens of options available with tar. The basic operations of tar, however, are used to create a backup archive (-c), extract files from an archive (-x), and update files in an archive (-u). You can also append files to (-r or -A) or list the contents of (-t) an archive .

> **NOTE** *Although the tar command is available on nearly all UNIX and BSD systems, it behaves differently on many systems. For example, Solaris does not support -z to manage tar archives compressed in gzip format. The Star (pronounced ess-tar) command supports access control lists (ACLs) and file flags (for extended permissions used by Samba).*

In addition to being used for backups, tar files are popular ways to distribute source code and binaries from software projects. That's because you can expect every BSD and UNIX-like system to contain the tools you need to work with tar files.

> **NOTE** *One quirk of working with the tar command results from the fact that tar was created before there were standards regarding how options are entered. Although you can prefix tar options with a dash, it isn't always necessary. For example, you might see a command that begins tar xvf with no dashes to indicate the options.*
>
> *A classic example of using the tar command might combine old-style options and pipes for compressing the output:*
>
> ```
> $ tar cf - *.txt | gzip -c > myfiles.tar.gz   Make archive, zip it and output
> ```

The preceding example illustrates a two-step process you might find in documentation for older UNIX systems. The tar command creates (c) an archive from all .txt files in the current directory. Instead of writing to the default tape device (/dev/sa0), the f option says to direct output to a file (or, in this case, "-" for standard output). The output is piped to the gzip command, and output to stdout (-c), and then redirected to the myfiles.tar.gz file. Note that tar is one of the few commands that doesn't require options to be preceded by a dash (-).

New tar versions, on modern BSD systems, can **create the archive and compress the output** in one step:

```
$ tar czf myfiles.tar.gz *.txt     Create gzipped tar file of .txt files
$ tar czvf myfiles.tar.gz *.txt    Be more verbose creating archive
a textfile1.txt
a textfile2.txt
```

In the examples just shown, note that the new archive name (myfiles.tar.gz) must immediately follow the f option to tar (which indicates the name of the archive). Otherwise, the output from tar will be directed to the default tape device (/dev/sa0) or stdout (if you use "-" instead of a filename). The z option says to do gzip compression, and v produces verbose descriptions of processing.

104

When you want to **return the files to a file system** (unzipping and untarring), you can also do that as either a one-step or a two-step process, using the `tar` and optionally the `gunzip` command:

```
$ gunzip -c myfiles.tar.gz | tar xf -          Unzips and untars archive
```

Alternately, try the following command line instead:

```
$ gunzip myfiles.tar.gz ; tar xf myfiles.tar   Unzips then untars archive
```

The preceding command removes the `tar.gz` file, leaving only the `.tar` file. To do that same procedure in one step, you could use the following command:

```
$ tar xzvf myfiles.tar.gz
x textfile1.txt
x textfile2.txt
```

The results of the previous commands are the same: The archived `.txt` files are copied from the archive to the current directory. The `x` option extracts the files, `z` uncompresses (unzips) the files, `v` makes the output, and `f` indicates that the next option is the name of the archive file (`myfiles.tar.gz`).

Using Compression Tools

Compression is an important aspect of working with backup files. It takes less disk space on your backup medium (CD, DVD, tape, and so on) or server to store compressed files. It also takes less time to transfer the archives to other media or download the files over a network.

Although compression can save a lot of storage space and transfer times, it can significantly increase your CPU usage. You can consider using hardware compression on a tape drive (see `http://tinyurl.com/5z6olt`).

> **NOTE** *See the man page of the `mt` command for details on how compression can be set via software for most magnetic tape drives.*

In the examples shown in the previous section, `tar` calls the `gzip` command, but `tar` can work with many compression tools. Out of the box on Mac OS X, `tar` will work with `gzip` and `bzip2`. The former is faster, but the latter offers more compression.

If you are archiving and compressing large amounts of data, the time it takes to compress your backups can be significant. However, with each compression command, you can choose different compression levels, to balance the need for more compression with the time that compression takes.

To use the `tar` command with **bzip2 compression,** use the `-j` option:

```
$ tar cjvf myfiles.tar.bz2 *.txt    Create archive, compress with bzip2
```

You can also **uncompress (-j) a bzip2 compressed file** as you extract files (-x) using the `tar` command:

```
$ tar xjvf myfiles.tar.bz2    Extract files, uncompress bzip2 compression
```

Compressing with gzip

As noted, you can **use any of the compression commands alone** (as opposed to within the `tar` command line). The following example uses the `gzip` command to create and work with `gzip`-compressed files:

```
$ gzip myfile                 gzips myfile and renames it myfile.gz
```

The next command provides the same result but with verbose output:

```
$ gzip -v  myfile             gzips myfile with verbose output
myfile: 86.0% -- replaced with myfile.gz
$ gzip -tv myfile.gz          Tests integrity of gzip file
myfile.gz:    OK
$ gzip -lv myfile.gz          Get detailed info about gzip file
method  crc    date  time     compressed    uncompr.  ratio uncompressed_name
defla 0f27d9e4 Jul 10 04:48      46785         334045  86.0% myfile
```

Use any one of the following commands to **compress all files in a directory:**

```
$ gzip -rv mydir      Compress all files in a directory
mydir/file1: 39.1% -- replaced with mydir/file1.gz
mydir/file2: 39.5% -- replaced with mydir/file2.gz
$ gzip -1 myfile      Fastest compression time, least compression
$ gzip -9 myfile      Slowest compression time, most compression
```

Add a dash before a number from 1 to 9 to set the compression level. As illustrated previously, -1 is the fastest (least) compression and -9 is the slowest (most) compression. The default for `gzip` is level 6. The `lzop` command has fewer levels: 1, 3 (the default), 7, 8, and 9. Compression levels for `bzip2` behave differently.

To **uncompress a gzipped file,** you can use the `gunzip` command. Use either of the following examples:

```
$ gunzip -v myfile.gz       Unzips myfile.gz and renames it myfile
myfile.gz:       86.0% -- replaced with myfile
$ gzip -dv myfile.gz        Same as previous command line
```

Although the examples just shown refer to zipping regular files, the same options can be used to compress `tar` archives.

Compressing with bzip2

The **bzip2 command** is considered to provide the highest compression among the compression tools described in this chapter. Here are some examples of bzip2:

```
$ bzip2 myfile            Compresses file and renames it myfile.bz2
$ bzip2 -v myfile         Same as previous command, but more verbose
  myfile:  9.529:1, 0.840 bits/byte, 89.51% saved, 334045 in, 35056 out.
$ bunzip2 myfile.bz2      Uncompresses file and renames it myfile
$ bzip2 -d myfile.bz2     Same as previous command
$ bunzip2 -v myfile.bz2   Same as previous command, but more verbose
  myfile.bz2: done
```

Listing, Joining, and Adding Files to tar Archives

So far, all we've done with tar is create and unpack archives. Also available are options for listing the contents of archives, joining archives together, adding files to an existing archive, and deleting files from an archive.

To **list an archive's contents,** use the -t option:

```
$ tar tvf myfiles.tar            List files from uncompressed archive
-rw-r--r-- root/root     9584 2008-07-05 11:20:33 textfile1.txt
-rw-r--r-- root/root     9584 2008-07-09 10:23:44 textfile2.txt
$ tar tzvf myfiles.tgz           List files from gzip compressed archive
```

Use the -r option to **add one or more files to an existing archive.** In the following example, myfile is added to the archive.tar archive file:

```
$ tar rvf archive.tar myfile    Add a file to a tar archive
```

You can use wildcards to **match multiple files to add** to your archive:

```
$ tar rvf archive.tar *.txt     Add multiple files to a tar archive
```

Backing Up over a Network

After you have backed up your files and gathered them into a tar archive, what do you do with that archive? The primary reason for creating a backup is in case something bad happens (such as a hard disk crash) and you need to restore your files from that backup. Methods you can employ to keep those backups safe include the following:

❑ **Copying to removable media** such as tape, CD, or DVD (as described later in this chapter)

❑ **Copying to another machine** over a network

Fast and reliable networks; inexpensive, high-capacity hard disks; and the security that comes with moving your data off-site have all made network backups a popular practice. For an individual backing up personal data or for a small office, combining a few simple commands may be all that is needed to create efficient and secure backups. This approach represents a direct application of the UNIX philosophy: joining together simple programs that do one thing to get a more complex job done.

Although just about any command that can copy files over a network can be used to move your backup data to a remote machine, some utilities are especially good for the job. Using OpenSSH tools such as ssh and scp, you can set up secure passwordless transfers of backup archives and encrypted transmissions of those archives.

Tools such as the rsync command can save resources by backing up only files (or parts of files) that have changed since the previous backup. The following sections describe some of these techniques for backing up your data to other machines over a network.

> **NOTE** *A similar tool that might interest you is the* rsnapshot *command* (pkg_
> add -r rshapshot). *The* rsnapshot *command* (www.rsnapshot.org/) *can
> work with* rsync *to make configurable hourly, daily, weekly, or monthly snapshots
> of a file system. It uses hard links to keep a snapshot of a file system, which it can
> then synchronize with changed files.*

Backing Up tar Archives over ssh

OpenSSH (www.openssh.org/) provides tools to securely perform remote login, remote execution, and remote file copy over network interfaces. By setting up two machines to share encryption keys, you can transfer files between those machines without entering passwords for each transmission. That enables you to create scripts to back up your data from an SSH client to an SSH server, without any manual intervention.

From a central BSD system, you can **gather backups from multiple client machines** using OpenSSH commands. The following example runs the tar command on a remote site (to archive and compress the files), pipes the tar stream to standard output, and uses the ssh command to catch the backup locally (over ssh) with tar:

```
$ mkdir mybackup ; cd mybackup
$ ssh kafka@server1 'tar cf - myfile*' | tar xvf -
kafka@server1's password: ******
myfile1
myfile2
```

In the example just shown, all files beginning with myfile are copied from the home directory of kafka on server1 and placed in the current directory. Note that the left side of the pipe creates the archive, and the right side expands the files from the archive to the current directory. (Keep in mind that ssh might overwrite local files if they exist, which is why we created an empty directory in the example.)

108

To reverse the process and **copy files from the local system to the remote system**, run a local `tar` command first. This time, however, we add a `cd` command to put the files in the directory of our choice on the remote machine:

```
$ tar cf - myfile* | ssh kafka@server1 \
        'cd /Users/kafka/myfolder; tar xvf -'
kafka@server1's password: ******
myfile1
myfile2
```

In this next example, we're not going to untar the files on the receiving end, but instead **write the results to tgz files:**

```
$ ssh kafka@server1 'tar czf - myfile*' | cat > myfiles.tgz
$ tar cvzf - myfile* | ssh kafka@server1 'cat > myfiles.tgz'
```

The first example takes all files beginning with `myfile` from the kafka user's home directory on server1, tars and compresses those files, and directs those compressed files to the `myfiles.tgz` file on the local system. The second example does the reverse by taking all files beginning with `myfile` in the local directory and sending them to a `myfiles.tgz` file on the remote system.

The examples just shown are good for copying files over the network. Besides providing compression, they also enable you to use any `tar` features you choose, such as incremental backup features.

Backing Up Files with rsync

A more feature-rich command for doing backups is `rsync`. What makes `rsync` so unique is the `rsync` algorithm, which compares the local and remote files one small block at a time using checksums, and transfers only the blocks that are different. This algorithm is so efficient that it has been reused in many backup products.

The `rsync` command can work either on top of a remote shell (`ssh`) or by running an `rsyncd` daemon on the server end. The following example uses `rsync` over ssh to **mirror a directory:**

```
$ rsync -avz --delete marlowe@server1:/Users/marlowe/pics/ mypics/
```

The preceding command is intended to mirror the remote directory structure (`/Users/marlowe/pics/`) to a directory on the local system (`mypices/`). The `-a` says to run in archive mode (recursively copying all files from the remote directory), the `-z` option compresses the files, and `-v` makes the output verbose. The `--delete` option tells `rsync` to delete any files on the local system that no longer exist on the remote system.

For ongoing backups, you can have rsync do seven-day incremental backups. Here's an example:

```
# mkdir /mnt/backups
# rsync --delete --backup                              \
    --backup-dir=/mnt/backups/backup-`date +%A` \
    -avz marlowe@server1:/Users/marlowe/Personal/     \
    /mnt/backups/current-backup/
```

When the above command runs, all the files from /Users/marlowe/Personal on the remote system server1 are copied to the local directory /mnt/backups/current-backup. The first time the command is run, all files are backed up to the current backup directory. The next time the command runs (on the next day), all files modified that day are copied to a directory named after the current day of the week, such as /mnt/backups/backup-Monday. Over a week, seven directories will be created that reflect changes over each of the past seven days.

Another trick for rotated backups is to **use hard links instead of multiple copies** of the files. This two-step process consists of rotating the files and then running rsync:

```
# rm -rf /mnt/backups/backup-old/
# mv /mnt/backups/backup-current/ /mnt/backups/backup-old/
# rsync --delete --link-dest=/mnt/backups/backup-old -avz \
    marlowe@server1:/Users/marlowe/Personal/ /mnt/backups/backup-current/
```

In the previous procedure, the existing backup-current directory replaces the backup-old directory, deleting the two-week-old full backup with last week's full backup. When the new full backup is run with rsync using the --link-dest option, if any of the files being backed up from the remote Personal directory on server1 existed during the previous backup (now in backup-old), then a hard link between the file in the backup-current directory and backup-old directory is created.

You can save a lot of space by having hard links between files in your backup-old and backup-current directories. For example, if you had a file named file1.txt in both directories, you could check that both were the same physical file by listing the files' inodes as follows:

```
$ ls -i /mnt/backups/backup*/file1.txt
260761   /mnt/backups/backup-current/file1.txt
260761   /mnt/backups/backup-old/file1.txt
```

Backing Up to CD or DVD

By default, if you put a blank CD or DVD into a Mac OS X system, the system will prompt you for an action. You can change this default behavior by selecting System Preferences ⇨ CDs and DVDs, and configuring responses to different behaviors (such as inserting a blank CD).

Backing up to a CD or DVD via the GUI is a three-step process:

1. Control-click or right-click on your Desktop and choose Create Burn Folder.

2. Select the items you want to move to the CD and drag them to your newly created Burn Folder.

3. Open the Burn Folder in Finder and click Burn when you're ready to back up to the CD or DVD (see Figure 8-1).

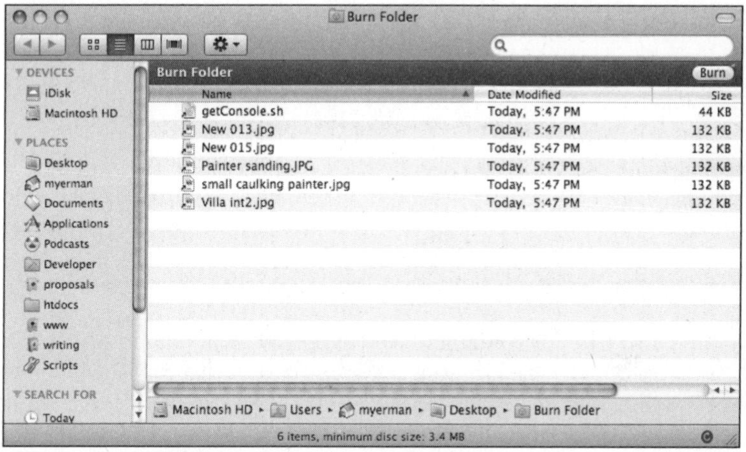

Figure 8-1: Backing up to CD using a burn folder

To back up using the command line, create a disk image using the hdiutil command-line utility in Terminal. For example, you can create an image of one of the subdirectories in your home directory using the following command:

```
hdiutil create  -srcdir ~/documents/www ~/Desktop/backup.dmg
```

Depending on how many files you are processing, this command may take a while to run. After it's completed, you can burn the disk image to disc with the following command:

```
hdiutil burn ~/Desktop/backup.dmg
```

You will be prompted to insert a disc.

Working with Time Machine and Time Capsule

The simplest way to run backups of your entire Mac OS X installation is to run Time Machine. From the GUI, simply set up your preferences for Time Machine and then attach a Firewire- or USB-attached hard drive, a network-attached drive (such as Time Capsule), or another storage device.

Time Machine will first make a backup copy of your entire Mac OS X volume to the destination drive, and then make hourly backups of any changes made on the system.

However, some users will want to either change the frequency of backups (say, every four hours instead of every hour) or exclude certain directories from the backup process. Many developers use SVN or some other system for maintaining source code and associated media files, and therefore don't need the protection provided by an hourly backup.

If you're running on Leopard (Mac OS X 10.5), download a nice piece of freeware called Time Machine Scheduler (available at www.klieme.com/TimeMachineScheduler.html) and install it. Time Machine Scheduler enables you to change the backup intervals, skip backups during certain time periods, and run manual backups.

Note that some users will still need to start Time Machine backups from the command line—say, over an SSH session from remote. To do that, use the following command:

```
/System/Library/CoreServices/backupd.bundle/Contents/Resources/backupd-helper &
```

You could also add this command to an iCal event, making it possible to run manual backups at specified times. Simply create an AppleScript with the following in it, and then attach it to an iCal event:

```
do shell script "/System/Library/CoreServices/backupd.bundle/Contents/Resources/
backupd-helper &"
```

You can reset Time Machine's interval with the following command:

```
sudo defaults write /System/Library/LaunchDaemons/com.apple.backupd-auto
StartInterval -int 7200
```

The default interval for backing up is 3,600 seconds (one hour). You will need to know the sudo password in order to make this command work.

Summary

BSD and its predecessor UNIX systems handled data backups by combining individual commands that each handled a discrete set of features. Backups of your critical data can still be done in this way. In fact, many of the tools you can use will perform more securely and efficiently than ever before.

The tape archiver utility (tar command) has expanded well beyond its original job of making magnetic tape backups of data files. Because nearly every BSD, Linux, and UNIX system includes tar, it has become a standard utility for packaging software and backing up data to compressed archives. Those archives can then be transported and stored in a variety of ways.

To move backed up data to other machines over a network, you can use the remote execution features of OpenSSH tools (such as ssh). You can also use an excellent utility called rsync. With rsync, you can save resources by backing up only the files (or parts of files) that have changed. The hdiutil program enables you to burn files to a CD from the command line, augmenting the native GUI functions for doing the same work.

Mac OS X backup features such as Time Machine and Time Capsule are also available to the UNIX power user. You can use the default options for doing hourly backups, or you can add command-line options and AppleScripting to your arsenal of tricks to schedule additional backups.

9

Checking and Running Processes

When an executable program starts up, it runs as a process that is under the management of your system's process table. Every Mac OS X system provides all the tools you need to view and change the processes running on your system.

The ps and top commands are great for viewing information on your running processes. There are literally dozens of options to ps and top to help you view process information exactly the way you want.

There are commands such as nice and renice for raising and lowering processor priority for a process. You can move processes to run in the background (bg command) and move them back to the foreground (fg command).

Sending signals to a process is a way of changing its behavior or killing it altogether. Using the kill and killall commands, you can send signals to processes by PID or name, respectively. You can also send other signals to processes to do such things as reread configuration files or continue with a stopped process.

IN THIS CHAPTER

Viewing active processes with ps and top

Finding and controlling processes

Adjusting CPU priority with nice and renice

Moving processes to background (bg) or foreground (fg)

Killing and signaling processes with kill and killall

Using at and batch to run commands

Scheduling commands to run repeatedly with cron

To run commands at scheduled times or to ensure that they are not tied to your shell session, you can use the at and batch commands. To run commands repetitively at set times, there are the cron and anacron facilities.

Listing Active Processes

To see which processes are currently running on a system, most people use the ps and top commands. The ps command gives you a snapshot (in a simple list) of processes running at the moment. The top command offers a screen-oriented, constantly updated listing of running commands, sorted as you choose (by CPU use, I/O, UID, and so on).

Viewing Active Processes with ps

Every BSD system (as well as every system derived from UNIX, such as Linux, Mac OS X, and others) includes the ps command. Over the years, however, many slightly different versions of ps have appeared, offering slightly different options. Because ps dates back to the first UNIX systems, it also supports nonstandard ways of entering some options (for example, enabling you to drop the dash before an option in some cases).

The different uses of ps shown in this chapter will work on FreeBSD, OpenBSD, NetBSD, and most other UNIX and Linux systems. Here are some examples you can run to **show processes running for the current user** (Table 7-1 contains column descriptions of ps output):

```
$ ps                          List processes of current user at current shell
  PID TT  STAT    TIME  COMMAND
  810 v0  I+    0.00.09  -sh (sh)
 1117 v2  S     0.00.02  -sh (sh)
 1125 v2  R+    0.00.00  ps
$ ps U marlowe                Show all marlowe's running processes (simple output)
  PID TT  STAT    TIME  COMMAND
 1132 ??  S     0:00.01  sshd: marlowe@ttyp0 (sshd)
  810 v0  I+    0.00.09  -sh (sh)
 1117 v2  S     0.00.02  -sh (sh)
 1125 v2  R+    0.00.00  ps -U chris
 1133 p0  Ss+   0.00.00  -sh (sh)
 ...
$ ps uU marlowe               Show all marlowe's running processes (with CPU/MEM)
USER      PID %CPU %MEM   VSZ   RSS  TT  STAT STARTED      TIME COMMAND
chris    1132  0.0  1.3  6252  3312  ??  S    4:52PM  0:00.03 sshd: marlowe@ttyp0
chris     810  0.0  0.6  1756  1400  v0  I+   3:30PM  0:00.09 -sh (sh)
chris    1117  0.0  0.6  1752  1396  v2  I+   4:45PM  0:00.05 -sh (sh)
chris    1133  0.0  0.6  1756  1396  p0  Ss   4:52PM  0:00.03 -sh (sh)
chris    1204  0.0  0.4  1460  1036  p0  R+   5:07PM  0:00.00 ps -U marlowe -u
 ...
$ ps vU marlowe               Show all marlowe's running processes (with SL and RE)
  PID STAT    TIME  SL  RE PAGEIN   VSZ   RSS  LIM TSIZ %CPU %MEM COMMAND
 1132 S    0:00.16   0 127      0  6252  3312    -  168  0.0  1.3 sshd: marlowe
  810 I+   0:00.09 127 127      2  1756  1400    -  100  0.0  0.6 -sh (sh)
 1133 Ss   0:00.08   0 127      0  1756  1400    -  100  0.0  0.6 -sh (sh)
 ...
```

```
1244 I+   0:00.02  47 110      0  1752  1392      -  100  0.0  0.6 -sh (sh)
1264 R+   0:00.01   0   0      0  1460  1044      -   24  0.0  0.4 ps -vU
...
```

These examples illustrate some of the processes from a user logged in locally and remotely (over sshd). The first example shows ps alone being run from a Terminal window, so you only see the processes for the current shell running in that window. Other examples enable you to display different information for each process. The SL and RE columns show how many seconds the process has been sleeping and how long it has been in core memory, respectively (127 means forever).

Here are ps examples showing output for **every process currently running on the system**:

```
$ ps x | less       Show running processes, even without controlling terminals
  PID  TT  STAT     TIME COMMAND
    0  ??  WLs    0:00.00 [swapper]
    1  ??  ILs    0:00.01 /sbin/init --
    2  ??  DL     0:00.49 [g_event]
  ...

$ ps xl | less      Show long listing of processes
 UID   PID  PPID CPU PRI NI    VSZ    RSS MWCHAN STAT  TT       TIME COMMAND
   0     0     0   1  96  0      0      0 -      WLs   ??    0:00.00 [swapper]
   0     1     0   0   8  0    772    388 wait   ILs   ??    0:00.01 /sbin/init
   0     2     0   0  -8  0      0      8 -      DL    ??    0:00.49 [g_event]
  ...

$ ps xj | less      Show running process, with user name/process group
USER   PID  PPID  PGID   SID JOBC STAT  TT       TIME COMMAND
root     0     0     0     0    0 WLs   ??    0:00.00 [swapper]
root     1     0     1     1    0 ILs   ??    0:00.01 /sbin/init --
root     2     0     0     0    0 DL    ??    0:00.56 [g_event]
  ...

$ ps aux | less    Show running process, long BSD style
USER   PID %CPU %MEM    VSZ   RSS  TT  STAT STARTED       TIME COMMAND
root    10 99.0  0.0      0     8  ??  RL   3:30PM 209:34.30 [idle]
root     0  0.0  0.0      0     0  ??  WLs  3:30PM  0:00.00 [swapper]
root     1  0.0  0.2    772   388  ??  ILs  3:30PM  0:00.01 /sbin/init --
  ...

$ ps auwx         Show every running process, long BSD style, wide format
$ ps auwwx        Show every running process, long BSD style, unlimited width
```

The previous two commands are useful if you want to see the entire output of ps entries. When output extends beyond your column width, it will wrap instead of truncating.

If you prefer personalized views of ps output, you can select exactly which columns of data to display with ps using the -o option. Table 9-1 shows available column output and the options to add to -o to have each column print with ps.

Table 9-1: Selecting and Viewing ps Column Output

Option	Column Head	Description
%cpu	%CPU	Percentage of CPU use
%mem	%MEM	Percentage of memory use
acflag	ACFLG	Accounting flag
args	COMMAND	Command and arguments
comm	COMMAND	Command only
command	COMMAND	Command and arguments (same as args)
cpu	CPU	Short-term CPU usage factor (for scheduling)
etime	ELAPSED	Elapsed runtime
flags	F	Process flags, in hexadecimal (same as f)
inblk	INBLK	Total blocks read (same as inblock)
jid	JID	Jail ID
jobc	JOBC	Job control count
ktrace	KTRACE	Tracing flags
label	LABEL	MAC label
lim	LIM	Memory use limit
lockname	LOCK	Lock currently blocked on (as a symbolic name)
logname	LOGIN	Login name of user who started the session
lstart	STARTED	Time started
majflt	MAJFLT	Total page faults
minflt	MINFLT	Total page reclaims
msgrcv	MSGRCV	Total messages received (pipes/sockets reads)
msgsnd	MSGSND	Total messages sent (pipes/sockets writes)
mwchan	MWCHAN	Wait channel or lock currently blocked on
nice	NI	Nice value (same as ni)
nivcsw	NIVCSW	Total involuntary context switches

Table 9-1: Selecting and Viewing ps Column Output *(continued)*

Option	Column Head	Description
nsigs	NSIGS	Total signals taken (same as nsignals)
nswap	NSWAP	Total swaps in and out
nvcsw	NVCSW	Total voluntary context switches
nwchan	NWCHAN	Wait channel (as an address)
oublk	OUBLK	Total blocks written (same as oublock)
paddr	PADDR	Swap address
pagein	PAGEIN	Pageins (same as majflt)
pgid	PGID	Process group number
pid	PID	Process ID
ppid	PPID	Parent process ID
pri	PRI	Scheduling priority
re	RE	Core residency time, in seconds (127 means infinity)
rgid	RGID	Real group ID
rgroup	RGROUP	Group name (associated with real group ID)
rss	RSS	Resident set size
rtprio	RTPRIO	Real-time priority (101 means it is not a real-time process)
ruid	RUID	Real user ID
ruser	RUSER	Username (associated with real user ID)
sid	SID	Session ID
sig	PENDING	Pending signals (same as pending)
sigcatch	CAUGHT	Caught signals (same as caught)
sigignore	IGNORED	Ignored signals (same ignored)
sigmask	BLOCKED	Blocked signals (same as blocked)
sl	SL	Sleep time, in seconds (127 means infinity)
start	STARTED	Time started

Continued

119

Table 9-1: Selecting and Viewing ps Column Output *(continued)*

Option	Column Head	Description
state	STAT	Symbolic process state (same as stat)
svgid	SVGID	Saved gid from a setgid executable
svuid	SVUID	Saved UID from a setuid executable
tdev	TDEV	Control terminal device number
time	TIME	Accumulated CPU time, user + system (same as cputime)
tpgid	TPGID	Control terminal process group ID
tsid	TSID	Control terminal session ID
tsiz	TSIZ	Text size, in Kbytes
tt	TT	Control terminal name, two-letter abbreviation
tty	TTY	Full name of control terminal
uprocp	UPROCP	Process pointer
ucomm	UCOMM	Name to be used for accounting
uid	UID	Effective user ID
upr	UPR	Scheduling priority from system call (same as usrpri)
user	USER	Username (from user ID)
vsz	VSZ	Virtual size, in Kbytes (same as vsize)
wchan	WCHAN	Wait channel as a symbolic name
xstat	XSTAT	Exit or stop status (stopped or zombie processes only)

Note that some values that are meant to print usernames may still print numbers (UIDs) instead if the name is too long to fit in the given space. To see the values, use ps -L:

```
$ ps L        List column options for ps output
%cpu %mem acflag acflg args blocked caught comm command cpu cputime emul etime
f flags ignored inblk inblock jid jobc ktrace label lim lockname login logname
lstart lwp majflt minflt msgrcv msgsnd mwchan ni nice nivcsw nlwp nsignals nsigs
nswap nvcsw nwchan oublk oublock paddr pagein pcpu pending pgid pid pmem ppid
pri re rgid rgroup rss rtprio ruid ruser sid sig sigcatch sigignore sigmask sl
start stat state svgid svuid tdev time tpgid tsid tsiz tt tty ucomm uid upr
uprocp user usrpri vsize vsz wchan xstat
```

Using a comma-separated list of column options, you can produce your own custom output. Here are some examples of **custom views of running processes**:

```
$ ps xo ppid,user,%mem,tsiz,vsz,comm      Display process ID, user, memory, etc.
PPID USER  %MEM TSIZ   VSZ COMMAND
1129 chris  1.3  168  6252 sshd
$ ps xo ppid,user,start,time,%cpu,args  Display PID, user, start, time, etc.
PPID USER  STARTED       TIME %CPU COMMAND
1129 chris  4:52PM   0:00.82  0.0 sshd: chris@ttyp0 (sshd)
$ ps xo ppid,user,nice,cputime,args      Display PID, user, nice, CPU time, etc.
PPID USER  NI     TIME COMMAND
1129 chris  0   0:00.84 sshd: chris@ttyp0 (sshd)
$ ps xo ppid,user,stat,tty,sid,etime,args  Display PID, user, tty, sid, etc.
PPID USER  STAT TTY      SID    ELAPSED COMMAND
1129 chris S    ??      1129   06:39:23 sshd: chris@ttyp0 (sshd)
```

Here are a few other **extraneous examples of the ps command**:

```
$ ps aux -r | less                              Sort by CPU usage
USER    PID %CPU %MEM  VSZ   RSS  TT  STAT STARTED     TIME COMMAND
root     10 87.4  0.0    0     8  ??  RL   3:30PM 503:12.85 [idle]
root   2551  7.8  0.4 1384   916  v3  R   11:55PM  0:02.50 find .
root      4  1.0  0.0    0     8  ??  DL   3:30PM  0:08.73 [g_down]
$ ps -m | less                                  Sort by memory usage
USER    PID %CPU %MEM  VSZ   RSS  TT  STAT STARTED     TIME COMMAND
root   1307  0.0  1.2 4928  3004  v3  I    5:31PM  0:00.58 -csh (csh)
root    745  0.0  1.1 3504  2804  ??  Ss   3:30PM  0:01.04 sendmail:
$ ps -t ttyp0                                   Show ttyp0 processes
 PID  TT  STAT    TIME COMMAND
1133  p0  Ss   0:00.38 -sh (sh)
2595  p0  R+   0:00.00 ps -t ttyp0
$ ps -p 1129 -o pid,ppid,time,args          Display info for PID 1129
 PID PPID     TIME COMMAND
1129  739  0:08.08 sshd: chris [priv] (sshd)
$ ps -U marlowe,kafka -o pid,ruser,tty,stat,args  See info for two users
PID RUSER    TTY    STAT COMMAND
1132 chris    ??     S   sshd: marlowe@ttyp0 (sshd)
2480 francois ??     S   sshd: kafka@ttyp1 (sshd)
```

Watching Active Processes with top

If you want to **see the processes running on your system on an ongoing basis**, you can use the top command. The top command runs a screen-oriented view of your running processes that is updated continuously. If you start the top command with no options, it displays your system's uptime, tasks, CPU usage, and memory usage, followed by a list of your running processes, sorted by CPU usage. Here's an example:

```
$ top
Processes:  75 total, 4 running, 2 stuck, 69 sleeping… 375 threads
10:43:16
Load Avg:  0.83,  0.38,  0.31    CPU usage: 40.09% user,  7.93% sys, 51.98% idle
```

```
SharedLibs: num =    7, resident =   53M code, 1240K data, 3932K linkedit.
MemRegions: num = 29859, resident =  631M +   14M private,  273M shared.
PhysMem:  253M wired, 1075M active,  556M inactive, 1891M used,  157M free.
VM: 13G + 371M   595820(0) pageins, 466528(0) pageouts

  PID COMMAND     %CPU   TIME   #TH #PRTS #MREGS RPRVT  RSHRD  RSIZE  VSIZE
92555 top         11.6% 0:01.28  1    18    30  1120K   188K  1712K    18M
92383 cupsd        0.0% 0:00.02  2    30    31   452K   228K  1360K    19M
92355 mdworker     0.0% 0:00.14  3    50    32   604K  6612K  2664K    35M
90021 mdworker     0.0% 0:00.75  4    73    89  2404K    10M  8348K    42M
88407 bash         0.0% 0:00.26  1    14    20   324K   692K  1000K    18M
```

Here are examples of other options you can use to **start top to continuously display running processes**:

$ **top -s 5**	*Change update delay to 5 seconds (from default 3)*
$ **top -U marlowe**	*Only see processes of effective user name marlowe*
$ **top -S**	*Display system processes, as well as other processes*
$ **top -d 10**	*Refresh the screen 10 times before quitting*
$ **top -b**	*Run in non-interative non-screen-oriented batch mode*

This last example (top -b) formats the output of top in a way that is suitable for output to a file, as opposed to redrawing the same screen for interactive viewing. This can be used to create a log of processes—for example, when hunting down that runaway process that eats up all your resources in the middle of the night. Here's how to **run top and log the output** for 10 hours:

```
$ top -b -d 12000 > myprocesslog &
```

When top is running, you can **update and sort the process list in different ways**. To **immediately update the process list**, press Space. Press **O** and then type **cpu** to **sort by CPU and weighted CPU time.**

There are several ways to **change the behavior of top as it's running**. Press **s** and type a number representing seconds to **change the delay between refreshes**. Press **u** and enter a username to **display only processes for the selected user**. To **view only a select number of processes**, type **n** and type the number you want to see. Press Ctrl+L at any point to **redraw the screen.**

You can **act on any of the running processes** in different ways. To **signal (kill) a running process**, type **k** followed by the PID of the process to which you want to send the signal. This sends the default 15 signal (TERM), which enables the process to close in an orderly way. To **give a process a higher or lower run priority**, type **r** and then add either a negative number (to increase priority) or a positive number (to reduce priority), followed by the process ID of the process you want to change.

If you want to **find more information about how to use top**, type **?** during a top session. The man page also has a lot of information about how to use top:

```
$ man top          View the top man page
```

When you are done using top, type **q** to exit.

Finding and Controlling Processes

Changing a running process first means finding the process you want to change, and then modifying the processing priority or sending the process a signal to change its behavior. If you are looking for a particular process, you might find it tough to locate in a long list of processes output by ps or top.

The pgrep command offers ways of searching through your active processes for the ones you are looking for. The renice command enables you to change the processing priority of running processes. The kill, pkill, and killall commands enable you to send signals to running processes (including signals to end those processes).

Using grep and pgrep to Find Processes

In its most basic form, you can use grep to search for a command name (or part of one) and produce the process ID of any process that includes that name, as shown in the following example:

```
$ ps | grep http          Show info for any process including 'http' string
myerman  19416  0.0  0.0  112568   988  ??  S    3:46PM  0:00.00 /
Applications/MAMP/Library/bin/httpd -k start
...
```

If you need more control over finding processes, you can download proctools from sourceforge.net/projects/proctools. The proctools package will give you the pgrep command-line tool.

In its most basic form, you can use pgrep to search for a command name (or part of one) and produce the process ID of any process that includes that name, as shown in this example:

```
$ pgrep init          Show PID for any process including 'init' string
2617
1
```

Because you know there is only one init command running, you next use the -1 option to see each process's command name (to learn why two processes showed up):

```
$ pgrep -1 init        Show PID and name for any process including 'init' string
2617 xinit
1 init
```

You can also **search for processes that are associated with a particular user:**

```
$ pgrep -lu kafka      List all processes owned by user kafka
2803 vim
2552 bash
2551 sshd
```

Probably the most useful way to use pgrep is to have it **find the process IDs of the running processes and pipe those PIDs to another command** to produce the output. Here are some examples (look for other commands if Metacity or Firefox isn't running):

```
$ ps -p `pgrep metacity`       Search for metacity and run ps (short)
  PID TT    STAT    TIME COMMAND
  2617 ??   Is    00:07.02 /usr/local/bin/metacity --sm-client-id=default0
$ ps -fp `pgrep xinit`         Search for xinit and run ps (full)
  PID  TT STAT     TIME COMMAND
  2617 v2 I+      0:00.01 /usr/X11R6/bin/xinit /home/chris/.xinitrc
# renice -5 `pgrep safari`   Search for safari, improve its priority
20522: old priority 0, new priority -5
20557: old priority 0, new priority -5
```

Any command that can take a process ID as input can be combined with pgrep in these ways. As the previous example of pgrep illustrates, you can use commands such as renice to change how a process behaves while it is running.

Using fuser to Find Processes

Another way to locate a particular process is by what the process is accessing. The fuser command can be used to find which processes currently have a file or a socket open. After the processes are found, fuser can be used to send signals to those processes. The fuser command is most useful for determining whether files are being held open by processes on mounted file systems (such as local hard disks or Samba shares). Finding those processes enables you to close them properly (or just kill them if you must) so the file system can be unmounted cleanly.

Here are some examples of the fuser command for **listing processes that have files open on a selected file system:**

```
# fuser -cu /Users/myerman       Output of processes with /Users/myerman open
(with user name)
/Users/myerman: 12958c (myerman)
```

The example just shown displays the process ID for one running process associated with /Users/myerman. It might indicate an open file, an open shell, or a child process of a shell with the current directory in /Users/myerman or its subdirectories. The -c option causes /Users/myerman to be treated as the mount point (so anything below that point is matched), and -u causes the owner of each process to be listed.

Letters between the process IDs and the usernames indicate how the files being held open are being used. In these examples, an x indicates that the file is the executable text of the process, and a c says that the file is the current working directory of the process. Other possible letters include r (the file is in the process's root directory), j (the file is the jail root of the process), t (the file is the kernel tracing file of the process), y (the process uses the file as its controlling tty), m (the file is mmapped), w (the file is open for writing), a (the file is open as append only), s (the file has a shared lock), and e (the file has an exclusive lock).

Here are other examples using fuser to **show processes with files open:**

```
# fuser -c -m /boot    Show PIDs/symbols for processes opening /boot
# fuser -u /boot        Show PIDs/symbols/user of /boot, not subdirectories
```

After you know which processes have files open, you can close those processes manually or kill them. Close processes manually if at all possible, as simply killing processes can leave files in an unclean state! Here are examples of using fuser to **kill or send other signals to all processes with files open to a file system:**

```
# fuser -k /tmp/my.txt    Kill processes with /tmp/my.txt open (SIGKILL)
```

Even after a process is running, you can change its behavior in different ways. With the renice command, shown earlier, you can adjust a running process's priority in your system's scheduler. With the nice command, you can determine the default priority and set a higher or lower priority at the time you launch a process.

Another way you can change how a running process behaves is to send a signal to that process. The kill and killall commands can be used to send signals to running processes. Likewise, the pkill command can send a signal to a process.

Adjusting Processor Priority with nice

Every running process has a *nice* value that can be used to tell the process scheduler what priority should be given to that process. Positive values of niceness actually give your process a lower priority. The concept came about during the days of large, multi-user UNIX systems; you could be "nice" by running a non-urgent process at lower priority so other users had a shot at the CPU.

Niceness doesn't enforce scheduling priority; it's merely a suggestion to the scheduler. The default nice value is 0. You can use the nice command to run a process at a higher or lower priority than the default. The priority number can range from −35 (most favorable scheduling priority) to 19 (least favorable scheduling priority). Although the root user can raise or lower any user's nice value, a regular user can only lower the priorities of a process (setting a higher nice value).

> **WARNING** *Proceed with caution when assigning negative nice values to processes. This can possibly crash your machine if critical system processes lose their high priority.*

Here are a few examples of starting a command with `nice` to change a command's nice value:

```
$ nice -n 12 nroff -man a.roff | less   Format man pages at low priority
# nice -n -10 designer                  Launch QT Designer at higher priority
```

When a process is already running, you can change the process's nice value using the renice command. Here are some examples of the `renice` command:

```
$ renice +2 -u kafka              Renice kafka's processes +2
$ renice +5 4737                  Renice PID 4737 by +5
# renice -3 `find / -name \*.html -print`   Renice find process -3
9688: old priority -1, new priority -3
20279: old priority -1, new priority -3
20282: old priority -1, new priority -3
```

The backticks are used in the previous command line to indicate that the output of the `find` command (presumably all .html files on the volume) should be fed to the `renice` command.

The niceness settings for your processes are displayed by default when you run `top`. You can also see niceness settings using `-o nice` when you produce custom output from the `ps` command.

Running Processes in the Background and Foreground

When you run a process from a shell, it is run in the foreground by default. That means you can't type another command until the first one is done. By adding an ampersand (&) to the end of a command line, you can run that command line in the background. Using the `fg`, `bg`, and `jobs` commands, along with various control codes, you can move commands between background and foreground.

The following sequence of commands starts the GIMP image program from a Terminal window. After that is a series of control keys and commands to stop and start the process and move it between foreground and background:

```
$ gimp                    Run gimp in the foreground
<Ctrl+Z>                  Stop process and place in background
[1]+  Stopped       gimp
$ bg 1                    Start process running again in background (bash)
```

```
$ bg %1                    Start process running again in background (sh)
$ fg 1                     Continue running process in foreground (bash)
$ fg %1                    Continue running process in foreground (sh)
gimp
<Ctrl+C>                   Kill process
```

Note that processes placed in the background are given a job ID number (in this case, 1). By placing a percentage sign in front of the number (for example, %1) you can identify a particular background process to the bg and fg commands. You can do the same thing in the bash shell by typing the number with the command (as in fg 1). With one or more background jobs running at the current shell, you can **use the jobs command to manage your background jobs:**

```
$ jobs                     Display background jobs for current shell
[1]     Running               gimp &
[2]     Running               xmms &
[3]-    Running               gedit &
[4]+    Stopped               gtali
$ jobs -1                  Display PID with each job's information
[1]   31676 Running           gimp &
[2]   31677 Running           xmms &
[3]- 31683 Running            gedit &
[4]+ 31688 Stopped            gtali
$ jobs -1 %2               Display information only for job %2
[2]   31677 Running           xmms &
```

The processes running in the jobs examples might have been done while you were logged in (using ssh) to a remote system, but you wanted to **run remote GUI applications on your local desktop.** By running those processes in the background, you can have multiple applications running at once, while still having those applications associated with your current shell.

> **NOTE** With fg or bg, if you don't indicate which process to act on, the current job is used. The current job has a plus sign (+) next to it.

The fg and bg commands manipulate running processes by moving those processes to the foreground or background. Another way to manipulate running commands is to send signals directly to those processes. A common way to send signals to running processes is with the kill and killall commands.

Killing and Signaling Processes

You can stop or change running processes by sending signals to those processes. Commands such as kill and killall can send signals you select to running processes, which, as their names imply, are often signals to kill the process.

Signals are represented by numbers (9, 15, and so on) and strings (SIGKILL, SIGTERM, and so on). Table 9-2 describes standard signals you can send to processes in BSD systems.

Table 9-2: Standard Signals to Send to Processes

Signal Number	Signal Name	Description
1	SIGHUP	Hang up from Terminal or controlling process died
2	SIGINT	Interrupt program
3	SIGQUIT	Quit program
4	SIGILL	Illegal instruction
5	SIGTRAP	Trace trap
6	SIGABRT	Abort sent from abort function
7	SIGEMT	Emulate instruction executed
8	SIGFPE	Floating point exception
9	SIGKILL	Kill signal
10	SIGBUS	Bus error
11	SIGSEGV	Segmentation violation
12	SIGSYS	Non-existent system call invoked
13	SIGPIPE	Pipe broken (nothing to read write to pipe)
14	SIGALRM	Timer signal from alarm system call
15	SIGTERM	Termination signal
16	SIGURG	Discard signal
17	SIGSTOP	Stop the process
18	SIGTSTP	Stop typed at Terminal
19	SIGCONT	Continue if process is stopped
20	SIGCHLD	Child status changed
21	SIGTTIN	Terminal tries to read background process
22	SIGTTOU	Terminal tries to write to background process

The kill command can send signals to processes by process ID or job number, whereas the killall command can signal processes by command name. Here are some examples:

```
$ kill 28665          Send SIGTERM to process with PID 28665
$ kill -9 4895        Send SIGKILL to process with PID 4895
```

```
$ kill -SIGCONT 5254        Continue a stopped process (pid 5254)
$ kill %3                   Kill the process represented by job %3
$ killall spamd             Kill all spamd daemons currently running
$ killall -SIGHUP sendmail  Have sendmail processes reread config files
```

The SIGKILL (9) signal, used generously by trigger-happy novice administrators, should be reserved as a last resort. It does not allow the targeted process to exit cleanly but forces it to end abruptly. This can potentially result in loss or corruption of data handled by that process. The SIGHUP signal was originally used on UNIX systems to indicate that a terminal was being disconnected from a mainframe (such as from a hang-up of a dial-in modem). However, daemon processes, such as sendmail and httpd, were implemented to catch SIGHUP signals as an indication that those processes should reread configuration files.

Running Processes Away from the Current Shell

If you want a process to continue to run even if you disconnect from the current shell session, there are several ways to go about doing that. You can use the nohup command to **run a process in a way that it is impervious to a hang-up signal:**

```
$ nohup mylongscript.sh &       Run mylongscript.sh with no ability to interrupt
# nohup nice -9 gcc hello.c &    Run gcc uninterrupted and higher priority
```

Using nohup is different from running the command with an ampersand alone, because with nohup the command will keep running, even if you exit the shell that launched the command.

The nohup command was commonly used in the days of slow processors and dial-up connections (so you didn't have to stay logged into an expensive connection while a long compile completed). In addition, using tools today such as screen (described in Chapter 14) you can keep a shell session active even after you disconnect your network connection to that shell.

Scheduling Processes to Run

Commands associated with the cron facility can be used to set a command to run at a specific time (including now) so that it is not connected to the current shell. The at command **runs a command at the time you set.** Enter the at command, type the commands you want to run at the later time, and press Ctrl+D to queue the job:

```
# at now +1 minute          Start command running in one minute
ls -R /usr/ports > /tmp/portlist.txt
<Ctrl+D> <EOT>
job 5 at Thu Mar 20 20:37:00 2008
# at teatime                Start command at 4pm today
# at now +5 days            Start a command in five days
# at 06/25/08               Start a command at current time on June 25, 2008\
```

Another way to run a command that's not connected with the current shell is with the `batch` command. With `batch`, you can **set a command to start as soon as the processor is ready** (load average below .8):

```
# batch                Start command running immediately
find /mnt/isos | grep jpg$ > /tmp/mypics
<Ctrl+D> <EOT>
```

Note that after the `at` or `batch` commands, you see a secondary prompt. Type the command you want to run at that prompt and press Enter. After that, you can continue to enter commands. When you are done, press Ctrl+D on a line by itself to queue the commands you entered to run.

When the commands are entered, you can **check the queue of at and batch jobs that are set to** run by typing the `atq` command:

```
$ atq
Date                        Owner     Queue     Job#
Tue Dec 29 16:00:00 CST 2008    root      c         4
Sat Aug  2 19:24:00 CST 2008    root      c         5
```

Regular users can't view queued jobs. The root user can see everyone's queued at jobs. If you want to **delete an at job from the queue,** use the `atrm` command:

```
# atrm 5                Delete at job number 5
```

The `at` and `batch` commands are for queuing up a command to run as a one-shot deal. You can use the cron facility to **set up commands to run repeatedly.** These commands are scripted into cron jobs, which are scheduled in crontab files. There is one system crontab file (`/etc/crontab`). In addition, each user can create a personal crontab file that can launch commands at times that the user chooses. To **create a personal crontab file,** type the following:

```
$ crontab -e           Create a personal crontab file
```

The `crontab -e` command opens your crontab file (or creates a new one) using the vi text editor. Here are examples of several entries you could add to a crontab file:

```
15 8 * * Mon,Tue,Wed,Thu,Fri mail kafka < /var/project/stats.txt
* * 1 1,4,7,10 * find /doc | grep .doc$ > /var/sales/documents.txt
```

The first crontab example shown sends a mail message to the user named `kafka` by directing the contents of `/var/project/stats.txt` into that message. That mail command is run Monday through Friday at 8:15 a.m. In the second example, on the first day of January, April, July, and October, the `find` command runs to look for every `.doc` file in `/doc` and sends the resulting list of files to `/var/sales/documents.txt`.

The last part of each crontab entry is the command that is run. The first five fields represent the time and date the command is run. The fields from left to right are as follows: minute (0 to 59), hour (0 to 23), day of the month (0 to 31), month (0 to 12 or Jan, Feb, Mar, Apr, May, Jun, Jul, Aug, Sep, Oct, Nov, or Dec), and day of the week (0 to 7 or Sun, Mon, Tue, Wed, Thu, Fri, or Sat). An asterisk (*) in a field means to match any value for that field.

Here are some **other options with the crontab command**:

```
# crontab -eu marlowe        Edit another user's crontab (root only)
$ crontab -l                 List contents of your crontab file
15 8 * * Mon,Tue,Wed,Thu,Fri mail chris < /var/project/stats.txt
* * 1 1,4,7,10 * find / | grep .doc$ > /var/sales/documents.txt
$ crontab -r                 Delete your crontab file
```

An alternative to the cron facility is the anacron facility (pkg_add -r anacron). With anacron, as with cron, you can configure commands to run periodically. However, anacron is most appropriate for machines that are not on all the time. If a command is not run because the computer was off during the scheduled time, then the next time the computer is on, the anacron facility makes sure that the commands that were missed during the down time are run after the system resumes.

Summary

Watching and working with the processes that run on your Mac OS X system are important activities to ensure that your system is operating efficiently. Using commands such as ps and top, you can view the processes running on your system.

With commands such as nice and renice, you can adjust the recommended priorities at which selected processes run. When a process is running, you can change how it is running or kill the process by sending it a signal from the kill or killall commands.

After launching a command from the current shell, you can set that command's process to run in the background (bg) or foreground (fg). You can also stop and restart the process using different control codes.

To schedule a command to run at a later time, you can use the at or batch commands. To set up a command to run repeatedly at set intervals, you can use the cron or anacron facilities.

10

Managing the System

Without careful management, the demands on your Mac OS X system can sometimes exceed the resources you have available. Being able to monitor your system's activities (memory, CPU, and device usage) over time can help you ensure that your machine has enough resources to do what you require. Likewise, managing other aspects of your system, such as the device drivers it uses and how the boot process works, can help avoid performance problems and system failures.

This chapter is divided into several sections that relate to ways of managing your Mac OS X system. The first section can help you monitor the resources (processing power, devices, and memory) on your system. The next section describes how to check and set your system clock. Descriptions of the boot process and subsequent run levels follow. The last sections describe how to work with the kernel and related device drivers, as well as how to view information about your computer's hardware components.

IN THIS CHAPTER

Checking memory use with top and vmstat

Viewing CPU usage with iostat, systat, and top

Monitoring storage devices with iostat and lsof

Working with dates/time using date, cal, and NTP

Shutting down the system with reboot, halt, and shutdown

Monitoring Resources

FreeBSD, OpenBSD, NetBSD, and other UNIX-like systems do a wonderful job of keeping track of what they do, and Mac OS X is no different. If you care to look, you can find a lot of information about how your CPU, hard disks, virtual memory, and other computer resources are being used.

Of course, you can use commands to view information about how your computer's virtual memory, processor, storage devices, and network interfaces are being used on your system. There are commands that can monitor several different aspects of your system's resources. Because this book is not just a man page, however, we have divided the following sections by topic (monitoring memory, CPU, storage devices) rather than by the commands that do them (top and iostat).

Monitoring Memory Use

Few things will kill system performance faster than running out of memory. Commands such as top enable you to see basic information about how your RAM and swap are being used.

The top command provides a means of watching the currently running processes, with those processes sorted by CPU usage or memory (see Chapter 9 for a description of top for watching running processes). However, you can also use top to watch your memory usage in a screen-oriented way. Here is an example:

```
$ top
last pid:  1619;  load averages:  0.61,  0.85,  0.62  up 0+02:23:09  17:23:49
85 processes:  2 running, 83 sleeping
CPU states: 37.5% user,  0.0% nice, 15.4% system,  0.8% interrupt, 46.3% idle
Mem: 76M Active, 31M Inact, 79M Wired, 2476K Cache, 34M Buf, 53M Free
Swap: 484M Total, 25M Used, 459M Free, 5% Inuse

  PID USERNAME    THR PRI NICE    SIZE    RES STATE     TIME    WCPU COMMAND
 1618 marlowe       3 117       0 51964K 35352K RUN       0:07   7.96% totem
 1462 marlowe       1  96       0 85016K 15968K select    0:33   5.66% Xorg
 1491 marlowe       1  98       0 12812K  8008K select    0:05   1.03% metacity
 1494 marlowe       1  96       0 27880K 12088K select    0:08   0.44% gnome-panel
```

To exit top, press q. The top command shows the total memory usage for RAM (Mem:) and swap space (Swap:). However, because top is screen oriented and provides ongoing monitoring, you can watch memory usage change every two seconds (by default). The most useful column to analyze a process's memory usage is RES, which shows the process's actual physical RAM usage, also known as *resident size*. Run top -orsize, and running processes will be displayed in resident memory use order (to sort by the RES column):

```
$ top -orsize
   ...
  PID USERNAME    THR PRI NICE    SIZE    RES STATE     TIME    WCPU COMMAND
 1673 kafka         3 112       0 56288K 38660K RUN       0:22   0.00% totem
 1615 kafka         1  96       0 27060K 15428K select    0:03   0.00% kview
 1462 kafka         1 100       0 84900K 13388K select    1:51  10.60% Xorg
 1496 kafka         3  20       0 33072K 10928K kserel    0:05   0.00% nautilus
```

To see the total size of memory consumed by a process (including text, data, and stack), you can sort by the SIZE column. To do that, type top -ovsize:

```
$ top -ovsize
   ...
```

```
 PID USERNAME     THR PRI NICE   SIZE    RES STATE   TIME   WCPU COMMAND
1462 marlowe        1 100     0 85036K 12528K RUN    3:41 10.94% Xorg
1764 kafka          3 114     0 56124K 38712K RUN    0:31  0.00% totem
1496 kafka          3  20     0 33072K  8100K kserel 0:05  0.00% nautilus
1494 marlowe        1  96     0 27880K  9384K select 0:10  0.00% gnome-panel
```

Monitoring CPU Usage

An overburdened CPU is another obvious place to look for performance problems on your system. The iostat command can generate detailed reports of CPU utilization. The top command can be used to view which processes are consuming the most processing time.

Here are two examples of using iostat to **display a CPU utilization report:**

```
$ iostat -w 3       CPU stats every 3 seconds (starting apps)
disk0       cpu     load average
  KB/t tps  MB/s  us sy id   1m   5m  15m
 17.06   6  0.10   6  4 90  0.31 0.44 0.44
  0.00   0  0.00   9  4 87  0.29 0.43 0.43
  0.00   0  0.00   9  3 88  0.29 0.43 0.43
  0.00   0  0.00   8  3 89  0.26 0.42 0.43
  0.00   0  0.00   8  2 89  0.32 0.43 0.43
  0.00   0  0.00   9  3 89  0.32 0.43 0.43
  0.00   0  0.00  12  5 83  0.30 0.42 0.43
```

The preceding iostat example shows load averages and CPU consumption.

Here is an example of using iostat to **print CPU utilization reports for a set number of instances:**

```
$ iostat -w 2 -C 10     Repeat every 2 seconds for 10 times
```

If you want to find out specifically which processes are consuming the most processing time, you can use the top -mcpu command. Type top, and then press c to toggle between CPU usage and weighted CPU usage:

```
$ top -ocpu             Display running processes and sort by CPU usage
Processes:  75 total, 3 running, 2 stuck, 70 sleeping… 374 threads
11:15:32
Load Avg:  0.50,  0.50,  0.46   CPU usage: 14.94% user,   9.13% sys, 75.93% idle
SharedLibs: num =     7, resident =    50M code, 1068K data, 3928K linkedit.
MemRegions: num = 29856, resident =   633M +   13M private,  249M shared.
PhysMem:  257M wired, 1014M active,  456M inactive, 1733M used,   315M free.
VM: 13G + 371M   599883(0) pageins, 476960(0) pageouts

  PID COMMAND      %CPU   TIME   #TH #PRTS #MREGS RPRVT  RSHRD  RSIZE  VSIZE
94741 top         15.9% 0:01.79   1    20     30 1120K   188K  1708K    18M
```

```
12958 Terminal     12.5%  0:30.94   3  105-   184 3756K   15M   10M   366M
13088 firefox-bi    8.5%  2:13:50  17  298-   955  98M-   30M  128M-  563M-
87734 LaunchCFMA    6.1% 15:03.12  12  211-   791 129M-   31M  174M-  916M-
   82 WindowServ    2.0% 41:02.95   5  345   1532  14M    80M   77M   556M
    0 kernel_tas    1.6%  3:32:08  54    2   1301 6560K    0   164M   309M
  426 Cyberduck     1.4% 99:38.32  24  739-  4115  30M-   17M   44M- 1024M-
87430 Safari        0.6%  2:33.84  16  302-  1319 123M-   33M  136M-  607M-
13050 Mail          0.2% 40:22.35  46  367-  1858  63M-   34M   98M-  600M
```

The full output would show many more processes, all sorted by current weighted CPU usage (WCPU column). In this example, the top command (15.9 percent) and Terminal (12.5 percent) are consuming most of the CPU. If you decided you wanted to kill the Terminal process, you could type k and the process ID (12958) to kill the process (if for some reason you couldn't just close the Terminal window normally).

Monitoring Storage Devices

Basic information about storage space available to your Mac OS X file systems can be viewed using commands such as du and df (as described in Chapter 7). If you want details about how your storage devices are performing, other commands can be useful.

For example, if you want to find out **what files and directories are currently open on your storage devices**, you can use the lsof command. This command can be particularly useful if you are trying to unmount a file system that keeps telling you it is busy. You can check what open file is preventing the unmount and decide if you want to kill the process holding that file open and force an unmount of the file system. Here is an example of lsof:

```
# lsof | less      List processes holding files and directories open
COMMAND      PID     USER    FD     TYPE    DEVICE  SIZE/OFF      NODE NAME
loginwind     24 myerman    cwd      DIR     14,2       1462         2 /
loginwind     24 myerman    txt      REG     14,2     938352   8559653 /System/Libra
ry/CoreServices/loginwindow.app/Contents/MacOS/loginwindow
loginwind     24 myerman    txt      REG     14,2     600128   7038652 /System/Libra
ry/PrivateFrameworks/Admin.framework/Versions/A/Admin
loginwind     24 myerman    txt      REG     14,2     332016   8557715 /System/Libra
ry/PrivateFrameworks/URLMount.framework/Versions/A/URLMount
loginwind     24 myerman    txt      REG     14,2    5988576   8549420 /System/Libra
ry/PrivateFrameworks/DiskImages.framework/Versions/A/DiskImages
loginwind     24 myerman    txt      REG     14,2    4493952  10677411 /usr/lib/libx
ml2.2.dylib
```

When you are looking at the lsof output, you want to see the name of the file or directory that is open (NAME), the command that has it open (COMMAND) and the process ID of that running command (PID). In fact, instead of piping lsof output to less or grep, here are a few other ways you can find what you are looking for from lsof output:

```
# lsof -c csh          List files open by C shell (csh) shells
# lsof -d cwd          List directories open as current working directory
# lsof -u marlowe      List files and directories open by user marlowe
# lsof /var            List anything open on /var file system
# lsof +d /var/log     List anything open under /var/log directory
```

Mastering Time

Keeping correct time on your Mac OS X system is critical to the system's proper functioning. You can set the time on your system in several different ways. System time can be viewed and set manually (with the date command) or automatically (with ntpdate or the ntpd service). Another time-related command is uptime, which shows you how long your system has been up.

Changing Time Zone

Your Mac OS X system's time zone is set based on the contents of the /etc/localtime file. You can set a new time zone immediately by copying the file representing your time zone from a subdirectory of /usr/share/zoneinfo. For example, to change the current time zone to that of America/Chicago, you could do the following:

```
# cp /usr/share/zoneinfo/America/Chicago /etc/localtime
```

This can also be accomplished by creating a symlink:

```
# ln -s /usr/share/zoneinfo/America/Chicago /etc/localtime
```

Displaying and Setting Time and Date

The date command is the primary command-based interface for viewing and changing date and time settings, if you are not having that done automatically with NTP (Network Time Protocol). Here are examples of date commands for displaying dates and times in different ways:

```
$ date                           Display current date, time and time zone
Tue Aug 12 01:26:50 CDT 2008
$ date '+%A %B %d %G'            Display day, month, day of month, year
Tuesday August 12 2008
$ date '+The date today is %F.'  Add words to the date output
The date today is 2008-08-12.
$ date "+TIME: %H:%M:%S%nDATE: %Y-%m-%d"  Display TIME and DATE on separate lines
TIME: 06:29:10
DATE: 2008-12-18
```

```
$ date -u                        Display Coordinated Universal Time (UTC)
Mon Dec 29 15:19:12 UTC 2008
```

Although our primary interest in this section is time, because we are on the subject of dates as well, the `cal` command is a quick way to **display dates by month**. Here are examples:

```
$ cal                    Show current month calendar (today is highlighted)
      October 2008
Su Mo Tu We Th Fr Sa
          1  2  3  4
 5  6  7  8  9 10 11
12 13 14 15 16 17 18
19 20 21 22 23 24 25
26 27 28 29 30 31
$ cal 2009               Show entire year's calendar
                     2009

    January                 February                  March
Su Mo Tu We Th Fr Sa    Su Mo Tu We Th Fr Sa     Su Mo Tu We Th Fr Sa
             1  2  3      1  2  3  4  5  6  7      1  2  3  4  5  6  7
 4  5  6  7  8  9 10      8  9 10 11 12 13 14      8  9 10 11 12 13 14
11 12 13 14 15 16 17     15 16 17 18 19 20 21     15 16 17 18 19 20 21
18 19 20 21 22 23 24     22 23 24 25 26 27 28     22 23 24 25 26 27 28
25 26 27 28 29 30 31                              29 30 31
...
$ cal -j                 Show Julian calendar (numbered from January 1)
      October 2008
 Su  Mo  Tu  We  Th  Fr  Sa
             275 276 277 278
279 280 281 282 283 284 285
286 287 288 289 290 291 292
293 294 295 296 297 298 299
300 301 302 303 304 305
```

The `date` command can also be used to change the system date and time. (Be careful, however, because randomly changing the date could crash your system.) Here are examples:

```
# date 0812152100              Set date/time to Aug, 12, 2:21PM, 2008
Mon Dec 15 21:00:00 CST 2008
# date -v +2H                  Adjust time to 2 hours later
Sun Aug 12 11:42:33 CDT 2008
# date -v +3m                  Adjust date/time to one month earlier
Wed Nov 12 11:42:38 CDT 2008
```

The next time you boot FreeBSD, the system time will be reset based on the value of your hardware clock (or your NTP server, if NTP service is enabled); and the next time you shut down, the hardware clock will be reset to the system time, in order to preserve that time while the machine is powered off. One way to ensure that you always get the correct time set for your system is to use the NTP.

Using Network Time Protocol to Set Date/Time

When you install Mac OS X, you are given the opportunity to set your time zone and to see whether your system clock reflects local or UTC time. Your system displays the date and time based on your hardware clock and time zone. As noted earlier, one way to ensure that your system's time doesn't drift is to use the NTP.

The ntpd daemon is installed with the Mac OS X system. Its configuration file is at /etc/ntp.conf and will likely have an entry in it like the following:

```
server time.apple.com minpoll 12 maxpoll 17
```

In other words, poll the server time.apple.com every 12 to 17 seconds to keep the time accurate on the system. However, just having this setting enabled isn't enough. You need to also toggle the automatic updates.

To do that, click System Preferences in your Dock, and then click Date and Time. From the Date & Time tab, shown in Figure 10-1, check the box next to "Set date & time automatically."

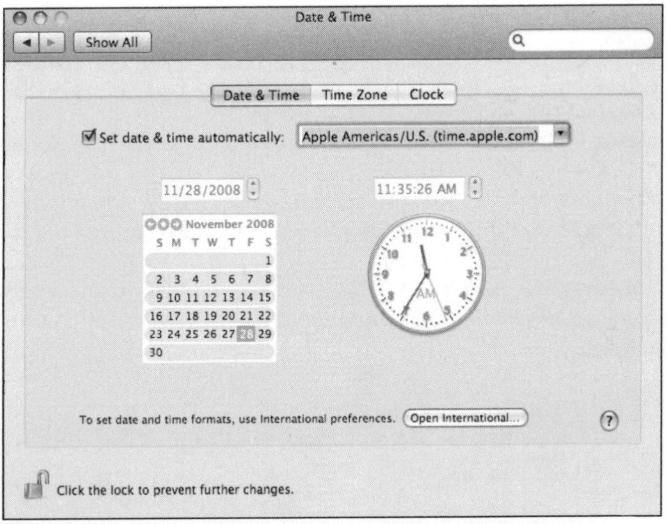

Figure 10-1: Setting the date and time automatically

Checking Uptime

A matter of pride among BSD and other Linux and UNIX enthusiasts is how long they can keep their systems running without having to reboot. Like other BSD systems, Mac OS X systems have been known to run for years without having to reboot.

The length of time that a Mac OS X system has been running since the previous reboot is referred to as *uptime*. You can **check your system's uptime** as follows:

```
$ uptime               Check how long your system has been running
  6:53pm  up 196 days, 14:25,   3 users,   load average: 1.66, 0.88, 0.35
```

The output of uptime shows the current time, how many days and hours the system has been up, and how many users are currently logged in. After that, uptime shows the system load over the past 1-, 5-, and 15-minute time periods.

Starting and Stopping Your System

On most BSD and Linux machines, you can use the init command to start and stop the system, including init 0 (shut down) and init 6 (reboot). On Mac OS X, you use more specific commands for stopping the system. The advantages of commands such as halt, reboot, or shutdown are that they include options that enable you **to stop some features before shutdown occurs.** Here is an example:

> **WARNING** *Don't try the following commands if you don't intend to actually turn off your system, especially on a remote system.*

```
# reboot              Reboot the computer
# halt -n             Don't run sync to sync hard drives before shutdown
# halt -p             The system will power down, if possible
# shutdown +10        Shutdown in ten minutes after warning the users
# shutdown -r 06:08   Reboot at 6:08 am
# shutdown +10 'Bye!' Send custom message to users before shutdown
```

You can also shut down a Mac OS X system by clicking the Apple icon in the upper-left corner of the screen and selecting Shut Down from the menu, as shown in Figure 10-2.

In the rare event that your Mac OS X system is hanging or won't respond to any commands, you can force a reboot by holding down the power button until the system starts up again.

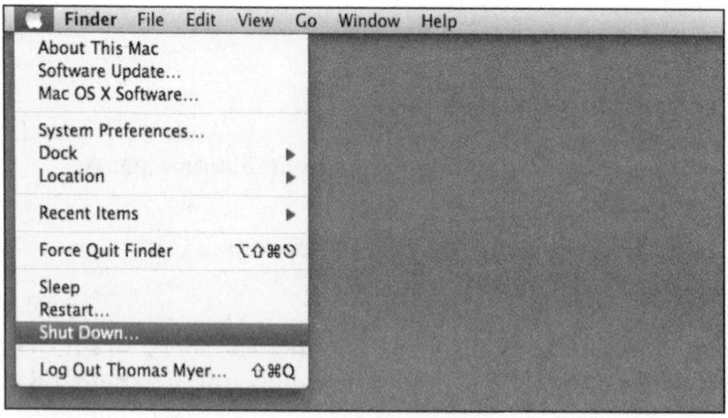

Figure 10-2: Shutting down via the menu

Straight to the Kernel

In general, when the kernel starts up on your Mac system, you shouldn't have to do too much with it. However, there are tools for checking the kernel that is in use and for viewing information about how the kernel started up. In addition, if something goes wrong or you need to add some extra support to the kernel, tools are available for those situations.

To find out **what version of Mac OS X you are running,** type the following:

```
$ uname -r          Display name of current release
9.5.0
$ uname -a          Display all name and release information
Darwin Macintosh 9.5.0 Darwin Kernel Version 9.5.0: Wed Sep  3 11:29:43 PDT
2008; root:xnu-1228.7.58~1/RELEASE_I386 i386
```

You can **control kernel parameters with the system running** using the sysctl command. You can also add parameters permanently to the /etc/sysctl.conf file, which enable them to load as a group or at each reboot. Here are some examples:

```
# sysctl -a | less          List all kernel parameters
kern.ostype = Darwin
kern.osrelease = 9.5.0
kern.osrevision = 199506
kern.version = Darwin Kernel Version 9.5.0: Wed Sep  3 11:29:43 PDT 2008;
root:xnu-1228.7.58~1/RELEASE_I386
kern.maxvnodes = 33792
kern.maxproc = 532
kern.maxfiles = 12288

...
# sysctl kern.hostname              List value of particular parameter
kern.hostname: macintosh
# sysctl kern.geom.debugflags=16   Set value of kernel.geom.debugflags to 16
```

As noted earlier, if you want to change any of your kernel parameters permanently, you should add them to the /etc/sysctl.conf file. Parameter settings in that file are in the form *parameter = value*.

Summary

Like other BSD and Linux systems, Mac OS X systems make it easy for you to watch and modify many aspects of your running system to ensure that it is operating at peak performance. Commands such as top and iostat enable you to view how your system is using its memory, CPU, and storage devices. Using commands such as date and cal, as well as services such as NTP, you can watch and manage your system's date and time settings.

11

Managing Network Connections

Connecting to a network from a Mac OS X system is often as easy as attaching your computer's network interface card (NIC) to your ISP's hardware (such as a DSL or cable modem) and allowing the system to auto-detect the connection. However, if your network interface doesn't come up or requires some manual intervention, many commands are available for configuring network interfaces, checking network connections, and setting up special routing.

This chapter covers many useful commands for configuring and working with your network interface cards, such as `sysinstall` and `ifconfig`. In particular, it covers ways of configuring wired, wireless, and modem network hardware. You will also learn about commands such as `netstat`, `dig`, and `ping` for getting information about your network when your hardware is connected and the network interfaces are in place.

IN THIS CHAPTER

Getting network statistics

Managing network connections

Checking DNS name resolution with dig, host, and hostname

Checking connectivity with ping and arping

Tracing connections with traceroute and route

Watching the network with netstat

Configuring Network Interfaces

To configure network interfaces on Mac OS X, click the System Preferences icon on your Dock and then click Network. Click Advanced and you can configure settings for AirPort (wireless networking), DNS servers, DHCP, and more (see Figure 11-1).

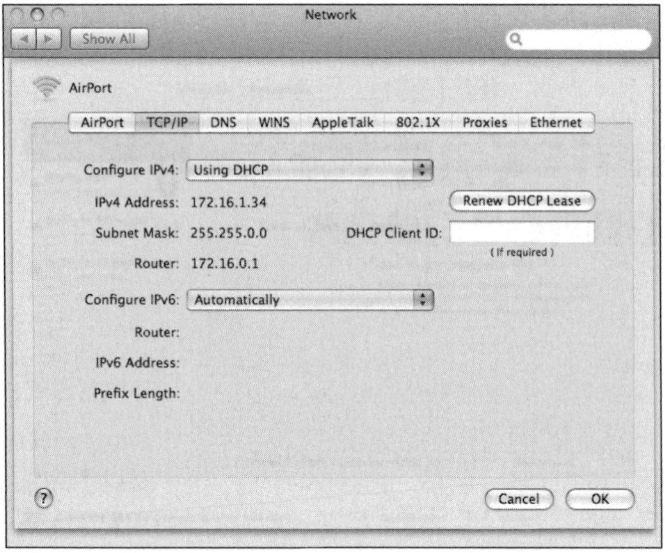

Figure 11-1: Configuring network Interfaces on Mac OS X

More than likely, you won't need to make any changes, as Mac OS X is pretty good about auto-detecting any newly installed NICs and keeping track of the wireless and wired network interfaces that you have.

Ninety percent of the work you'll do configuring network interfaces can be done from the System Preferences area, but much of the material that follows provides you with the information you need to configure, manage, and monitor network interface cards from the command line.

> **NOTE** *The interface names for your Ethernet NICs are based on the driver used to support that NIC. If you are coming from a Linux environment, you might expect Ethernet interfaces to be named eth0, eth1, and so on. In Mac OS X, the names might be lo0, en0, en1, fw0, or something else. Examples in this chapter use lo0 to represent a wireless Ethernet NIC interface.*

Managing Network Interface Cards

If the network hardware on your computer didn't immediately appear and let you connect to the Internet, try the following steps to troubleshoot the problem:

1. Check that your network interface card (NIC) is properly installed and that the cable is connected to your network (ISPs CPE, switch, and so on).

2. After the cable is connected, make sure you have a link with no speed or duplex mismatches.

3. If all else fails, consider replacing your NIC with a known-good spare to isolate a hardware failure.

To check the link from your BSD system and to set speed and duplex, the `ifconfig` command provides these and many other features.

> **NOTE** *If you are used to tools such as* `ethtool` *and* `mii-tool`, *coming from Linux or other UNIX environments, the* `ifconfig` *command contains many of the same features you would get from those two commands.*

To **view the syntax of the ifconfig command**, type any invalid option:

```
# ifconfig -?          View options to the ifconfig command
ifconfig: illegal option -- ?
usage: ifconfig [-L] [-C] interface address_family [address [dest_address]]
                [parameters]
       ifconfig interface create
       ifconfig -a [-L] [-C] [-d] [-m] [-u] [-v] [address_family]
       ifconfig -l [-d] [-u] [address_family]
       ifconfig [-L] [-C] [-d] [-m] [-u] [-v]
```

To **display just the names of every available network interface,** use the `-l` option. The following example shows that there is an Ethernet NIC (fxp0), a parallel port (plip0) and a loopback (lo0):

```
# ifconfig -l          List names of network interfaces
lo0 gif0 stf0 en0 fw0 en1
```

To **display settings for a specific Ethernet card,** add the interface name to the command. For example, to view card information for fxp0 (the first wired Ethernet NIC), type the following:

```
# ifconfig lo0                 See settings for NIC at lo0
lo0: flags=8049<UP,LOOPBACK,RUNNING,MULTICAST> mtu 16384
   inet6 fe80::1%lo0 prefixlen 64 scopeid 0x1
   inet 127.0.0.1 netmask 0xff000000
   inet6 ::1 prefixlen 128
```

To **display a capabilities list for a particular network card,** use the `-m` option:

```
# ifconfig -m lo0      Display driver information for NIC
lo0: flags=8049<UP,LOOPBACK,RUNNING,MULTICAST> mtu 16384
   inet6 fe80::1%lo0 prefixlen 64 scopeid 0x1
   inet 127.0.0.1 netmask 0xff000000
   inet6 ::1 prefixlen 128k
```

The `ifconfig` command can be used to **change NIC settings** as well as to display them.

To **hard-set the NIC to 100Mpbs with full duplex,** type this command:

```
# ifconfig lo0 media 100baseTX mediaopt full-duplex   Change speed/duplex
# ifconfig lo0                                         View new NIC settings
lo0: flags=8843<UP,BROADCAST,RUNNING,SIMPLEX,MULTICAST> mtu 1500
        options=8<VLAN_MTU>
```

```
inet 10.0.0.204 netmask 0xffffff00 broadcast 10.0.0.255
ether 00:d0:b7:79:a5:35
media: Ethernet 100baseTX <full-duplex>
status: active
```

To **hard-set the speed to 10Mpbs,** use the following:

```
# ifconfig lo0 media 10baseT/UTP        Change speed
# ifconfig lo0                          View new NIC settings
lo0: flags=8843<UP,BROADCAST,RUNNING,SIMPLEX,MULTICAST> mtu 1500
        options=8<VLAN_MTU>
        inet 10.0.0.204 netmask 0xffffff00 broadcast 10.0.0.255
        ether 00:d0:b7:79:a5:35
        media: Ethernet 10baseT/UTP <full-duplex>
        status: active
```

To **change the IP address and netmask,** type this:

```
# ifconfig lo0 inet 10.0.0.208 netmask 255.0.0.0 Change IP and netmask
# ifconfig lo0                                   View new NIC settings
lo0: flags=8843<UP,BROADCAST,RUNNING,SIMPLEX,MULTICAST> mtu 1500
        options=8<VLAN_MTU>
        inet 10.0.0.208 netmask 0xff000000 broadcast 10.255.255.255
        ether 00:d0:b7:79:a5:35
        media: Ethernet 10baseT/UTP <full-duplex>
        status: active
```

The changes just made to your NIC settings are good for the current session. When you reboot, however, those settings will be lost. To **make the current settings stick at the next reboot** or network restart, add the options to the ifconfig_fxp0 line in the /etc/rc.conf file (change fxp0 to the appropriate interface name if it isn't the first Ethernet NIC interface). For example:

```
ifconfig_fxp0="inet 10.0.0.208 netmask 255.0.0.0 media 100baseTX"
```

The netstat command provides many ways to **get network interface statistics.** With no options, netstat **shows active network connections and active sockets** as follows:

```
$ netstat              Show active connections and sockets
Active Internet connections
Proto Recv-Q Send-Q  Local Address          Foreign Address         (state)
tcp4       0      0  Macintosh.50492        channel03.01.05..http   ESTABLISHED
tcp4       0      0  Macintosh.50409        ug-in-f111.googl.imaps  ESTABLISHED
tcp4       0      0  Macintosh.50408        ug-in-f111.googl.imaps  ESTABLISHED
tcp4       0      0  Macintosh.50407        ug-in-f111.googl.imaps  ESTABLISHED
tcp4       0      0  Macintosh.49517        64.233.183.111.imaps    ESTABLISHED
udp4       0      0  *.rockwell-csp2        *.*
udp4       0      0  *.*                    *.*
udp4       0      0  *.54101                *.*
    ...
```

To **show quick statistics on all network interfaces,** use `netstat` as follows:

```
$ netstat -i              Get network interface statistics for all interfaces
netstat -i
Name  Mtu   Network      Address           Ipkts Ierrs   Opkts Oerrs  Coll
lo0   16384 <Link#1>                         215     0     215     0     0
lo0   16384 localhost    fe80::1             215     -     215     -     -
lo0   16384 127             localhost        215     -     215     -     -
lo0   16384 localhost    ::1                 215     -     215     -     -
gif0* 1280  <Link#2>                           0     0       0     0     0
...
```

Use the `-w` option to instruct `netstat` to **refresh network interface statistics every second:**

```
$ netstat -w 2 -I fxp0         Refresh network statistics every 2 seconds
            input       (Total)           output
    packets  errs     bytes    packets  errs      bytes colls
        13     0       266         12     0        244      0
         2     0      5938          1     0      84282      0
        92     2      6676        116     0     115574      0
       183     3     16862        225     0     369602      0
       152     2     13642        191     0     264566      0
       137     4      6836        169     0     103890      0
       113     0     10276        139     0     144936      0
```

You can **check whether there are active connections to your computer** from `netstat` with the `-p` option, as follows:

```
$ netstat -p tcp               Display active TCP connections
Active Internet connections
Proto Recv-Q Send-Q  Local Address      Foreign Address        (state)
tcp4     0      0    Macintosh.50501    channel03.01.05..http  ESTABLISHED
tcp4     0      0    Macintosh.50409    ug-in-f111.googl.imaps ESTABLISHED
tcp4     0      0    Macintosh.49517    64.233.183.111.imaps   ESTABLISHED
```

As the output indicates, the `netstat` command returns three connections. Here are some other quick examples of the `netstat` command:

```
$ netstat -r                   Display kernel routing tables for IPv4 and IPv6
$ netstat -rs                  Display routing stats (bad routes, dynamic routes)
$ netstat -s -p tcp | less     Display detailed statistics for TCP interfaces
$ netstat -n                   Display output with IP addresses, not hostnames
$ netstat -m                   Display information on network memory buffers
```

Managing Network Connections

Starting and stopping the network interfaces for your wired Ethernet connections to your LAN or the Internet are usually handled automatically at the time you boot and shut down your Mac OS X system. However, you can run scripts from the `/etc/rc.d` directory to start and stop your network interfaces anytime you want, or edit the /etc/rc.conf file to specify whether or not your network services start automatically.

The ifconfig command can also be used to configure, activate, and deactivate interfaces.

Starting and Stopping Network Connections

You can use the ifconfig command to bring network interfaces up and down, as shown here:

```
# ifconfig en0 down       Turn off network interface for Ethernet card (en0)
# ifconfig -d             List interfaces that are down
gif0: flags=8010<POINTOPOINT,MULTICAST> mtu 1280
stf0: flags=0<> mtu 1280
    ...
# ifconfig en0 up         Turn on network interface for Ethernet card (fxp0)
# ifconfig -u             List interfaces that are up
lo0: flags=8049<UP,LOOPBACK,RUNNING,MULTICAST> mtu 16384
inet6 fe80::1%lo0 prefixlen 64 scopeid 0x1
inet 127.0.0.1 netmask 0xff000000
inet6 ::1 prefixlen 128
en0: flags=8863<UP,BROADCAST,SMART,RUNNING,SIMPLEX,MULTICAST> mtu 1500
ether 00:1b:63:1e:24:21
media: autoselect status: inactive
supported media: autoselect 10baseT/UTP <half-duplex> 10baseT/UTP <full-duplex>
10baseT/UTP <full-duplex,hw-loopback> 10baseT/UTP <full-duplex,flow-control>
100baseTX <half-duplex> 100baseTX <full-duplex> 100baseTX <full-duplex,hw-
loopback> 100baseTX <full-duplex,flow-control> 1000baseT <full-duplex> 1000baseT
<full-duplex,hw-loopback> 1000baseT <full-duplex,flow-control> none
fw0: flags=8863<UP,BROADCAST,SMART,RUNNING,SIMPLEX,MULTICAST> mtu 2030
lladdr 00:1b:63:ff:fe:67:b7:20
media: autoselect <full-duplex> status: inactive
supported media: autoselect <full-duplex>
en1: flags=8863<UP,BROADCAST,SMART,RUNNING,SIMPLEX,MULTICAST> mtu 1500
inet6 fe80::21b:63ff:fec3:8cbb%en1 prefixlen 64 scopeid 0x6
inet 172.16.1.34 netmask 0xffff0000 broadcast 172.16.255.255
ether 00:1b:63:c3:8c:bb
media: autoselect status: active
supported media: autoselect
    ...
```

Note that the network interfaces will appear as active after running ifconfig with the down option. However, the words UP and RUNNING will no longer appear when you list the interface, and no data will be able to go in either direction across that interface.

When your network interfaces are up, there are tools you can use to view information about those interfaces and associated NICs.

Starting and Stopping Network Services

You can start and stop services associated with your network interfaces in much the same way that you use the `netif` script to start and stop the interfaces. Services such as the Secure Shell (`sshd`) and Network File System (`nfsd`) can be manually started using the `/sbin/service` script.

To find out which services can be started this way, type the following command:

```
# /sbin/service —list          Check options available
/sbin/service --list
bootps
com.apple.airportd
com.apple.airportPrefsUpdater
com.apple.alf.agent
com.apple.AOSHelper
com.apple.AppleFileServer
com.apple.atrun
com.apple.ATSServer
com.apple.audio.coreaudiod
com.apple.autofsd
com.apple.automountd
com.apple.backupd-attach
com.apple.backupd-auto
com.apple.backupd-wake
com.apple.backupd
com.apple.blued
com.apple.bootlog
com.apple.bsd.dirhelper
com.apple.configd
com.apple.configureLocalKDC
com.apple.CoreRAID
com.apple.coreservicesd
com.apple.dashboard.advisory.fetch
...
```

Here are some examples of starting and using services:

```
# /sbin/service ssh start     Start the SSH service
# /sbin/service ssh stop      Stop the SSH service
# /sbin/service finger start  Start the finger service
```

Checking Name Resolution

Because IP addresses are numbers, and people prefer to address things by name, TCP/IP networks (such as the Internet) rely on DNS to resolve hostnames into IP addresses. FreeBSD provides several tools for looking up information related to DNS name resolution.

Typically, DNS entries are added automatically from a DHCP server on Mac OS X. That information is then stored in the /etc/resolv.conf file. It looks something like the following:

```
nameserver 11.22.33.44
nameserver 22.33.44.55
```

The preceding numbers are replaced by real IP addresses of computers that serve as DNS name servers. When you can connect to working DNS servers, you can use commands to query those servers and look up host computers.

You can use the dig command (which should be used instead of the deprecated nslookup command) to look up information from a DNS server. The host command can be used to look up address information for a hostname or domain name.

To **search your DNS servers for a particular hostname** (in the following examples www.example .com), use the dig command as follows:

```
$ dig www.example.com    Search DNS servers set in /etc/resolv.conf
; <<>> DiG 9.4.2-P2 <<>> www.google.com
;; global options:  printcmd
;; Got answer:
;; ->>HEADER<<- opcode: QUERY, status: NOERROR, id: 28730
;; flags: qr rd; QUERY: 1, ANSWER: 5, AUTHORITY: 0, ADDITIONAL: 0
;; WARNING: recursion requested but not available

;; QUESTION SECTION:
;www.example.com.  IN   A
...
```

Instead of using your assigned name server, you can **query a specific name server**. This is useful if you believe that your name server is not resolving the address of a particular host properly and you want to check different servers to see how the name resolves. The following example queries the DNS server at 1.1.2.5:

```
$ dig www.example.com 1.1.2.5
```

Using dig, you can also **query for a specific record type**:

```
$ dig example.com mx   Queries for the mail exchanger
$ dig example.com ns   Queries for the authoritative name servers
```

Use the +trace option to **trace a recursive query** from the top-level DNS servers down to the authoritative servers:

```
$ dig +trace www.example.com   Recursively trace DNS servers
```

If you just want to see the IP address of a host computer, use the +short option:

```
$ dig +short www.example.com    Display only name/IP address pair
turbosphere.com.
66.113.99.70
```

You can use dig to do a reverse lookup to find DNS information based on IP address:

```
$ dig -x 10.1.1.1               Get DNS information based on IP address
```

Use host to do a reverse DNS lookup as well:

```
$ host 10.1.1.1
10.1.1.1.in-addr.arpa domain name pointer www.example.com.
```

To get hostname information for the local machine, use the hostname and dnsdomainname commands:

```
$ hostname                      View the local computer's full DNS host name
macintosh.local
$ hostname -s                   View the local computer's short host name
macintosh
```

You can also use hostname to set the local hostname temporarily (until the next reboot). Here's an example:

```
# hostname server1.example.com    Set local hostname
```

Note that changing the hostname of a running machine may adversely affect some running daemons. Instead, we recommend you set the local hostname so it is set each time the system starts up. One way to do that is to set the hostname option in the /etc/rc.conf file. For the previous example, the hostname line would appear as follows:

```
hostname="server1.example.com"
```

Troubleshooting Network Problems

Troubleshooting networks is generally done from the bottom layer up. As discussed at the beginning of this chapter, the first step is to ensure that the physical network layer components (cables, NICs, and so on) are connected and working. Next, verify that the links between physical nodes are working. After that, many tools are available for checking the connectivity to a particular host.

Checking Connectivity to a Host

When you know you have a link and no duplex mismatch, the next step is to ping your default gateway. You should have configured the default gateway (gw), whether you did that manually or had it set automatically by DHCP when the network started. To check your default gateway in the actual routing table, use the route command to find a host on the other side of that gateway as follows:

```
# route get example.com
   route to: www.example.com
destination: default
       mask: default
    gateway: 10.0.0.1
  interface: en0
      flags: <UP,GATEWAY,DONE,STATIC>
recvpipe  sendpipe  ssthresh  rtt,msec   rttvar  hopcount     mtu    expire
      0         0         0          0        0         0    1500         0
```

The gateway for the default route is 10.0.0.1. To ensure that there is IP connectivity to that gateway, use the ping command as follows:

```
$ ping 10.0.0.1
PING 10.0.0.1 (10.0.0.1) 56 data bytes
64 bytes from 10.0.0.1: icmp_seq=0 ttl=64 time=1.43 ms
64 bytes from 10.0.0.1: icmp_seq=1 ttl=64 time=0.382 ms
64 bytes from 10.0.0.1: icmp_seq=2 ttl=64 time=0.313 ms
64 bytes from 10.0.0.1: icmp_seq=3 ttl=64 time=0.360 ms

--- 10.0.0.1 ping statistics ---
4 packets transmitted, 4 received, 0% packet loss
round-trip min/avg/max/stddev = 0.313/0.621/1.432/0.469 ms
```

> **NOTE**   Some hosts are configured to ignore ping requests, so not getting a reply doesn't indicate that the host or gateway is down.

By default, ping continues until you press Ctrl+C. Other ping options include the following:

```
$ ping -a 10.0.0.1          Add an audible ping as ping progresses
$ ping -c 4 10.0.0.1        Ping 4 times and exit (default in Windows)
$ ping -q -c 5 10.0.0.1     Show summary of pings (works best with -c)
# ping -f 10.0.0.1          Send a flood of pings (must be root)
$ ping -i 3 10.0.0.1        Send packets in 3-second intervals
# ping -s 1500 10.0.0.1     Set packet size to 1500 bytes (must be root)
PING 10.0.0.1 (10.0.0.1) 1500 data bytes
```

Use the ping flood option with caution. By default, ping sends small packets (56 bytes). Large packets (such as the 1,500-byte setting just shown) are good to make faulty NICs or connections stand out. Only the root user can send a flood of pings, or pings with byte sizes over the default 56 bytes.

Checking Address Resolution Protocol (ARP)

If you're not able to ping your gateway, you may have an issue at the Ethernet MAC layer. The Address Resolution Protocol (ARP) can be used to find information at the MAC layer. To view and configure ARP entries, use the arp command. This example shows arp listing computers in the ARP cache by hostname:

```
# arp -a          List all current ARP entries
ritchie   (10.0.0.1) at 00:10:5a:ab:f6:a7 on fxp0 [ethernet]
einstein  (10.0.0.50) at 00:0b:6a:02:ec:98 on fxp0 [ethernet]
thompson  (10.0.0.204) at 00:d0:b7:79:a5:35 on fxp0 permanent [ethernet]
```

In this example, you can see the names of other computers that the local computer's ARP cache knows about, and the associated hardware address (MAC address) of each computer's NIC. To **delete an entry from the ARP cache,** use the -d option:

```
# arp -d 10.0.0.50          Delete address 10.0.0.50 from ARP cache
```

Instead of just letting ARP dynamically learn about other systems, you can **add static ARP entries to the cache** using the -s option:

```
# arp -s 10.0.0.51 00:0B:6A:02:EC:95    Add IP and MAC addresses to ARP
```

To **query a subnet to see whether an IP is already in use,** and to find the MAC address of the device using it, use the arping command (pkg_add -r arping). The arping command can be used to check for IP conflicts before bringing an Ethernet NIC up. Here are examples:

```
# arping 10.0.0.50          Query subnet to see if 10.0.0.50 is in use
ARPING 10.0.0.50
60 bytes from 00:0b:6a:02:ec:98 (10.0.0.50): index=0 time=9.966 msec
60 bytes from 00:0b:6a:02:ec:98 (10.0.0.50): index=1 time=9.930 msec
60 bytes from 00:0b:6a:02:ec:98 (10.0.0.50): index=2 time=9.930 msec
60 bytes from 00:0b:6a:02:ec:98 (10.0.0.50): index=3 time=9.931 msec
^C
--- 10.0.0.50 statistics ---
4 packets transmitted, 4 packets received,   0% unanswered
# arping -I fxp0 10.0.0.50    Specify interface to query from
```

Like the ping command, the arping command continuously queries for the address until the command is ended by typing Ctrl+C. Typically, you just want to know whether the target is alive, so you can run the following command:

```
# arping -c 1 10.0.0.51   Query 10.0.0.50 and stop after 2 counts
```

153

Tracing Routes to Hosts

After ensuring that you can ping your gateway and even reach machines that are outside your network, you may still have issues reaching a specific host or network. If so, you can **use traceroute to find the bottleneck or point of failure:**

```
$ traceroute www.google.com   Follow the route taken to a host
traceroute: Warning: www.google.com has multiple addresses; using 74.125.95.147
traceroute to www.l.google.com (74.125.95.147), 64 hops max, 40 byte packets
 1  homeportal.gateway.org (1.16.0.1)  2.477 ms  2.707 ms  1.633 ms
 2  71.145.159.254 (71.145.159.254)  13.803 ms  14.842 ms  13.397 ms
 3  99.171.168.34 (99.171.168.34)  13.350 ms  14.395 ms  13.702 ms
 4  bb2-10g0-0.aus2tx.sbcglobal.net (151.164.243.247)  14.092 ms  14.768 ms
13.793 ms
 5  69.220.8.57 (69.220.8.57)  19.688 ms  24.126 ms  20.747 ms
 6  72.14.197.109 (72.14.197.109)  19.501 ms  21.329 ms  19.592 ms
 7  66.249.94.94 (66.249.94.94)  19.384 ms  20.664 ms  23.572 ms
 8  216.239.47.121 (216.239.47.121)  29.388 ms  30.792 ms  29.511 ms
 9  209.85.253.173 (209.85.253.173)  54.357 ms  54.148 ms  53.407 ms
10  209.85.241.27 (209.85.241.27)  53.030 ms  54.153 ms 209.85.241.29
(209.85.241.29)  53.179 ms
11  209.85.240.45 (209.85.240.45)  60.877 ms 72.14.239.193 (72.14.239.193)
54.391 ms 209.85.240.45 (209.85.240.45)  55.040 ms
12  iw-in-f147.google.com (74.125.95.147)  53.183 ms  53.144 ms  53.083 ms
```

Sometimes the last hops look like this:

```
28  * * *
29  * * *
30  * * *
```

The lines of asterisks (*) at the end of the trace can be caused by firewalls that block traffic to the target. However, if you see several asterisks before the destination, those can indicate heavy congestion or equipment failures and point to a bottleneck.

By default, traceroute uses UDP packets, which provide a more realistic performance picture than ICMP. That's because some Internet hops give lower priority to ICMP traffic. If you'd still like to trace using ICMP packets, try this command:

```
# traceroute -I www.google.com   Use ICMP packets to trace a route
```

To **trace a route to a remote host using TCP packets,** use the -T option to traceroute:

```
# traceroute -P TCP www.google.com   Use TCP packets to trace a route
```

By default, traceroute connects to port 80. You can **set a different port** using the -p option:

```
# traceroute -P TCP -p 25 www.google.com   Connect to port 25 in trace
```

You can **view IP addresses instead of hostnames** by disabling name resolution of hops:

```
$ traceroute -n www.google.com    Disable name resolution in trace
```

To view and manipulate the kernel's routing table, the `route` command has tradition-ally been the tool of choice. This is slowly being replaced by the `ip route` command in some Linux distributions, but `route` is still commonly used in BSD distributions.

You can use the `route` command to **display your local routing table**. Here are two examples of the `route` command, with and without DNS name resolution:

```
# route get apple.com           Display local routing table information
 route to: 17.149.160.49
destination: default
      mask: default
   gateway: homeportal.gateway.org
 interface: en1
     flags: <UP,GATEWAY,DONE,STATIC,PRCLONING>
recvpipe  sendpipe  ssthresh  rtt,msec    rttvar  hopcount      mtu     expire
       0         0         0         0         0         0      1500          0
```

```
# route -n get apple.com        Display routing table without DNS lookup
 route to: 17.149.160.49
destination: default
      mask: default
   gateway: 172.16.0.1
 interface: en1
     flags: <UP,GATEWAY,DONE,STATIC,PRCLONING>
recvpipe  sendpipe  ssthresh  rtt,msec    rttvar  hopcount      mtu     expire
       0         0         0         0         0         0      1500          0
```

To **change the default route on your system,** use the `add default` options as follows:

```
# route add default 10.0.0.2         Change the default route
```

You can **add a new route to your network** by specifying the destination and the IP address of the gateway (such as `10.0.0.100`):

```
# route add -net 192.168.0.0 netmask 255.255.255.0 gw 10.0.0.100
```

To **delete a route,** use the `delete` option:

```
# route delete -net 192.168.0.0 Delete a route
```

To **make a new route permanent,** create a `defaultrouter` entry in the `/etc/rc.conf` file. For example, to set the default route to `10.0.0.2` at each system reboot, you could add the following entry to the file `/etc/rc.conf`:

```
defaultrouter="10.0.0.2"
```

Displaying netstat Connections and Statistics

Another command that can display information about the routing table is the net-stat command. However, netstat can also **display information about packets sent between transport-layer protocols** (TCP and UDP) and ICMP.

To use netstat to **display the routing table,** type the following:

```
# netstat -rn            Display the routing table
Routing tables
Internet:
Destination      Gateway           Flags    Refs     Use  Netif Expire
default          10.0.0.1          UGS      0        681  fxp0
10.0.0.1         00:10:5a:ab:f6:a7 UHLW     2        0    fxp0   268
10.0.0.50        00:0b:6a:02:ec:98 UHLW     2        980  fxp0   690
127.0.0.1        127.0.0.1         UH       0        32   lo0
...
```

To use netstat to **display detailed summaries of activities for TCP, ICMP, UDP, and protocols,** type the following:

```
$ netstat -s | less      Show summary of TCP, ICMP, UDP activities
tcp:
        21156 packets sent
                19743 data packets (1184618 bytes)
                207 data packets (44928 bytes) retransmitted
                62 data packets unnecessarily retransmitted
                0 resends initiated by MTU discovery
                964 ack-only packets (149 delayed)
                0 URG only packets
                0 window probe packets
    ...
```

You can **view a list of TCP statistics for each interface** by typing the following:

```
# netstat -i -p tcp         View TCP activities
Name   Mtu Network    Address           Ipkts Ierrs   Opkts Oerrs  Coll
fxp0   1500 <Link#1>  00:d0:b7:79:a5:35  38600     0   36776     0    0
plip0  1500 <Link#2>                         0     0       0     0    0
lo0   16384 <Link#3>                        40     0      40     0    0
lo0   16384 fe80:3::1  fe80:3::1            0     -       0     -    -
lo0   16384 localhost.loc ::1              4     -       4     -    -
...
```

You can also **view information about active sockets.** This includes information on server processes listening for requests from the network:

```
# netstat -AanW -p tcp
Active Internet connections (including servers)
Socket   Proto Recv-Q Send-Q  Local Address    Foreign Address    (state)
```

```
c24e0000 tcp4    0    0  127.0.0.1.6010    *.*                LISTEN
c24c6910 tcp4    0    0  10.0.0.204.22     10.0.0.50.45664    ESTABLISHED
c24c6570 tcp4    0    0  127.0.0.1.25      *.*                LISTEN
c24c6ae0 tcp4    0    0  *.22              *.*                LISTEN
c24c5000 tcp4    0    0  *.949             *.*                LISTEN
c24c51d0 tcp4    0    0  *.897             *.*                LISTEN
c24c5740 tcp4    0    0  *.2049            *.*                LISTEN
c24c5ae0 tcp4    0    0  *.649             *.*                LISTEN
c24c5cb0 tcp4    0    0  *.111             *.*                LISTEN
```

From the preceding output, you can see that there is one established connection (a remote login via ssh on port 22 from the host at address 10.0.0.50). Other sockets represent processes listening for a variety of service requests.

To **display how much data has been transferred over a particular interface (in bytes)**, use the -I and -b options. Here is an example:

```
# netstat -I en0 -b
Name  Mtu    Network    Address           Ipkts Ierrs Ibytes  Opkts Oerrs   Obytes  Coll
en0   1500   <Link#4>   00:1b:63:1e:24:21 0 0      0      0     0       342    0
```

Summary

Nearly every aspect of the network connections from your Mac OS X system can be configured, checked, and monitored using command-line tools. You can view and change settings of your NICs using the ifconfig command. You can view network statistics with netstat.

To start and stop your network, commands such as netif and ifconfig are easy to manage. When a connection is established, you can see statistics about that connection using netstat and route commands.

To check DNS name resolution, use the dig, host, and hostname commands. Commands for checking connectivity and routes to a host include ping, arp, traceroute, and arping.

12

Accessing Network Resources

In the time it takes to fire up a graphical
FTP client, you could already have downloaded a few dozen files from a remote
server using command-line tools. Even
when a GUI is available, commands for
transferring files, web browsing, sharing
directories, and reading mail can be quick
and efficient to use. When no GUI is available, they can be lifesavers.

This chapter covers commands for accessing resources (files, e-mail, shared directories, and online chats) over the network.

IN THIS CHAPTER

Wget, curl, lftp, and scp
for file transfers

Sharing directories with
NFS, Samba, and SSHFS

IRC chats with irssi

Using the mail e-mail client

Transferring Files

Commands available with Mac OS X for downloading files from remote
servers (HTTP, HTTPS, FTP, or SSH) are plentiful and powerful. You
might choose one command over another because of the specific options
you need. For example, you may want to perform a download over an
encrypted connection, resume an aborted download, or do recursive
downloads. This section describes how to use wget, ftp, scp, and sftp.

Downloading Files with wget

Sometimes you need to **download a file from a remote server** using the command line. For example, you find a link to a software package but the
link goes through several HTTP redirects that prevent rpm from installing straight from HTTP; or you may want to script the automated download of a file, such as a log file, every night.

The wget command can download files from web servers (HTTP and
HTTPS) and FTP servers. You will need to install wget with the fink

package (`fink install wget`). With a server that doesn't require authentication, a wget command can be as simple as wget plus the location of the download file:

```
$ wget http://upload.wikimedia.org/wikipedia/commons/2/2c/Chokladbollar.jpg
```

If, for example, an **FTP server requires a login and password,** you can enter that information on the wget command line in the following forms:

```
$ wget ftp://user:password@ftp.example.com/path/to/file
$ wget —user=user —password=password ftp://ftp.example.com/path/to/file
```

For example:

```
$ wget ftp://chris:mykuulpwd@ftp.linuxtoys.net/home/chris/image.jpg
$ wget --user=chris --password=mykuulpwd \
        ftp://ftp.linuxtoys.net/home/chris/image.jpg
```

You can **use wget to download a single web page** as follows:

```
$ wget http://www.google.com        Download only the Web page
```

If you open the resulting `index.html`, you'll have all sorts of broken links. To download all the images and other elements required to render the page properly, use the -p option:

```
$ wget -p http://www.google.com     Download Web page and other elements
```

When you open the resulting `index.html` in your browser, chances are good you will still have all the broken links even though all the images were downloaded. That's because the links need to be translated to point to your local files, so instead do this:

```
$ wget -pk http://www.google.com    Download pages and use local file names
```

If you want wget to keep the original file and also do the translation, use the following:

```
$ wget -pkK http://www.google.com   Rename to local names, keep original
```

Sometimes an HTML file you download does not have an `.html` extension, but ends in `.asp` or `.cgi` instead. That may result in your browser not knowing how to open your local copy of the file. You can have wget append `.html` to those files using the -E option:

```
$ wget -E http://www.aspexamples.com    Append .html to downloaded files
```

With the wget command, you can **recursively mirror an entire website.** While copying files and directories for the entire depth of the server's file structure, the -m option adds time stamping and keeps FTP directory listings. (Use this with caution, because it can take a lot of time and space):

```
$ wget -m http://www.linuxtoys.net
```

Using some of the options just described, the following command line results in the most usable local copy of a website:

```
$ wget -mEkK http://www.linuxtoys.net
```

If you have ever had a large file download (such as a CD or DVD image file) disconnect before it completed, you may find the -c option to wget to be a lifesaver. Using -c, wget resumes where it left off, continuing an interrupted file download. For example:

```
$ wget http://example.com/DVD.iso          Begin downloading large file
...
95%[==========  ] 685,251,583 55K/s     Download killed before completion
$ wget -c http://example.com/DVD.iso    Resume download where stopped
...
HTTP request sent, awaiting response… 206 Partial Content
Length: 699,389,952 (667), 691,513 (66M) remaining [text/plain]
```

Because of the continue feature (-c), wget can be particularly useful for those with slow Internet connections who need to download large files. If you have ever had a download take several hours, only to be killed just before it finished, you'll know what we mean. (Note that if you don't use -c when you mean to resume a file download, the file will be saved to a different file: the original name with a .1 appended to it.)

Transferring Files with curl

The *client for URLs* application (curl command) provides similar features to wget for transferring files using web and FTP protocols. However, the curl command can also transfer files using other popular protocols, including SSH protocols (SCP and SFTP), LDAP, DICT, Telnet, and File.

Instead of supporting large, recursive downloads (as wget does), curl is designed for *single-shot file transfers*. It does, however, support more protocols (as noted) and some neat advanced features. Here are a few interesting examples of file transfers with curl for downloading a three-disc set of ISO images for FreeBSD:

```
$ curl -O \
ftp.freebsd.org/pub/FreeBSD/ISO-IMAGES-i386/6.3/6.3-RELEASE-i386-disc[1-3].iso
$ curl -OO \
ftp.freebsd.org/pub/FreeBSD/ISO-IMAGES-i386/6.3/6.3-RELEASE-i386-disc{1,2,3}.iso
```

The commands just shown illustrate how to use square brackets to indicate a range [1-3], and curly brackets for a list {1,2,3}, of characters or numbers to match files.

The following set of `curl` commands illustrates how to download, upload, and delete files from password-protected servers:

```
$ curl -O ftp://chris:MyPasswd@ftp.example.com/home/chris/fileA \
    -Q '-DELE fileA'
$ curl -T install.log ftp://chris:MyPasswd@ftp.example.com/tmp/ \
    -Q "-RNFR install.log" -Q "-RNTO Xinstall.log"
$ curl ftp://ftp.freebsd.org/pub/FreeBSD/doc/en/books/    List books contents
```

The first command line adds a username and password (`chris:MyPasswd`), downloads a file (`fileA`) from the server, and then deletes the file on the server when the download is done (`-Q '-DELE fileA'`). The next example uploads (`-T`) the file `install.log` to an FTP server. Then it renames the remote file to `Xinstall.log`. The last example tells `curl` to list the contents of the `/pub/FreeBSD/doc/en/books/` directory at `ftp.freebsd.org`.

Transferring Files with FTP Commands

Most BSD systems, and Mac OS X is no different, come with the standard FTP client (`ftp` command), which works the same way it does on most UNIX and Windows systems. We recommend using the full-featured user-friendly `lftp` instead (`fink install lftp`).

With these FTP clients, you open a session to the FTP server (as opposed to just grabbing a file, as you do with `wget` and `curl`). Then you navigate the server much as you would a local file system, getting and putting documents across the network connection. The following examples show how to **connect to an FTP server with lftp**:

```
$ lftp ftp.freebsd.org                  Anonymous connection
lftp ftp.freebsd.org:~>
$ lftp marlowe@example.com              Authenticated connection
lftp example.com:~>
$ lftp -u marlowe example.com           Authenticated connection
Password: ******
lftp example.com:~>
$ lftp -u marlowe,Mypwd example.com     Authentication with password
lftp example.com:~>
$ lftp                                  Start lftp with no connection
lftp :~> open ftp.freebsd.org           Start connection in lftp session
lftp ftp.freebsd.org:~>
```

> **WARNING** *The fourth example should be avoided in real life. Passwords that are entered in a command line end up stored in clear text in your* `~/.bash_history` *if you use the* bash *shell. They may also be visible to other users in the output of* `ps auwx`.

When a connection is established to an FTP server, you can use a set of commands during the FTP session. FTP commands are similar to shell commands. Just as in a bash shell, you can press Tab to autocomplete filenames. In a session, `lftp` also supports sending multiple jobs to the background (Ctrl+Z) and returning them to the foreground (`wait` or `fg`). These are useful if you want to continue traversing the FTP site while files are downloading or uploading. Background jobs run in parallel. Type `jobs` to see a list of running background jobs. Type `help` to see a list of `lftp` commands.

The following sample `lftp` session illustrates **useful commands when downloading**:

```
$ lftp ftp.freebsd.org
lftp ftp.freebsd.org:~> pwd                            Check current directory
ftp://ftp.freebsd.org
lftp ftp.freebsd.org:~> ls                             List current directory
drwxr-xr-x   3 ftpuser  ftpuser     512 Jun  5  2007 pub
drwxr-xr-x   3 ftpuser  ftpuser     512 Jun  5  2007 sup
lftp ftp.freebsd.org:~> cd /pub/FreeBSD/doc/en/books/faq  Change directory
lftp ftp.freebsd.org:…> get book.pdf.bz2               Download a file
book.pdf.bz2 at 776398 (1%) 467.2K/s eta:26m {Receiving data]
lftp ftp.freebsd.org:…> <Ctrl+z>                       Send download to background
lftp ftp.freebsd.org:…> cd /pub/FreeBSD/doc/en/articles/explaining-bsd
lftp ftp.freebsd.org:…> mget *                         Get all from explaining-bsd
lftp ftp.freebsd.org:…> !ls                            Run local ls
lftp ftp.freebsd.org:…> bookmark add article           Bookmark location
lftp ftp.freebsd.org:…> quit                           Close lftp
```

This session logs in as the anonymous user at `ftp.freebsd.org`. After changing to the directory containing the document I was looking for, I downloaded it using the `get` command. By typing Ctrl+Z, the download could continue while I did other activities. Next, the `mget` command (which allows wildcards such as *) downloaded all files from the `explaining-bsd` directory.

Any command preceded by an exclamation mark (such as `!ls`) is executed by the local shell. The `bookmark` command saves the current location (in this case, the directory `/pub/FreeBSD/doc/en/articles/explaining-bsd` on the `freebsd.org` FTP site) under the name `article`, so next time I can run `lftp article` to return to the same location. The `quit` command ends the session.

Here are some **useful commands during an authenticated lftp upload session**. This assumes you have the necessary file permissions on the server:

```
$ lftp kafka@example.com
Password: *******
lftp example.com:~> lcd /home/kafka/songs       Change to a local directory
lftp example.com:~> cd pub/uploads              Change to server directory
lftp example.com:~> mkdir songs                 Create directory on server
lftp example.com:~> chmod 700 songs             Change remote directory perms
lftp example.com:~> cd songs                    Change to the new directory
lftp example.com:~> put song.mp3 tune.mp3       Upload files to server
3039267 bytes transferred
lftp example.com:~> mput /var/songs/*           Upload matched files
lftp example.com:~> quit                        Close lftp
```

The lftp session illustrates how you can use shell command names to operate on remote directories (provided you have permission). The mkdir and chmod commands create a directory and leave permissions open only to your user account. The put command uploads one or more files to the remote server. The mput command can use wildcards to match multiple files for download. Other commands include mirror (to download a directory tree) and mirror -R (to upload a directory tree).

lftp also provides a shell script for **non-interactive download sessions**: lftpget. The syntax of lftpget is similar to that of the wget command:

```
$ lftpget ftp://ftp.freebsd.org:/pub/FreeBSD/doc/en/books/handbook/book.pdf.bz2
```

Keep in mind that standard FTP clients are insecure because they do all their work in clear text. Your alternative, especially when security is a major issue, is to use SSH tools to transfer files.

Using SSH Tools to Transfer Files

Because SSH utilities are among the most important tools in a system administrator's arsenal of communications commands, some of the more complex uses of configuring and using SSH utilities are covered in Chapter 13. However, in their most basic form, SSH utilities are the tools you should use most often for basic file transfer.

In particular, the scp command will do most of what you need to get a file from one computer to another, while making that communication safe by encrypting both the password stage and the data transfer stage of the process. The scp command replaces the rcp command as the most popular tool for host-to-host file copies.

> **WARNING**   *You do not get a warning before overwriting existing files with* scp, *so ensure that the target host doesn't contain any files or directories you want that are in the path of your* scp *file copies.*

Copying Remote Files with scp

To use scp to transfer files, the SSH service (usually the sshd server daemon) must be running on the remote system. Here are some examples of **useful scp commands**:

```
$ scp myfile kafka@server1:/tmp/        Copy myfile to server1
Password: ******
$ scp server1:/tmp/myfile .             Copy remote myfile to local working dir
Password: ******
```

Use the -p option to **preserve permissions and timestamps** on the copied files:

```
$ scp -p myfile server1:/tmp/
```

If the SSH service is configured to listen on a port other than the default port 22, then use -P to **indicate another port** on the scp command line:

```
$ scp -P 12345 myfile server1:/tmp/     Connect to a particular port
```

To do **recursive copies** from a particular point in the remote file system, use the -r option:

```
$ scp -r mydir marlowe@server1:/tmp/     Copies all mydir to remote /tmp
```

Although scp is most useful when you know the exact locations of the file(s) you need to copy, sometimes it's more helpful to browse and transfer files interactively.

Copying Remote Files in sftp and lftp Sessions

The sftp command enables you to use an ftp-like interface to **find and copy files over SSH protocols**. Here's an example of how to start an sftp session:

```
$ sftp kafka@server1
kafka@server1's password: *****
sftp>
```

Use sftp in the same manner as you use regular ftp clients. Type ? for a list of commands. You can change remote directories (cd), change local directories (lcd), check current remote and local directories (pwd and lpwd), and list remote and local contents (ls and lls). Depending on the permissions of the user you logged in as, you may be able to create and remove directories (mkdir and rmdir), and change permissions (chmod) and ownership/group (chown and chgrp) of files and directories.

You can also use lftp (discussed earlier in this chapter) as an sftp client. Using lftp adds some user-friendly features such as **path completion** using the Tab key:

```
$ lftp sftp://kafka@server1
Password: ********
lftp kafka@server1:~>
```

Sharing Remote Directories

The tools described up to this point in the chapter provide atomic file access, whereby a connection is set up and files are transferred in one shot. When more persistent, ongoing access to a remote directory of files is needed, services for sharing and mounting remote file systems can be most useful. Such services include Network File System (NFS) and Samba.

Sharing Remote Directories with NFS

Before sharing directories from your BSD system with NFS, you must start the NFS service. To do this in Mac OS X, simply run the following command:

```
sudo nfsd
```

You can control `nfsd` with the following commands:

```
sudo nfsd start       Start or restart NFS
sudo nfsd stop        Stop NFS
sudo nfsd disable     Disable the NFS service
sudo nsfd status      Get current status of NFS
```

When your system is running the NFS service, you can add entries to the `/etc/exports` file on the server to share directories with remote clients and use `showmount` commands to see available and mounted shared directories. Mounting a shared directory is done with special options to the standard `mount` command.

Please note that if you create an `/etc/exports` file, your Mac OS X automatically connects to an NFS share. This makes the NFS functionality more like other UNIX systems (the NetInfo Manager GUI utility has been removed from the Leopard release, so don't bother looking for it if you're on Mac OS X 10.5 or higher).

Here's a sample entry in the `/etc/exports` file:

```
/Users -maproot=kafka -network 10.0.0 -mask 255.255.255.0
```

Sharing Directories from an NFS Server

With the NFS server running as just described, directories can be shared from that server by using the `mount` command:

```
sudo mount nfsserver:/export/this /Users/myerman/mounts
```

This command will only work as long as you don't restart the Mac OS X system. If you want to automount, see the earlier note about creating an `/etc/exports` file.

Viewing and Exporting NFS Shares

From the BSD server system, you can use the `showmount` command to see what shared directories are available from the local system. For example:

```
# /usr/sbin/showmount -e
Export list for server.example.com
/export/myshare  client.example.com
/mnt/public      *
```

From a client BSD system, you can use the `showmount` command to see what shared directories are available from a selected computer. For example:

```
# /usr/sbin/showmount -e server2.example.com
Exports list on server2.example.com
/export/myshare client.example.com
/mnt/public     *
```

Mounting NFS Shares

Use the mount command to mount a remote NFS share on the local computer. Here is an example:

```
# mkdir /mnt/server-share
# mount server.example.com:/export/myshare /mnt/server-share
```

This example notes the NFS server (server.example.com) and the shared directory from that server (/export/myshare). The local mount point, which must exist before mounting the share, appears at the end of the command (/mnt/server-share).

Pass NFS-specific options to the mount command by adding them after the -o option:

```
# mount -o rw,hard,intr server.example.com:/export/myshare /mnt/server-share
```

The rw option mounts the remote directory with read-write permissions, assuming that permission is available. With hard set, someone using the share will see a server not responding message when a read or write operation times out. If that happens, having set the intr option enables you to interrupt a hung request to a remote server (type Ctrl+C).

Sharing Remote Directories with Samba

Samba is the open-source implementation of the Windows file and print-sharing protocol originally known as Server Message Block (SMB) and now called Common Internet File System (CIFS).

Viewing and Accessing Samba Shares

To scan your network for SMB hosts, type the following:

```
$ findsmb
                        *=DMB
                        +=LMB
IP ADDR         NETBIOS NAME  WORKGROUP/OS/VERSION
---------------------------------------------------------------------
192.168.1.1     SERVER1       +[MYWORKGROUP] [Unix] [Samba 3.0.25a-3.fc7]
```

To view a text representation of your network neighborhood (shared directories and printers), use smbtree:

```
# smbtree
Password: ******
MSHOME
  \\HOPE-HP          Hope's HP
  \\HOPE-HP\Printer      SnagIt 7
  \\HOPE-HP\C$           Default share
  \\HOPE-HP\ADMIN$       Remote Admin
  \\HOPE-HP\Printer2     PageManager PDF Writer
```

```
\\HOPE-HP\Printer4          Adobe PDF
\\HOPE-HP\SharedDocs
\\HOPE-HP\print$            Printer Drivers
\\HOPE-HP\D$                Default share
\\HOPE-HP\IPC$              Remote IPC
```

To **add an existing user as a Samba user,** use the `smbpasswd` command:

```
# smbpasswd -a kafka
New SMB password: ******
Retype new SMB password: ******
Added user francois
```

To **list services offered by a server to an anonymous user,** type the following:

```
$ smbclient -L server
Password: ******
Anynymous login successful
Domain=[MYGROUP] OS=[Unix] Server=Samba 3.0.23c
tree connect failed: NT_STSTUS_LOGON_FAILURE
```

Here's the output from `smbclient` for a specific user named myerman:

```
$ smbclient -L server -U myerman
Password: ******
Domain=[MYGROUP] OS=[Unix] Server=[Samba 3.0.23c]

    Sharename    Type    Comment
    ---------    ----    -------
    IPC$         IPC     IPC Service (Samba Server Version 3.0.23c)
    hp5550       Printer HP DeskJet 5550 Printer

        Server              Comment
        ---------           -------
        THOMPSON            Samba Server Version 3.0.23c

        Workgroup           Master
        ---------           -------
        MYGROUP             THOMPSON
```

To **connect to a Samba share ftp-style,** type the following:

```
$ smbclient //192.168.1.1/myshare -U marlowe
Password:
Domain=[MYWORKGROUP] OS=[Unix] Server=[Samba 3.0.23c]
smb: \>
```

As with most FTP clients, type help or ? to see a list of available commands. Likewise, you can use common shell-type commands, such as cd, ls, get, put, and quit, **to get around on the SMB host.**

You can also use the Mac OS X GUI to do the same work. For example, click the Finder icon in the Dock, and then select Go ⇨ Connect to Server from the menu.

In the Server Address field of the dialog that appears, type the URL of the Samba server using the smb://*ServerName*/*ShareName*/ syntax, as shown in Figure 12-1.

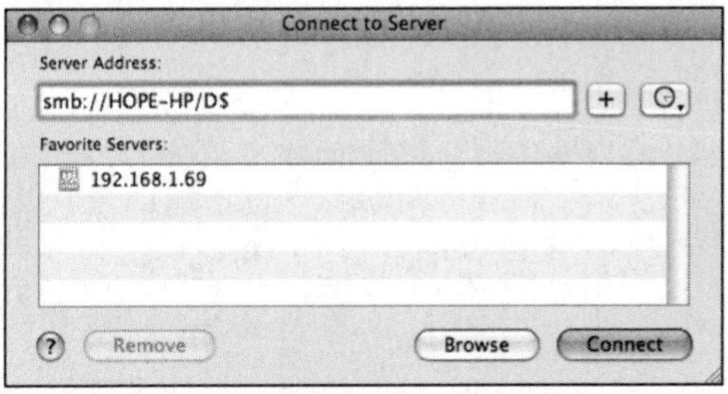

Figure 12-1: Connecting to a Samba share using Connect to Server

Mounting Samba Shares

You can **mount remote Samba shares on your local file system** much as you would a local file system or remote NFS file system. To mount the share, enter the following:

```
# mount -t smbfs //kafka@192.168.1.1/myshare /mnt/mymount/
```

> **NOTE** *The Samba file system (*smbfs*), while still available on FreeBSD, is deprecated on some Linux systems. If you are mounting a Samba share from a BSD system to a Linux system, indicate CIFS (*-t cifs*) as the file system type when you mount that remote Samba share.*

You can **see the current connections and file locks** on a server using the smbstatus command. This will tell you whether someone has mounted your shared directories or is currently using an smbclient connection to your server:

```
# smbstatus
Samba version 3.0.23c
PID     Username    Group     Machine
-------------------------------------------
 5466   francois    francois 10.0.0.55   (10.0.0.55)

Service   pid   machine    Connected at
-------------------------------------------
myshare   5644  10.0.0.55  Tue Jun  3 15:08:29 2008

No locked files
```

To see **briefer output**, use the -b option:

```
$ smbstatus -b
```

Looking Up Samba Hosts

NetBIOS names are used to identify hosts in Samba. You can **determine the IP address of a computer** using the nmblookup command to broadcast for a particular NetBIOS name on the local subnet as follows:

```
$ nmblookup thompson
querying thompson on 192.168.1.255
192.168.1.1 server1<00>
```

To **find the IP address for a server on a specific subnet,** use the -U option:

```
$ nmblookup -U 192.168.1.0 server1
querying server1 on 192.168.1.255
192.168.1.1 server1<00>
```

Checking Samba Configuration

If you are unable to use a Samba share or you have other problems communicating with your Samba server, you can test the Samba configuration on the server. The testparm command can be used to **check your main Samba configuration file** (smb.conf):

```
$ testparm
Load smb config files from /private/etc/smb.conf
Processing section "[homes]"
Processing section "[printers]"
Loaded services file OK.
Server role: ROLE_STANDALONE
Press enter to see a dump of your service definitions
```

After pressing Enter as instructed, you can see the settings from your smb.conf file. Here's how my entries appear in the smb.conf file:

```
[global]
dos charset = 437
unix charset = UTF-8-MAC
display charset = UTF-8-MAC
realm = LKDC:SHA1.D5F61881A1E85AF1DED78D0FBA71CAEAAA61C759
server string = Thomas Myer's Computer
enable disk services = No
enable print services = No
auth methods = guest, odsam
map to guest = Bad User
obey pam restrictions = Yes
passdb backend = odsam
lanman auth = No
use kerberos keytab = Yes
log level = 1
debug pid = Yes
max xmit = 131072
name resolve order = lmhosts wins bcast host
max smbd processes = 10
```

```
printcap name = cups
os level = 2
preferred master = No
domain master = No
usershare allow guests = Yes
usershare allow full config = Yes
usershare max shares = 1000
usershare owner only = No
usershare path = /var/samba/shares
idmap domains = default
idmap alloc backend = odsam
idmap negative cache time = 5
com.apple:lkdc realm = LKDC:SHA1.D5F61881A1E85AF1DED78D0FBA71CAEAAA61C759
com.apple:filter shares by access = yes
darwin_streams:brlm = yes
idmap config default:backend = odsam
idmap config default:default = yes
ea support = Yes
stream support = Yes
use sendfile = Yes
printing = cups
print command =
lpq command = %p
lprm command =
include = /var/db/smb.conf
vfs objects = darwinacl, darwin_streams

[homes]
comment = User Home Directories
read only = No
create mask = 0750
browseable = No
com.apple:show admin all volumes = yes

[printers]
comment = All Printers
path = /tmp
create mask = 0700
printable = Yes
browseable = No
```

The previous example of `testparm` shows the entries you set in the `smb.conf` file. However, it doesn't **show all the default entries you didn't set.** You can view those using the `-v` option. Pipe it to the `less` command to page through the settings:

```
$ testparm -v | less
```

If you want to **test a configuration file before it goes live,** you can tell `testparm` to use a file other than `/etc/samba/smb.conf`:

```
$ testparm /etc/samba/test-smb.conf
```

Chatting with Friends in IRC

Despite the emergence of instant messaging, Internet Relay Chat (IRC) is still used by a lot of people today. freenode.net has a ton of chat rooms dedicated to supporting major open-source software projects. In fact, many people stay logged into them all day and just watch the discussions of their favorite UNIX projects scroll by, a behavior known as *lurking*.

The xchat utility is a good graphical, multi-operating system IRC client (to install, type **fink install xchat**). Once the xchat package is installed, simply double-click its icon in the Applications folder. The elite way to use IRC is to run a text-mode client in screen on an always-on machine, such as an old server. Another similar option is to use an IRC proxy client, also known as a *bouncer*, such as dircproxy.

The original IRC client was ircII. It allowed the addition of scripts—in some ways similar to macros found in productivity suites—that automated some of the commands and increased usability. The most popular was PhoEniX by Vassago. Then came BitchX, which started as an ircII script and then became a full-blown client. Today, most people use irssi. To **install and launch irssi** from Mac OS X, type the following:

```
# fink install irssi
$ irssi -n JayJoe200x
```

In this example, the username (nick) is set to JayJoe200x (you should choose your own, of course). You should see a blue status bar at the bottom of the screen indicating that you are in Window 1, the status window. IRC commands are preceded with a / character. For example, to **connect to the freenode server**, type the following:

```
/connect chat.freenode.net
```

If you don't add your username on the command line, you are connected to chat.freenode.net under the username you are logged in under. On IRC, a chat room is called a *channel* and has a pound sign (#) in front of the name. Next, try **joining the #freebsd IRC channel**:

```
/join #freebsd
```

Your screen should look similar to the one shown in Figure 12-2.

You are now in the channel in Window 2, as indicated in the status bar. Switch among the irssi windows by typing Alt+1, Alt+2, and so on (or Ctrl+N and Ctrl+P). To **get help** at any time, type /help. To **get help for a command**, type /help *command*, where *command* is the name of the command for which you want more information. Help text will output in the status window, not necessarily the current window.

To add to the IRC chat, simply type a message and press Enter to **send a message** to those in the channel. Type /part to leave a channel. Type /quit to **exit the program**.

There is a lot more to `irssi`. You can customize it and improve your experience significantly. Refer to the `irssi` documentation (`www.irssi.org/documentation`) for more information about how to use `irssi`.

```
                              thompson
File  Edit  View  Terminal  Tabs  Help
Irssi v0.8.10 - http://irssi.org/help/
06:02 - - -
06:02 - - - freenode is a service of Peer-Directed Projects Center, an
06:02 - - - IRS 501(c)(3) not-for-profit organization.  Our yearly
06:02 - - - fundraiser will begin soon; if you'd like to donate early,
06:02 - - - please see http://freenode.net/pdpc_donations.shtml for more
06:02 - - - information.  Thank you for using freenode!
06:02 - - End of /MOTD command.
06:02 freenode-connect [freenode@freenode/bot/connect] requested CTCP VERSION from jayjoe200x:
06:02 - - Mode change [+i] for user JayJoe200x
06:03 - - #freebsd ##freebsd Forwarding to another channel
06:03 - -
  06:08  JayJoe200x( i)  1:freenode (change with ^X)
[(status)]
```

Figure 12-2: irssi connected to #freebsd on freenode

Using Text-Based E-mail Clients

Most *mail user agents (MUAs)* are GUI-based these days, so if you began using e-mail in the past decade or so, you probably think of Evolution, KMail, Thunderbird, Mail. app (on Mac OS X), or (on Windows systems) Outlook, when it comes to e-mail clients. On the first UNIX and BSD systems, however, e-mail was handled by text-based applications.

Although you'll likely be using Mail.app or another graphical e-mail client, it's worth your time to become familiar with the text-based mail tools.

If you find yourself needing to check e-mail on a remote server or other text-based environment, venerable text-based mail clients are available and still quite useful. In fact, some hard-core geeks still use text-based mail clients exclusively, touting their efficiency and scoffing at HTML-based messages.

The mail clients described in this chapter assume that your messages are stored in standard MBOX format on the local system. That means that you are either logged into the mail server or you have already downloaded the messages locally (for example, by using POP3 or similar).

> **NOTE** *Text-based mail clients can be used to read mail already downloaded by other mail clients. For example, you could open your Evolution mail Inbox file by typing* mail -f $HOME/.evolution/mail/local/Inbox.

The oldest, and easiest, command to use when you just want a quick check for messages in the root user's mailbox on a remote server, is the mail command (/bin/mail). If your $MAIL variable is set, just log in as root and type mail. Otherwise, use the -f option, as noted earlier, to identify the mailbox file directly (mail -f /var/mail/root).

Although `mail` can be used interactively, it is often used for **sending script-based e-mails**. Here are some examples:

```
$ uname -a | mail -s 'My OS X version' kafka@example.com
$ ps auwx | mail -s 'My Process List' marlowe@example.com
```

The two `mail` examples just shown provide quick ways to mail off some text without having to open a GUI mail application. The first example sends the output from the `uname -a` command to the user `kafka@example.com`. The subject (`-s`) is set to `'My OS X Version'`. In the second example, a list of currently running processes (`ps auwx`) is sent to the same user with a subject of `'My Process List'`.

Used interactively, by default the `mail` command opens the mailbox set by your current shell's `$MAIL` value. For example:

```
# echo $MAIL
/var/mail/root
# mail
Mail version 8.1 6/6/93.  Type ? for help.
"/var/mail/root": 25 messages 25 new
>N  1 root@thompson.locald  Tue Jan  8 03:02  41/1193  "X5 security run output"
 N  2 root@thompson.locald  Tue Jan  8 03:02  73/2504  "X5 daily run output"
 N  3 root@thompson.locald  Sat Jan 19 03:02  35/1119  "X5 security run output"
 N  4 root@thompson.locald  Sat Jan 19 03:02  70/2419  "X5 daily run output"
&
```

The current message has a greater-than sign (>) next to it. New messages have an N at the beginning; unread (but not new) have a U; and if there is no letter, the message has been read. The prompt at the bottom (&) is ready to accept commands.

At this point, you are in command mode. You can use simple commands to **move around** and **perform basic mail functions** in `mail`. Type **?** to see a list of commands, or type the number of the message you want to see. Type **v3** to open the third message in the `vi` editor. Type **h18** to see a list of message headers that begins with message 18. To reply to message 7, type **r7** (type your message, and then put a dot on a line by itself to send the message). Type **d4** to delete the fourth message (or **d4–9** to delete messages four through nine). Type **!bash** to escape to the shell (and then **exit** to return to `mail`).

You should understand that before you exit `mail`, any messages you view will be copied from your mailbox file to your `$HOME/mbox` file when you exit, unless you preserve them (`pre*`). To keep all messages in your mailbox, exit by typing **x**. To save your changes to the mailbox, type **q** to exit.

You can open any file that is in MBOX format when you use `mail`. For example, if you are logged in as the root user but want to open the mailbox for the user `kafka`, type the following:

```
# mail -f /var/mail/kafka
```

Summary

Network access commands provide quick and efficient ways to get content you need over a network. Dozens of commands are available to download files over FTP, HTTP, SSH, or other protocols, including `wget`, `curl`, `lftp`, and `scp`.

For ongoing access to remote directories of files, this chapter covers how to use NFS and Samba command tools. You can participate in IRC chats, which are popular among open-source projects, using the `irssi` command. For text-based e-mail clients, you have options such as the `mail` command.

13

Remote System Administration

Most professional UNIX administrators do not run a graphical interface on their Internet servers. As a result, when you need to access other computers for remote administration, you will almost surely need to work from the command line at some time. Luckily, there are many feature-rich UNIX commands to help you do so.

Tools associated with the Secure Shell (SSH) service not only enable remote login and file transfer, they also offer encrypted communication to keep your remote administration work secure. With tools such as Virtual Network Computing (VNC), you can have a server's remote desktop appear on your local client computer. These and other features for performing remote systems administration are described in this chapter.

Remote Login and Tunneling with SSH

BSD systems, like their big brother UNIX, grew up on university networks. At a time when the only users of these networks were students and professors, and with networks mostly isolated from one another, there was little need for security.

Applications and protocols that were designed in those times (the 1970s and 1980s) reflect that lack of concern for encryption and authentication. SMTP is a perfect example of that. This is also true of the first generation of UNIX remote tools: telnet, ftp (file transfer protocol), rsh (remote shell), rcp (remote copy), rexec (remote execution), and rlogin (remote login). These tools send user credentials and traffic in clear text, making them very dangerous to use on the public, untrusted Internet; they have become mostly deprecated and replaced with the Secure Shell (SSH) commands (ssh, scp, sftp commands, and related services).

Although there are still some uses for the legacy remote commands (see the "Using Legacy Communications Tools" sidebar), most of this section describes how to use SSH commands to handle the majority of your needs for remote communications.

Using Legacy Communications Tools

Despite the fact that SSH provides better tools for remote communications, legacy communications commands, sometimes referred to as *r commands*, are still included with most major BSD distributions. Some of these tools will perform faster than equivalent SSH commands because they don't need to do encryption. Therefore, some old-school UNIX administrators may use them occasionally on private networks or still include them in old scripts. Although for the most part you should ignore these legacy remote commands, one of these commands in particular can be useful in some cases: telnet.

The telnet command is still used to communicate with some network appliances (routers, switches, UPSs, and so on) that do not have the horsepower to run an ssh daemon. Even though telnet poses a security risk, some appliance manufacturers include support for it anyway.

One good way to use the telnet command is for troubleshooting many Internet protocols such as POP3, SMTP, HTTP, and others. Under the hood, these plain-text protocols are simply automated telnet sessions during which a client (such as a browser or mail user agent) exchanges text with a server. The only difference is the TCP port in use. Here is an example of how you could telnet to the HTTP port (80) of a web server:

```
$ telnet www.example.com 80
Trying 208.77.188.166…
Connected to www.example.com.
Escape character is '^]'.
GET /index.html
<!DOCTYPE html PUBLIC "-//W3C//DTD XHTML 1.1//EN"
 "http://www.w3.org/TR/xhtml11/DTD/xhtml11.dtd">
<html xmlns="http://www.w3.org/1999/xhtml" xml:lang="en">
        <head>
                <title>My Web server…
```

Similarly, you can telnet to a mail server on port 25 (SMTP) and 110 (POP3) and issue the proper commands to troubleshoot e-mail problems. For more complete descriptions of using the telnet command to troubleshoot network protocols, refer to the *Linux Troubleshooting Bible* (Wiley, 2004).

If you need to forcefully exit your telnet session, type the escape sequence (Ctrl+] by default). This will stop sending your keyboard input to the remote end and bring you to the telnet command prompt, where you can type quit or ? for more options.

Configuring SSH

Nowadays, the all-purpose tool of remote system administration is Secure Shell (SSH). SSH commands and services replace all the old remote tools and add strong encryption, public keys, and many other features. The most common implementation of SSH in the free and open-source software world is OpenSSH (www.openssh.com), maintained by the OpenBSD project. SSH is available natively on Mac OS X, so all you need to start using it is access to Terminal and a shell.

If you prefer to use graphical tools to administer your remote BSD system, you can enable *X11 tunneling* (also called *X11 port forwarding*). With X11 tunneling enabled (on both the SSH client and the server), you can start an X application on the server and have it displayed on the client. All communication across that connection is encrypted.

FreeBSD comes with X11 forwarding turned on (X11Forwarding yes) for the server (sshd daemon). You still need to enable it on the client side. To **enable X11 forwarding on the client for a one-time session**, connect with the following command:

```
$ ssh -X kafka@myserver
```

To **enable X11 forwarding permanently for all users**, add ForwardX11 yes to /etc/ssh/ssh_config. To enable it permanently for a specific user only, add the lines to that user's ~/.ssh/config. After those settings have been added, the -X option is no longer required in order to use X11 tunneling. Run ssh to connect to the remote system as you would normally. To test that the tunneling is working, run xclock after ssh'ing into the remote machine, and it should appear on your client desktop.

SSH tunneling is an excellent way to securely use remote graphical tools!

Logging in Remotely with SSH

To **securely log in to a remote host**, you can use either of two different syntaxes to specify the username:

```
$ ssh -l kafka myserver
$ ssh kafka@myserver
```

However, scp and sftp commands (discussed in Chapter 10) support only the *user@ server* syntax, so we recommend you get used to that one. If you don't specify the username, ssh will attempt to log in using the same user you are logged in as locally. When connected, if you need to **forcefully exit your SSH session**, type the escape sequence of a tilde followed by a period (~.).

Accessing SSH on a Different Port

For security purposes, a remote host may have its SSH service listening to a different port than the default port number 22. If that's the case, use the -p option to ssh to contact that service:

```
$ ssh -p 12345 kakfa@example.com    Connect to SSH on port 12345
```

Using SSH to Do Tunneling (X11 Port Forwarding)

With SSH tunneling configured as described earlier, the SSH service forwards X Window System clients to your local display. However, tunneling can be used with other TCP-based protocols as well.

Tunneling for X11 Clients

The following sequence of commands illustrates how to start an SSH session, and then start a few X applications so they appear on the local desktop:

```
$ ssh -x kafka@myserver                       Start ssh connection to myserver
kafka@myserver's password: *******
[kafka@myserver ~]$ echo $DISPLAY     Show the current X display entry
localhost:10.0                                SSH sets display to localhost:10.0
[kafka@myserver ~]$ xeyes&                    Show moving desktop eyes
[kafka@myserver ~]$ gnome-system-monitor&     Monitor system activities
[kafka@myserver ~]$ xcalc&                    Use a calculator
```

As more connections are requested, the $DISPLAY will be set to 11.0, 12.0, and so on.

Tunneling for CUPS Printing Remote Administration

X11 is not the only protocol that can be tunneled over SSH. You can forward any TCP port with SSH. This is a great way to configure secure tunnels quickly and easily. No configuration is required on the server side.

For example, myserver is a print server with the CUPS printing service's web-based user interface enabled (running on port 631). That GUI is only accessible from the local machine. On my MacBook Pro, I tunnel to that service using ssh with the following options:

```
$ ssh -L 1234:localhost:631 myserver
```

This example forwards port 1234 on my client PC to localhost port 631 on the server. I can now browse to http://localhost:1234 on my client PC. This will be redirected to cupsd listening on port 631 on the server. Note that you need root privilege to forward ports with numbers lower than 1024.

Tunneling to an Internet Service

Another example of using SSH tunneling is when your local machine is blocked from connecting to the Internet, but you can get to another machine (myserver) that has an

Internet connection. The following example enables you to visit the Google.com website (HTTP, TCP port 80) across an SSH connection to a computer named `myserver` that has a connection to the Internet:

```
$ ssh -L 12345:google.com:80 myserver
```

With this example, any connection to the local port 12345 is directed across an SSH tunnel to `myserver`, which in turn opens a connection to `Google.com` port 80. You can now browse to `http://localhost:12345` and use `myserver` as a relay to the Google.com website. Because you only intend to use `ssh` to forward a port, and not to obtain a shell on the server, you can add the `-N` option to **prevent the execution of remote commands**:

```
$ ssh -L 12345:google.com:80 -N myserver
```

Using SSH with Public Key Authentication

Up to this point, we've only used `ssh` with the default password authentication. The `ssh` command also supports public key authentication. This offers several benefits:

❑ **Automated logins for scripts and cron jobs:** By assigning an empty passphrase you can use `ssh` in a script to log in automatically. Although this is convenient, it is also dangerous, because anybody who gets to your key file can connect to any machine you can. Configuring for automatic login can also be done with a passphrase and a key agent. This is a trade-off between convenience and security, as explained next.

❑ **Two-factor authentication:** When using a passphrase-protected key for interactive logins, authentication is done using two factors (the key and the passphrase) instead of one.

Using Public Key Logins

Here's the process to **set up key-based communications** between two BSD systems. In the following example, we use empty passphrases for no-password logins. If you prefer to protect your key with a passphrase, simply enter it when prompted during the first step (key pair creation).

On the client system, run the following `ssh-keygen` command to **generate the key pair** while logged in as the user who needs to initiate communications:

```
$ ssh-keygen
Generating public/private rsa key pair.
Enter file in which to save the key (/home/chris/.ssh/id_rsa): <Enter>
Enter passphrase (empty for no passphrase): <Enter>
Enter same passphrase again: <Enter>
Your identification has been saved in /home/chris/.ssh/id_rsa.
Your public key has been saved in /home/chris/.ssh/id_rsa.pub.
The key fingerprint is:
ac:db:a4:8e:3f:2a:90:4f:05:9f:b4:44:74:0e:d3:db chris@host.domain.com
```

Note that at each prompt you press the Enter key to create the default key filename and to enter (and verify) an empty passphrase. You now have a private key that you need to keep very safe, especially because in this procedure you didn't protect it with a passphrase.

You also now have a public key (id_rsa.pub), which was created by the previous command. This public key needs to be installed on hosts to which you want to con-nect. The content of ~/.ssh/id_rsa.pub needs to be copied (securely) to ~/.ssh/authorized_keys for the user you want to ssh to on the remote server. The autho-rized_keys file can contain more than one public key if multiple users use ssh to connect to this account.

Log in to the *remote server* system as the user that you will want to ssh as with the key. If you don't already have a ~/.ssh directory, the first step is to create it as follows:

```
$ cd
$ mkdir .ssh
$ chmod 700 .ssh
```

The next step is to copy (securely) the public key file from the client and put it in an authorized keys file on the server. This can be accomplished using scp. For example, assuming the client system named myclient and the client user named chris, type the following on the server:

```
$ scp chris@myclient:/home/chris/.ssh/id_rsa.pub    Get client id_rsa.pub
$ cat id_rsa.pub >> ~/.ssh/authorized_keys          Add to your keys
$ chmod 600 ~/.ssh/authorized_keys                  Close permissions
$ rm id_rsa.pub                    Delete public key after copying its content
```

This procedure can also be accomplished by editing the ~/.ssh/authorized_keys text file on the server and copying and pasting the public key from the client. Be sure you do so securely over ssh, and do not insert any line breaks in the key. The entire key should fit on one single line, even if it wraps on your screen.

Next, from the client (using the client and server user accounts you just configured), you can just ssh to the server and the key will be used. If you set a passphrase, you will be asked for it, as you would for a password.

Saving Private Keys to Use from a USB Flash Drive

If you'd like to store your private key somewhere safer than your hard drive, you can use a USB flash drive (sometimes called a thumbdrive or pen drive):

```
$ mv ~/.ssh/id_rsa /Volumes/THUMBDRIVE1/myprivatekey
```

Then, when you want to use the key, insert the USB drive and type the following:

```
$ ssh -i /media/THUMBDRIVE1/myprivatekey marlowe@myserver
```

Using keys with passphrases is more secure than simple passwords, but also more cumbersome. To make your life easier, you can use `ssh-agent` to **store unlocked keys for the duration of your session.** When you add an unlocked key to your running `ssh-agent`, you can run `ssh` using the key without being prompted for the passphrase each time.

To see what the `ssh-agent` command does, run the command with no option. A three-line `bash` script appears when you run it, as follows:

```
$ ssh-agent
SSH_AUTH_SOCK=/tmp/ssh-SkEQZ18329/agent.18329; export SSH_AUTH_SOCK;
SSH_AGENT_PID=18330; export SSH_AGENT_PID;
echo Agent pid 18330;
```

The first two lines of the preceding output need to be executed by your shell. Copy and paste those lines into your shell now. You can avoid this extra step by starting `ssh-agent` and having the `bash` shell evaluate its output by typing the following:

```
$ eval `ssh-agent`
Agent pid 18408
```

You can now unlock keys and add them to your running agent. Assuming you have already run the `ssh-keygen` command to create a default key, now **add that default key** using the `ssh-add` command:

```
$ ssh-add
Enter passphrase for /home/chris/.ssh/id_rsa: *******
Identity added: /home/chris/.ssh/id_rsa (/home/chris/.ssh/id_rsa)
```

Next, you could add the key you stored on the USB thumbdrive:

```
$ ssh-add /media/THUMBDRIVE1/myprivatekey
```

Use the -l option to `ssh-add` to **list the keys stored in the agent:**

```
$ ssh-add -l
2048 f7:b0:7a:5a:65:3c:cd:45:b5:1c:de:f8:26:ee:8d:78 /home/chris/.ssh/id_rsa
(RSA)
2048 f7:b0:7a:5a:65:3c:cd:45:b5:1c:de:f8:26:ee:8d:78
/media/THUMBDRIVE1/myprivatekey (RSA)
```

To **remove one key from the agent**—for example, the one from the USB thumbdrive—run `ssh-add` with the -d option:

```
$ ssh-add -d /media/THUMBDRIVE1/myprivatekey
```

To **remove all the keys stored in the agent,** use the -D option:

```
$ ssh-add -D
```

Using screen: A Rich Remote Shell

The ssh command gives you only one screen. If you lose that screen, you lose all you were doing on the remote computer. That can be very bad if you were in the middle of something important, such as a 12-hour compile. In addition, if you want to do three things at once, such as vi httpd.conf, tail -f error_log, service httpd reload, you need to open three separate ssh sessions.

Essentially, screen is a terminal multiplexer. If you are a system administrator working on remote servers, screen is a great tool for managing a remote computer with only a command-line interface available. Besides allowing multiple shells sessions, screen also enables you to disconnect from it and then reconnect to that same screen session later.

The screen software package is available for Mac OS X via fink. To **create and install the screen package**, type the following from the Mac OS X server on which you want to use screen:

fink install screen

To **use screen**, run the ssh command from a client system to connect to the BSD server where screen is installed. Then simply type the following command:

$ **screen**

If you ran screen from a Terminal window, after you see the license message press Enter and you should see a regular bash prompt in the window. To control screen, press the Ctrl+A key combo, followed by another keystroke. For example, Ctrl+A followed by ? (noted as Ctrl+A, ?) displays the help screen. With screen running, here are some commands and control keys you can use to operate screen.

```
$ screen -ls                            List active screens
There is a screen on:
      7089.pts-2.myserver    (Attached)  Shows screen is attached
1 Socket in /var/run/screen/S-kafka.
$ Ctrl+A, A                             Change window title
Set window's title to: My Server          Type a new title
$ Ctrl+A, C                             Create a new window
$ Ctrl+A, "                               Show active window titles
Num Name                Flags
   0 My Server                            Up/down arrows change
windows
   1 bash
$ Ctrl+A, Ctrl+D                        Detach screen from terminal
$ screen -ls                            List active screens
There is a screen on:
      7089.pts-2.myserver    (Detached)  Shows screen is detached
1 Socket in /var/run/screen/S-kafka.
```

The `screen` session just shown resulted in two windows being created (each running a `bash` shell). You can create as many as you like and name them as you choose, and instead of detaching from the `screen` session, you could have just closed it by exiting the shell in each open window (type `exit` or Ctrl+D).

When the `screen` session is detached, you are returned to the shell that was opened when you first logged into the server. You can reconnect to that screen session as described in the following section, "Reconnecting to a screen Session."

Table 13-1 shows some other useful control key sequences available with `screen`.

Table 13-1: Control Keys for Using screen

Keys	Description
Ctrl+A, ?	Show help screen
Ctrl+A, C	Create new window
Ctrl+A, Ctrl+D	Detach `screen` from terminal. The `screen` session and its windows keep running.
Ctrl+A, "	View list of windows
Ctrl+A, '	Prompt for number or name of window to switch to
Ctrl+A, Ctrl+N	Go to next window, if multiple screen windows are open
Ctrl+A, n	View next window
Ctrl+A, P	View previous window
Ctrl+A, A	Rename current window
Ctrl+A, W	Show list of window names in the title bar

Reconnecting to a screen Session

After you detach from a screen session, you can return to that screen again later (even after you log out and disconnect from the server). **To reconnect** when only one screen is running, type the following:

```
$ screen -r
```

If several screen sessions are running, `screen -r` won't work. For example, this shows what happens when two detached screen sessions are running:

```
$ screen -r
There are several suitable screens on:
      7089.pts-2.myserver    (Detached)
```

```
       7263.pts-2.myserver     (Detached)
Type "screen [-d] -r [pid.]tty.host" to resume one of them.
```

As the output suggests, you could identify the screen session you want by its name (which, by default, is a combination of the session's process ID, tty name, and hostname). For example:

```
$ screen -r 7089.pts-2.myserver
```

Naming screen Sessions

Instead of using the default names, you can **create more descriptive names for your screen sessions** when you start screen. For example:

```
$ screen -S mysession
$ screen -ls
There is a screen on:
       26523.mysession (Attached)
```

Sharing screen Sessions

The screen command also allows the **sharing of screens**. This feature is great for tech support, because each person connected to the session can both type into and watch the current session! Creating a named screen, as in the preceding section, makes this easier. (Because you are sharing a screen, use either a temporary user account or a temporary password, for security reasons.) Now another person on a different computer can ssh to the server (using the same user name) and type the following:

```
$ screen -x mysession
```

Just as with screen -r, if only one screen is running, you don't need to specify which screen you are connecting to:

```
$ screen -x
```

Using a Remote Windows Desktop

Many system administrators who become comfortable using a Mac OS X desktop prefer to do administration of their Windows systems from Mac OS X whenever possible. There are various remote desktop and VNC clients available, among them CoRD. CoRD is available for download at cord.sourceforge.net.

To be able to **connect to your Windows system desktop from Mac OS X**, you have to enable Remote Desktop from your Windows system. To do that from Windows XP (and others), right-click My Computer and select Properties. Then choose the Remote tab from the System Properties window and select the "Allow users to connect remotely to this computer" checkbox. Select which users you want to let connect to the Windows box and click OK.

Now, from Mac OS X, you can start CoRD by clicking on its icon in the Applications folder. You can then add a connection by pressing ?N and entering the connection information (such as IP address or host name, username, password, and so on).

You should now be able to log in to the remote Windows machine and administer it as if you were at the console (Figure 13-1). CoRD also enables you to save sessions into the list of Saved Servers for future recall.

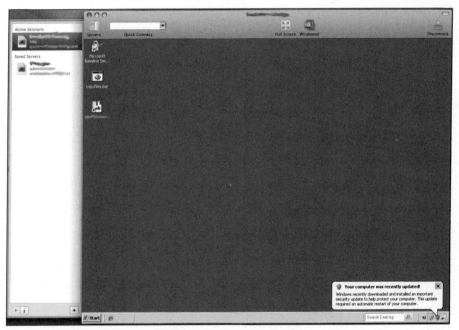

Figure 13-1: Connecting to a Windows server using CoRD

Using Remote Desktop and Applications

The X Window System (X) should not be run on typical production servers for security and performance reasons; but thanks to the client-server nature of X, you can run an X-enabled program on a remote machine and direct its graphical output to your desktop. In that relationship, the application running from the remote machine is referred to as the *X client*, and your desktop is the *X server*. When running remote X applications on untrusted networks or the Internet, use SSH forwarding as described earlier. On trusted LANs, do it without SSH, as described here.

By default, your X desktop will not allow remote X applications to connect (pop-up) on your desktop. You can **allow remote apps on your desktop** using the `xhost` command. On your local display, use the `xhost` command to control which remote machines can connect to X and display applications on your desktop. Here are examples of `xhost`:

> **NOTE** *Listening for remote X clients is disabled by default. Before you allow access to your X display, you need to start your X desktop with the `-listen_tcp` option. For example, start your desktop by typing **startx -listen_tcp**.*

```
$ xhost                      List allowed hosts
access control enabled, only authorized clients can connect
$ xhost +                    Disable access control (dangerous)
access control disabled, clients can connect from any host
$ xhost -                    Re-enable access control
access control enabled, only authorized clients can connect
$ xhost remotemachine        Add an allowed host
remotemachine being added to access control list
```

Access control should be completely disabled only for troubleshooting purposes. However, with access enabled for a particular host machine (*remotemachine* in this case), you can do the following from a shell on the remote computer to have X applications from that machine appear on the local desktop (in this case called *localmachine*):

```
$ export DISPLAY=localmachine:0      Set the DISPLAY to localmachine:0
$ xterm &                            Open remote Terminal on local
$ xclock &                           Open remote clock on local
$ gtali &                            Open remote dice game on local
```

After setting the DISPLAY variable on *remotemachine* to point to *localmachine*, any application run from that shell on *remotemachine* should appear on Desktop 0 on *localmachine*. In this case, we started Terminal window, clock, and game applications.

> **NOTE** *Sharing X applications in this way between BSD and other UNIX-like hosts is pretty easy. However, it is not trivial to use across other computer platforms. If your desktop runs Windows, you have to run an X server. A free solution is Cygwin, which includes an X server. There are also feature-rich commercial X servers but they can be very expensive. To share remote desktops across different operating system platforms, we suggest you use Virtual Network Computing (VNC).*

Sharing Your Desktop Using VNC

Virtual Network Computing (VNC) consists of server and client software that enables you to assume remote control of a **full desktop display from one computer on another**. In Mac OS X, VNC support is built right in, but it is put somewhat out of the way.

To turn on support for VNC, click System Preferences on your Dock, and then click Sharing. Next, select the Remote Management checkbox.

When you click this option, you'll get another set of options to configure, as shown in Figure 13-2. For example, do you allow remote users to open applications? Copy or delete files? Shut down your system? Check the appropriate boxes.

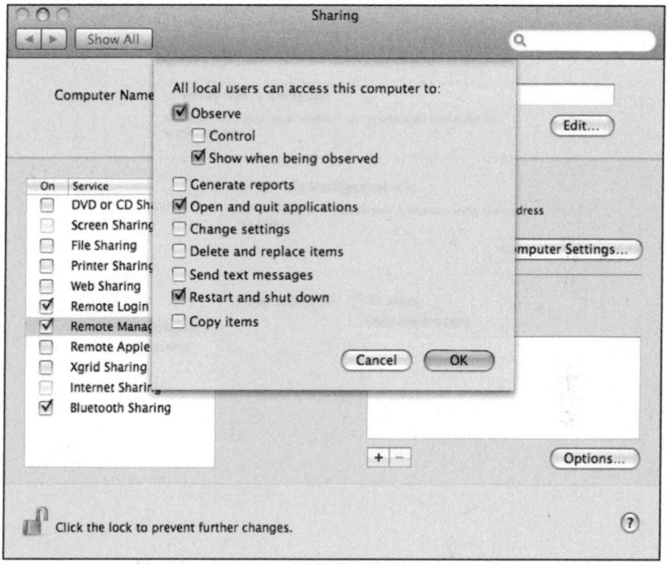

Figure 13-2: Setting options for remote management

Finally, make sure that you specify which users can perform these tasks. By default, the configuration is set for all users, but you can certainly limit the list to a group of users.

Having remote desktop management built in can be a huge boon to any group of system administrators who need to support numerous Mac users spread out through an office environment, especially one that consists of many buildings or regional sites.

Summary

If you ever find yourself in a position where you need to administer multiple BSD systems, you have a rich set of commands with BSD systems for doing remote system administration. The Secure Shell (SSH) facility offers encrypted communications between clients and servers for remote login, tunneling, and file transfer.

Virtual Network Computing (VNC) enables one BSD system to share its desktop with a client system so that the remote desktop appears right on the client's desktop.

14

Locking Down Security

Securing your Mac OS X system means many things. To be secure, you need to restrict access to the user accounts and services on the system. However, after that, security means checking that no one has gotten around the defenses you have set up.

FreeBSD, NetBSD, OpenBSD, and other systems based on BSD distributions are designed in many ways to be secure by default. That means that there are no user accounts with blank passwords, that the firewall is restrictive by default, and that most network services (Web, FTP, and so on) are off by default (even if the service's software is installed).

As someone setting up a BSD system, you can go beyond the default settings to make your system even more secure. For example, by setting up services in *chrooted jails* you can prevent an intruder from accessing parts of the computer system that are outside the compromised service. By encrypting critical data, you can make it nearly impossible for someone to use stolen data.

Although many of the commands covered in this book can be used to check and improve the security of your BSD system, some basic BSD features are particularly geared toward security. For example, secure user accounts with good password protection, a solid firewall, and consistent logging (and log monitoring) are critical to having a secure BSD system. Commands related to those features, plus some advanced features related to protecting network services, are covered in this chapter.

> **NOTE** *Although a lot of computer security efforts focus on protecting computers from outside attackers, policies protecting data from those inside a company have become a growing issue. The procedures covered in this chapter should be enhanced with policies that restrict internal users from accessing data they don't need for their jobs, and track improper access from those users.*

Working with Users and Groups

During installation, you are asked to assign a password to your user (for system administration). Unlike other BSD and UNIX systems, Mac OS X makes sure that the root user is disabled by default—the only way to get access to privileged functions or files is via the sudo command.

We encourage you to always log in as a regular user and only su or sudo to the root account when necessary. (In fact, by default, you are not allowed to log in remotely using ssh to a BSD system as root user.) When FreeBSD is installed, you can use commands or graphical tools to add more users, modify user accounts, and assign and change passwords.

Managing Users the GUI Way

In Mac OS X, you can manage user accounts by clicking System Preferences (see Figure 14-1) in the Dock, and then clicking Accounts.

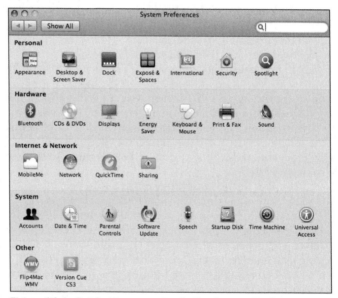

Figure 14-1: Getting to accounts via the System Preferences

You can then add more accounts to the system (see Figure 14-2) by clicking the plus symbol under the Accounts list and entering the necessary information (username, password, and more).

In Mac OS X, command-line options for adding, editing, or removing user accounts don't exist at all. You must use the GUI.

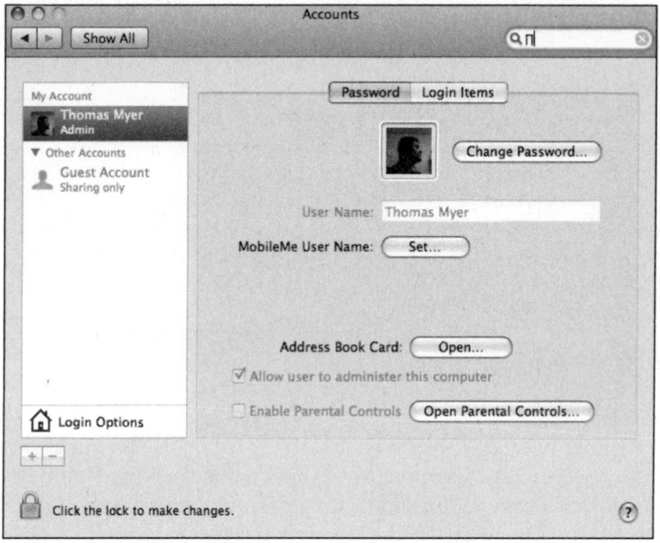

Figure 14-2: Adding user accounts with the GUI

Checking on Users

After you have created user accounts, and let those users loose on your system, you can use several commands to keep track of how they are using your system. Commands for checking on user activity on your BSD system that are covered in other chapters include the following:

❑ The find command to search the system for files anywhere on the system that are owned by selected users (see Chapter 4)

❑ The du command to see how much disk space has been used in selected users' home directories (see Chapter 7)

❑ Commands such as fuser, ps, and top to find out which processes users are running (see Chapter 9)

Aside from these commands, there are commands for checking such things as who is logged into your system and getting general information about the users with accounts on your system. Here are examples of commands for **getting information about people logging into your system:**

```
$ last                    List the most recent successful logins
myerman    ttys000                   Wed Nov 12 12:58    still logged in
myerman    console                   Wed Nov 12 11:29    still logged in
reboot     ~                         Wed Nov 12 11:29
shutdown   ~                         Wed Nov 12 11:29
myerman    console                   Wed Nov 12 11:21 - 11:29   (00:07)
```

```
reboot     ~                      Wed Nov 12 11:20
shutdown   ~                      Wed Nov 12 11:20
myerman    ttys000               Wed Nov 12 11:01 - 11:04  (00:02)
myerman    ttys000               Sun Nov  9 16:23 - 16:20 (1+23:57)
myerman    ttys000               Sat Nov  8 09:40 - 13:46  (04:05)
$ last -h thompson     List logins from host computer thompson
hope    ttyp0    thompson      Mon Oct  6 12:28 - 12:28  (00:00)
joe     ttyp0    thompson      Tue Sep 31 13:08 - 13:08  (00:00)
kafka   ttyp0    thompson      Fri Aug 22 17:23 - 17:23  (00:00)
$ who -u               List who is currently logged in (long form)
myerman  console  Nov 12 11:29   .         23
myerman  ttys000  Nov 12 12:58   .        298
$ users                List who is currently logged in (short form)
myerman kafka hope
```

With the last command, you can see when each user logged in (or opened a new shell) and either how long they were logged in or a note that they are still logged in. The ttyv1 and ttyv3 terminal lines show users working from virtual terminals on the console. The ttyp? lines indicate a person opening a shell from a remote computer (thompson) or local X display (:0.0). The -h option to the last command enables you to see who logged in most recently from a particular host computer. The who -u and users commands show information on currently logged-in users.

Here are some commands for **finding out more about individual users** on your system:

```
$ id                    Your identity (UID, GID and group for current shell)
uid=501(myerman) gid=501(myerman) groups=501(myerman),98(_lpadmin),80(admin)

$ who am i              Your identity (user, tty, login date, location)
myerman  ttys000  Nov 12 12:58
```

> **NOTE** *If you were to log in as a regular user such as myerman, then use* su *to get root permission, the output of* id *and* who *would show different users. That's because* id *reflects the permission you switched to (root) and* who *shows the user who logged in originally (myerman).*

```
$ finger -s myerman     User information (short)
Login     Name                TTY   Idle  Login  Time    Office   Phone
myerman   Thomas Myer        *con   2:26  Wed    11:29
myerman   Thomas Myer         s00         Wed    12:58
$ finger -1 myerman     User information (long)
Login: myerman
Name: Thomas Myer
Directory: /Users/myerman
Shell: /bin/bash
On since Wed Nov 12 11:29 (CST) on console, idle 2:26 (messages off)
On since Wed Nov 12 12:58 (CST) on ttys000
No Mail.
No Plan.
```

Besides displaying basic information about the user (login, name, home directory, shell, and so on), the `finger` command will display any information stored in special files in the user's home directory. For example, the contents of the user's ~/.plan and ~/.project files, if those files exist, are displayed at the end of the `finger` output. With a one-line .project file and a multi-line .plan file, output would appear as follows:

```
$ finger -l myerman    User information (long, .project and .plan files)
   ...
Project:
My project is to take over the world.
Plan:
My grand plan is
to take over the world
by installing Mac OS X on every computer
```

Configuring the Built-in Firewall

A firewall is a critical tool for keeping your computer safe from intruders over the Internet or other network. It can protect your computer by checking every packet of data that comes to your computer's network interfaces, making a decision about what to do with that packet based on parameters you have set.

The firewall in Mac OS X 10.5 (Leopard) is an application firewall. It enables you to control connections on a per-application basis instead of a per-port basis. This makes it easier for less-experienced users to benefit from security. Furthermore, you still have access to the `ipfw` command-line tool that gives you packet-level control over the firewall.

By default, Mac OS X systems ship with the firewall turned off. To change this, click System Preferences on your Dock, and then click Security. Select the Firewall tab. You have three levels of security, as shown in Figure 14-3.

❑ **Allow all incoming connections:** Mac OS X will not block any incoming connections to your computer.

❑ **Allow only essential services:** Mac OS X will allow incoming connections to a limited set of services (among them configd, mDNSResponder for Bonjour, and raccoon for IPSec).

❑ **Set access for specific services and applications:** This mode provides you with the most flexibility, as it enables you to choose whether to deny or allow incoming connections for any application on your system.

If you select the third option, you can click the Advanced button to set up logging of events and to put your Mac OS X system in "Stealth mode" (in other words, it won't respond to ICMP requests).

Once you've saved your changes to your firewall, you can use the `ipfw` command-line tool to get even more granular control over packet traffic going to your system. The command-line tool offers you control over a variety of rules for denying and allowing certain types of traffic on both UDP and TCP protocols.

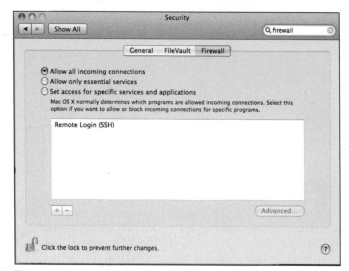

Figure 14-3: Setting up a firewall

Here are some commands for **checking out the state of your firewall**:

```
# ipfw list      List the current set of firewall rules
00100 allow ip from any to any via lo0
00200 allow ip from any to 127.0.0.0/8
...
# ipfw show      Show statistics for each matching packet rule
# ipfw -at list  List the current rules with statistics and timestamps
# ipfw zero      Zeros the counters so you can start with fresh statistics
```

If you want to add a rule directly to the firewall (until the next reboot), you can run the `ipfw` command directly with the add option. You should choose a rule number that is appropriate for the type of rule you are establishing:

```
# ipfw -q add 1550 allow tcp from any to 21 setup keep-state
              Allow outside connections to FTP service (port 21)
# ipfw -q delete 1550   Delete rule number 1550
```

There are many other features in `ipfw` for setting up and working with firewall rules. Refer to the `ipfw` man page for details.

Working with System Logs

Most BSD systems are configured to log many of the activities that occur on those systems. Those activities are then written to log files located in the /var/log directory or its subdirectories. This logging is done by the Syslog facility.

FreeBSD uses the syslogd (system log daemon) as part of the basic installed system to manage system logging. That daemon is started automatically from the syslogd initialization script (/etc/rc.d/syslogd). Information about system activities is then directed to files in the /var/log directory such as messages, security, cron, auth. log, and others, based on settings in the /etc/syslog.conf file.

You can check any of the log files manually (using vi or another favorite text editor).

You can also **send your own messages to the syslogd logging facility** using the logger command. Here are a couple of examples:

```
# logger Added new video card           Message added to messages file
# logger -p warn -t CARD -f /tmp/my.txt  Priority, tag, message file
```

In the first example, the words "Added new video card" are sent to the messages file. In the second example, the message priority is set to info and a tag of CARD is added to each line in the message. The message text is taken from the /tmp/my.txt file that I created before running the command. To see these log entries in real time, use tail -f or less as described in Chapter 5.

Summary

Although many tools are available for securing your Mac OS X system, the first line of security starts with securing both the user accounts and the services on your system.

Because most serious security breaches from outside your organization can come from intruders accessing your systems on public networks, setting up secure firewalls is important for any system connected to the Internet. The ipfw facility is one of several facilities in Mac OS X that provide the firewall features you can configure to meet your needs.

A

Using vi or Vim Editors

Although easy-to-use graphical text editors (such as TextEdit or BBEdit) are readily available on Mac OS X systems, most power users still use vi or Emacs to edit text files. Besides the fact that vi and Emacs will work from any shell (no GUI required), they offer other advantages, such as your hands never having to leave the keyboard and integration with useful utilities; and unlike GUI editors, text-based editors are usable over slow Internet connections such as dial-up or satellite.

This appendix focuses on features of the vi editor that not only help you with basic editing, but also help you do some advanced text manipulation. We chose to cover vi rather than Emacs because vi is more universal and leaner, and because vi keyboard shortcuts require only two arms. Because some UNIX-like systems use the Vim (Vi IMproved) editor instead of the older vi editor, the descriptions in this appendix are extended to cover Vim as well. Some features in Vim that are not in vi include multiple undo levels, syntax highlighting, and online help.

> **NOTE** *If you have never used vi or Vim before, try out the tutor that comes with the* vim6 *package. Run the* vimtutor *command and follow the instructions to step through many of the key features of vi and Vim. To see the differences between vi and Vim, type* :help vi_diff.txt *while running the* vim *command. To install the* vim6 *package, type the following as root user:* **pkg_add -r vim6**.

Depending on how your vim6 package was built, you may or may not get all the latest vim features working at first. In many cases, the compatible option is on, which causes conflicting behaviors between vi and vim to behave like vi (see the text on undo later in this appendix). To turn on the latest vim features, type **:set incompatible** while editing with vim or add this to your ~/.vimrc file:

```
set incompatible
```

Starting and Quitting the vi Editor

If you want to experiment with using vi, you should copy a text file to practice on. For example, enter the following:

```
$ cp /etc/services /tmp
```

Then open that file using the vi command as follows:

```
$ vi /tmp/services
```

To benefit from all the improvements of Vim, make sure you have the FreeBSD vim6 package installed. On many systems, vi is aliased to the vim command. You may want to double-check that, using the alias command. If you want to use vim directly, type **/usr/local/bin/vim**. If you specifically want to use the older-style vi command, use the full path to the vi command instead:

```
/bin/vi /tmp/text.txt
```

Here are a few other ways you can **start vi**:

```
$ vi +25 /tmp/services    Begin on line 25
$ vi + /tmp/services      Begin editing file on the last line
$ vi +/tty /tmp/services  Begin on first line with word "tty"
$ vi -r /tmp/services     Recover file from crashed edit session
$ view /tmp/services      Edit file in read-only mode
```

When you are done with your vi session, you have several different ways to save and quit. To **save the file before you are ready to quit**, type **:w**. To **quit and save changes**, type either **ZZ** or **:wq**. To **quit without saving changes**, type **:q!**. If you find that you can't write to the file you are editing, it may be opened in read-only mode. If that's the case, you can try forcing a write by typing **:w!** or you can **save the contents of the file to a different name**. For example, type the following to save the contents of the current file to a file named myfile.txt:

```
:w /tmp/myfile.txt
```

> **NOTE** It's important to understand that :w writes the current file out to another file, so if you continue editing you are still editing the original file. In the preceding example, if you started editing the services file, and then wrote the contents to myfile.txt, in order to continue editing myfile.txt you would have to change to it by typing **:e /tmp/myfile.txt**.

The vi editor also enables you to **line up several files at a time to edit**. For example, enter the following:

```
$ cd /tmp
$ touch a.txt b.txt c.txt
$ vi a.txt b.txt c.txt
```

In this example, vi will open the a.txt file first. You can **move to the next file** by typing **:n**. You may want to **save changes before moving to the next file (:w)** or **save changes as you move to the next file (:wn)**. To **abandon changes while moving to the next file,** type **:n!**. To go back to the previous file, type **:prev**.

You will probably find it easier to open multiple files using the vim feature for splitting your screen. When you're in vim and have a file open, you can **split your screen multiple times** either horizontally or vertically:

```
:split /etc/services
:vsplit /etc/hosts
```

Use <Tab> to complete the path to the files, just as you would in a bash shell. To **navigate between split windows**, press Ctrl+W, followed by the W key. To close the current window, use the usual vim exit command (:q).

Moving Around in vi

The first thing to get used to with vi is that you can't just start typing. Vi has multiple modes that enable you to perform different sets of tasks. You start a vi session in normal mode, where vi is waiting for you to type a command to get started. While you are in normal mode you can move around the file in order to establish your position in the file. To enter or modify text, you need to be in insert or replace modes.

Assuming vi is open with a file that contains several pages of text, Table A-1 shows some keys and combinations you can type to **move around the file while in normal mode**.

Table A-1: Keystroke Commands for Moving Around

Key	Result	Key	Result
PageDown or Ctrl+F	Move down one page	PageUp or Ctrl+B	Move up one page
Ctrl+D	Move down half page	Ctrl+U	Move up half page
G	Go to last line of file	:1	Go to first line of file (use any number to go to that line)
H	Move cursor to top of screen	L	Move cursor to screen bottom
M	Move cursor to middle of screen	Ctrl+L	Redraw screen (if garbled)

Continued

Table A-1: Keystroke Commands for Moving Around *(continued)*

Key	Result	Key	Result
Enter	Move cursor to beginning of the next line	-	Move cursor to beginning of the previous line
End or $	Move cursor to end of line	Home or ^ or 0	Move cursor to line beginning
(	Move cursor to beginning of previous sentence	)	Move cursor to beginning of next sentence
{	Move cursor to beginning of previous paragraph	}	Move cursor to beginning of next paragraph
w	Move cursor to next word (space, new line or punctuation)	W	Move cursor to next word (space or new line)
b	Move cursor to previous word (space, new line or punctuation)	B	Move cursor to previous word (space or new line)
e	Move cursor to end of next word (space, new line or punctuation)	E	Move cursor to end of next word (space or new line)
Left arrow or Backspace or h	Move cursor left one letter	Right arrow or l	Move cursor right one letter
k or up arrow	Move cursor up one line	j or down arrow	Move cursor down one line
/*string*	Find next occurrence of *string*	?*string*	Find previous occurrence of *string*
n or /	Find same string again (forward)	N or ?	Find same string again (backwards)

Changing and Deleting Text in vi

To begin changing or adding to text with vi, you can enter insert or replace modes, as shown in Table A-2. When you enter insert or replace mode, the characters you type will appear in the text document (as opposed to being interpreted as commands).

Press the Esc key to exit to normal mode after you are done inserting or replacing text.

Table A-2: Commands for Changing Text

Key	Result	Key	Result
i	Typed text appears before current character	I	Typed text appears at the beginning of current line
a	Typed text appears after current character	A	Typed text appears at the end of current line
o	Open a new line below current line to begin typing	O	Open a new line above current line to begin typing
s	Erase current character and replace with new text	S	Erase current line and enter new text
c?	Replace ? with l, w, $, c to change the current letter, word, end of line, or line	C	Erase from cursor to end of line and enter new text
r	Replace current character with the next one you type	R	Overwrite as you type from current character going forward

Table A-3 contains keys you type to delete or paste text.

Table A-3: Commands for Deleting and Pasting Text

Key	Result	Key	Result
x	Delete character under cursor	X	Delete character to left of cursor
d?	Replace ? with l, w, $, d to cut the current letter, word, or end of line from cursor or entire line	D	Cut from cursor to end of line
y?	Replace ? with l, w, $ to copy (yank) the current letter, word, or end of line from cursor	Y	Yank current line
p	Pastes cut or yanked text after cursor	P	Pastes cut or yanked text before cursor

Using Miscellaneous Commands

Table A-4 shows a few miscellaneous, but important, commands you should know.

Table A-4: Miscellaneous Commands

Key	Result
u	Type **u** to undo the previous change. Multiple u commands toggles the previous undo on and off. (In vim, typing **:set nocompatible** will allow multi-level undos. Use Ctrl-r to undo your undos.)
.	Typing a period (.) will repeat the previous command. For example, if you deleted a line, replaced a word, changed four letters, and so on, the same command will be done wherever the cursor is currently located. (Entering Input mode again resets it.)
J	Join the current line with the next line.
Esc	If you didn't catch this earlier, the Esc key returns you from an input mode back to command mode. This is one of the keys you will use most often.

Modifying Commands with Numbers

Nearly every command described so far can be modified with a number. In other words, instead of deleting one word, replacing one letter, or changing one line, you can delete six words, replace 12 letters, and change nine lines. Table A-5 shows some examples.

Table A-5: Modifying Commands with Numbers

Command	Result
7cw	Erase the next seven words and replace them with text you type.
d5d	Cut the next five lines (including the current line).
3p	Paste the previously deleted text three times after the current cursor.
9db	Cut the nine words before the current cursor.
10j	Move the cursor down 10 lines.
y2)	Copy (yank) text from the cursor to the end of the next two sentences.
5Ctrl+F	Move forward five pages.
6J	Join together the next six lines.

From these examples, you can see that most vi keystrokes for changing text, deleting text, or moving around in the file can be modified using numbers.

Using Ex Commands

The vi editor was originally built on an editor called Ex. Some of the vi commands you've seen so far start with a semicolon; these are known as *Ex* commands. To enter Ex commands, start from normal mode and type a semicolon (:). This switches you to command-line mode. In this mode, you can use the Tab key to complete your command or filename, and the arrow keys to navigate your command history, as you would in a bash shell. When you press Enter at the end of your command, you are returned to normal mode.

Table A-6 shows some examples of Ex commands.

Table A-6: Ex Command Examples

Command	Result
`:!bash`	Escape to a bash shell. When you are done, type **exit** to return to vi.
`:!date`	Run `date` (or any command you choose). Press Enter to return.
`:!!`	Rerun the command previously run.
`:20`	Go to line 20 in the file.
`:5,10w abc.txt`	Write lines 5 through 10 to the file abc.txt.
`:e abc.txt`	Leave the current file and begin editing the file abc.txt.
`:.r def.txt`	Read the contents of `def.txt` into the file below the current line.
`:s/UNIX/FreeBSD`	Substitute `FreeBSD` for the first occurrence of UNIX on the current line.
`:s/UNIX/FreeBSD/g`	Substitute `FreeBSD` for all occurrences of UNIX on the current line.
`:%s/UNIX/FreeBSD/g`	Substitute `FreeBSD` for the all occurrences of UNIX in the entire file.
`:g/FreeBSD /p`	List every line in the file that contains the string "FreeBSD ".
`:g/gaim/s//pidgin/gp`	Find every instance of `gaim` and change it to `pidgin`.

From the ex prompt you can also see and change settings related to your vi session using the set command. Table A-7 shows some examples.

Table A-7: set Commands in ex Mode

Command	Result
:set all	List all settings.
:set	List only those settings that have changed from the default.
:set number	Have line numbers appear to the left of each line. (Use set nonu to unset.)
:set ai	Sets auto-indent, so opening a new line follows the previous indent.
:set ic	Sets ignore case, so text searches will match regardless of case.
:set list	Show $ for end of lines and ^I for tabs.
:set wm	Causes vi to add line breaks between words near the end of a line.

Working in Visual Mode

The Vim editor provides a more intuitive means of selecting text called *visual mode*. To begin visual mode, move the cursor to the first character of the text you want to select and press the v key.

At this point, you can use any of your cursor movement keys (arrow keys, Page Down, End, and so on) to move the cursor to the end of the text you want to select. As the page and cursor move, you will see text being highlighted. When all the text you want to select is highlighted, you can press keys to act on that text. For example, d deletes the text, c enables you to change the selected text, :w /tmp/test.txt saves selected text to a file, and so on.

Summary

The vi command is one of the most popular text editors used for FreeBSD and UNIX systems. Using keystrokes, you go back and forth between command mode (where you can move around the file) and input or replace modes. For a vi that is more advanced, you can use the vim command. Using ex mode, you can read and write text from files, do complex search and replace commands, and temporarily exit to a shell or other command.

B

Special Shell Characters and Variables

Mac OS X offers several different shells you can use to enter commands and run scripts. Chapter 2 helps you become comfortable working in the shell. This appendix provides a reference of the numerous characters and variables that have special meaning to particular shells (such as the bash shell) or are available on most shells. Many of those elements are referenced in Table B-1 (Special Shell Characters) and Table B-2 (Shell Environment Variables).

IN THIS APPENDIX

Using special shell characters

Using shell variables

Using Special Shell Characters

You can use special characters from the shell to match multiple files, save some keystrokes, or perform special operations. Table B-1 shows some shell special characters that you may find useful.

Table B-1: Special Shell Characters

Character	Description
*	Match any string of characters.
?	Match any one character.
[...]	Match any character enclosed in the braces.
' ... '	Remove special meaning of characters between quotes. *Variables are not expanded.*
" ... "	Same as simple quotes except for the escape characters ($ ` and \) that preserve their special meaning.
\	Escape character to remove the special meaning of the character that follows.

Continued

Table B-1: Special Shell Characters *(continued)*

Character	Description
~	Refers to the $HOME directory.
~+	Value of the shell variable PWD or the working directory (bash only).
~-	Refers to the previous working directory (bash only).
.	Refers to the current working directory.
..	Refers to the directory above the current directory. Can be used repeatedly to reference several directories up.
$param	Used to expand a shell variable parameter.
cmd1 `cmd2` or cmd1 $(cmd2)	cmd2 is executed first. Then the call to cmd2 is substituted with the output of cmd2, and cmd1 is executed.
cmd1 >	Redirects standard output from command.
cmd1 <	Redirects standard input to command.
cmd1 >>	Append standard output to file from command, without erasing its current contents.
cmd1 | cmd2	Pipe output of one command to input of the next.
cmd &	Run the command in the background.
cmd1 && cmd2	Run first command, and if it returns a zero exit status, run the second command.
cmd1 || cmd2	Run first command, and if it returns a non-zero exit status, run the second command.
cmd1 ; cmd2	Run the first command, and when it completes run the second command.

Using Shell Variables

You identify a string of characters as a parameter (variable) by placing a $ in front of it (as in $HOME). Shell environment variables can hold information that is used by the shell itself, as well as by commands you run from the shell. Not all environment variables will be populated by default. Some of these variables you can change (such as the default printer in $PRINTER or your command prompt in $PS1). Others are managed by the shell (such as $OLDPWD). Table B-2 contains a list of many useful shell variables.

Table B-2: Shell Variables

Shell Variable	Description
BASH	Shows path name of the bash command (/bin/bash).
BASH_COMMAND	The command that is being executed at the moment.
BASH_VERSION	Version number of the bash command.
COLUMNS	Width of the terminal line (in characters).
DISPLAY	Identifies the X display where commands launched from the current shell will be displayed (such as :0.0). Can be a display on a remote host (such as example.com:0.0).
EUID	Effective user ID number of the current user. It is based on the user entry in /etc/passwd for the user who is logged in.
FCEDIT	Determines the text editor used by the fc command to edit history commands. The vi command is used by default.
GROUPS	Lists the primary group of which the current user is a member.
HISTCMD	Shows the current command's history number.
HISTFILE	Shows the location of your history file (usually located at $HOME/.bash_history).
HISTFILESIZE	Total number of history entries that will be stored (default is 1,000). Older commands are discarded after this number is reached.
HOME	Location of the current user's home directory. Typing the cd command with no options returns the shell to the home directory.
HOSTNAME	The current machine's hostname.
HOSTTYPE	Contains the computer architecture on which the BSD system is running (i386, i486, i586, i686, x86_64, ppc, or ppc64).
LESSOPEN	Set to a command that converts content other than plain text (images, zip files, and so on) so it can be piped through the less command.
LINES	Sets the number of lines in the current terminal.
LOGNAME	Holds the name of the current user.
MACHTYPE	Displays information about the machine architecture, company, and operating system (such as i686-portbld-freebsd6.2).
MAIL	Indicates the location of your mailbox file (typically the username in the /var/mail directory).

Continued

Table B-2: Shell Variables (continued)

Shell Variable	Description
MAILCHECK	Checks for mail in the number of seconds specified (default is 60).
OLDPWD	Directory that was the working directory before changing to the current working directory.
OSTYPE	Name identifying the current operating system (such as freebsd6.2).
PAGER	The program to use for man page display.
PATH	Colon-separated list of directories used to locate commands that you type (/bin, /usr/bin, and $HOME/bin are usually in the PATH).
PPID	Process ID of the command that started the current shell.
PRINTER	Sets the default printer, which is used by printing commands such as lpr and lpq.
PROMPT_COMMAND	Set to a command name to run that command each time before your shell prompt is displayed. (For example, PROMPT_COMMAND=ls lists commands in the current directory before showing the prompt.)
PS1	Sets the shell prompt. Items in the prompt can include date, time, username, hostname, and others. Additional prompts can be set with PS2, PS3, and so on.
PWD	Directory assigned as your current directory.
RANDOM	Accessing this variable generates a random number between 0 and 32767.
SECONDS	Number of seconds since the shell was started.
SHELL	Contains the full path to the current shell.
SHELLOPTS	Lists enabled shell options (those set to on).
SHLVL	Lists the shell levels associated with the current shell session.
TERM	Indicates the type of shell terminal window you are using. The default is xterm.
TMOUT	Set to a number representing the number of seconds the shell can be idle without receiving input. After the number of seconds is reached, the shell exits.
UID	User ID number assigned to the current username. The user ID number is stored in the /etc/password file.
USER	The current username.

C

Personal Configuration Files

In the home directory of every user account is a set of files and directories containing personal settings for that account. Because most configuration files and directories begin with a dot (.), you don't see them if you open a folder window to your home directory. Likewise, you typically need the -a option to `ls` to see those files when you list directory contents.

IN THIS APPENDIX

Shell configuration files

Browser and e-mail configuration files

Desktop configuration files

Network services configuration files

Music player configuration files

This appendix describes many of the dot files each user can work with on a Mac OS X system. After creating configuration files you like, you can, when appropriate, do such things as save them to `/usr/share/skel` (so every new user gets them) or save them if the user account moves to another machine.

> **NOTE** *Some of the files described in this appendix won't exist until you either start the application associated with the files or create the files manually.*

Bash shell files: Home directory files for storing and changing bash settings include the following:

❑ `.bash_profile`: Commands added to this file are executed when you invoke `bash` as a login shell or use `bash` as your default shell.

❑ `.bashrc`: Commands added to this file are executed when you start a `bash` shell that is not a login shell, and your default shell is not `bash`. (To have `.bashrc` sourced on login when your default shell is set to `bash`, add the following line to your `.bash_profile`: **test -f ~/.bashrc && . ~/.bashrc**.)

❑ `.bash_logout`: Commands added to this file are executed when you log out from a `bash` shell.

❑ `.bash_history`: Stores a history of commands run by the user from a `bash` shell.

C shell files: Besides systemwide `/etc/profile` and `/etc/csh.cshrc` files, home directory files for storing and changing C shell (`tcsh` and `csh`) settings include the following:

- ❑ `.login`: Commands added to this file are executed when you log in to a C shell.

- ❑ `.tcshrc` or `.cshrc`: Commands added to either of these files are executed when you start any C shell.

- ❑ `.history`: Stores a history of commands run by the user from a C shell.

Bourne shell files: If you are using the Bourne (sh) shell, which is the default for regular users in FreeBSD, the `.shrc` file in your home directory is important to know about. Commands in this file are run when the sh shell starts. The file sets several aliases for you and sets your command-line editor (Emacs by default). This is a good place to add directories to your $PATH or to change your shell prompt. (I always change the default editor to vi from Emacs.)

mail configuration files: Settings for the `mail` command are stored in the `.mailrc` and `.mail_aliases` files.

ncftp configuration files: If you use the `ncftp` FTP client, settings relating to your ncftp sessions are stored in the `.ncftp` directory in your home directory. The firewall file in that directory enables you to set firewalls, including information for using ncftp through a proxy server. The `history` file keeps a list of commands that were previously run during FTP sessions. The `log` file gathers error and informational messages. The `prefs_v3` file contains ncftp preferences.

Trusted hosts files: Although regular users can't change the systemwide `hosts.allow` or `hosts.deny` files, they can add a list of trusted hosts and, optionally, users from those hosts to their own `.rhosts` file in their home directories. If services such as `rlogin` or `rcp` are enabled (`/etc/inetd.conf`), a person from the trusted host can use those commands to log in or copy files to your machine without entering a password. This is a good thing to do if all of the computers on your network are wired together, in the same room, in a cabin in the Himalayas, with no outside connections. Otherwise, you should consider using trusted hosts in this way to be very insecure.

Secure Shell configuration files: If you use the secure shell (SSH) service, the `.ssh` directory in your home directory can be used to manage security settings. Here are examples:

- ❑ `known_hosts`: Keeps a list of host computers you have verified as authentic

- ❑ `identity`: Private authentication keys from SSH protocol version 1

- ❑ `id_rsa`: Private authentication keys from SSH protocol version 2

- ❑ `id_dsa`: Private authentication keys from SSH protocol version 2

- ❑ `identity.pub`, `id_dsa.pub`, `id_rsa.pub`: Public keys for the three private keys just described

- ❑ `authorized_keys`: File that contains public keys of remote clients

Virtual network computing files: If you use the `vncserver` utility to share your desktop with other computers on the network, settings for specifying how `vncserver` behaves are stored in your home directory's `.vnc` directory. The `xstartup` file in that directory contains applications that run on the VNC desktop when you start it up. The `vncpasswd` file holds the passwords stored for use by `vnserver`.

For each display that is started, a file named *host*:*#*.*log* is created (where *host* is the hostname and # is the display number). There is also a *host*:*#*.*pid* file for each display containing the process ID of the Xvnc process associated with the display.

X startup files: If you start your desktop interface using the `startx` command, the `.xinitrc` file can be used to indicate which desktop environment to start. For example, add `/usr/local/bin/gnome-session` to `.xinitrc` to start the GNOME desktop environment. Add `/usr/local/bin/startkde` to `.xinitrc` to have the KDE desktop environment start.

XMMS configuration files: If you use the XMMS music player, configuration files for that player are contained in the `.xmms` directory in your home directory. Subdirectories of that directory include Plugins (which hold audio plugins) and Skins (which holds available skins to use with the player). The `config` file in that directory holds preference settings for XMMS. The `xmms.m3u` file contains paths for songs the player has played.

213

D

AppleScript Command Summary

This appendix provides a brief summary of the commands available to perform actions in AppleScript scripts. Table D-1 lists each command by category and provides a brief description.

IN THIS APPENDIX

AppleScript commands

Table D-1: AppleScript commands

Command	Description
AppleScript Suite	
activate	Brings an application to the front, and opens it if it is on the local computer and not already running
log	In Script Editor, displays a value in the Event Log History window or in the Event Log pane of a script window
Clipboard Commands	
clipboard info	Returns information about the clipboard
set the clipboard to	Places data on the clipboard
the clipboard	Returns the contents of the clipboard
File Commands	
info for	Returns information for a file or folder
mount volume	Mounts the specified AppleShare volume
path to (application)	Returns the full path to the specified application
path to (folder)	Returns the full path to the specified folder
path to resource	Returns the full path to the specified resource

Continued

Table D-1: AppleScript commands *(continued)*

Command	Description
File Read/Write Operations	
close access	Closes a file that was opened for access
get eof	Returns the length, in bytes, of a file
open for access	Opens a disk file for the read and write commands
read	Reads data from a file that has been opened for access
set eof	Sets the length, in bytes, of a file
write	Writes data to a file that was opened for access with write permission
Internet Commands	
open location	Opens a URL with the appropriate program
Miscellaneous Commands	
current date	Returns the current date and time
do shell script	Executes a shell script using the sh shell
get volume settings	Returns the sound output and input volume settings
random number	Generates a random number
round	Rounds a number to an integer
set volume	Sets the sound output and/or input volume
system attribute	Gets environment variables or attributes of this computer
system info	Returns information about the system
time to GMT	Returns the difference between local time and GMT (Universal Time)
Scripting Commands	
load script	Returns a script object loaded from a file
run script	Runs a script or script file
scripting components	Returns a list of all scripting components
store script	Stores a script object into a file

Table D-1: AppleScript commands *(continued)*

Command	Description
Standard Suite	
copy	Copies one or more values into variables
count	Counts the number of elements in an object
get	Returns the value of a script expression or an application object
launch	Launches the specified application without sending it a run command
run	Launches an application, script, or script object
set	Assigns one or more values to one or more script variables or application objects
String Commands	
localized string	Returns the localized string for the specified key
offset	Finds one piece of text inside another
summarize	Summarizes the specified text or text file
User Interaction Commands	
beep	Beeps one or more times
choose application	Allows the user to choose an application
choose color	Allows the user to choose a color
choose file	Allows the user to choose a file
choose file name	Allows the user to specify a new file reference
choose folder	Allows the user to choose a folder
choose from list	Allows the user to choose one or more items from a list
choose remote application	Allows the user to choose a running application on a remote machine
choose URL	Allows the user to specify a URL
delay	Pauses for a fixed amount of time
display alert	Displays an alert
display dialog	Displays a dialog box, optionally requesting user input
say	Speaks the specified text

E

Fink Package Summary

This appendix provides a partial list of packages and tools available via Fink, the package management system. This is not a canonical list of the "best" or "most popular" packages, but merely a sample of the 2,500+ packages that are available via Fink.

IN THIS APPENDIX

Fink packages

All packages loaded with Fink are maintained in a separate folder hierarchy (/sw/bin). Fink downloads original source releases, patches them (if needed), configures them for Darwin, compiles them, and installs them.

Table E-1: Fink Packages

Package	Version	Description
agrep	2.04-18	Flexible egrep/fregrep replacement
anacron	2.3-6	Periodic command scheduler
analog	5.32-1	Program to measure usage on your web server
antiword	0.37-1	Display or convert MS-Word files
antlr	2.7.7-1001	ANother Tool for Language Recognition (formerly PCCTS)
apache-pm588		[virtual package]
apel	10.7-3	A Portable Emacs Library
apg	2.2.3-3	Automated password generator
barcode	0.98-12	Barcode generation library and CLI front end
base-files	1.9.8-1	Directory infrastructure
bash	2.05b-1013	The GNU Bourne Again Shell
bash-completion	20060301-3	Command-line completions for bash

Continued

Table E-1: Fink Packages (continued)

Package	Version	Description
bbkeys	0.8.4-1022	Key-binding handler for Blackbox
bbmail	0.8.3-1002	E-mail watcher designed for use with Blackbox
bbpager	0.3.1-1001	Pager tool for the Blackbox window manager
bcel	5.2-1	Byte Code Engineering Library
berkeleydb-pm586	0.31-1001	Perl interface to Berkeley DB library
berkeleydb-pm588	0.31-1001	Perl interface to Berkeley DB library
bidwatcher	1.3.17-1012	GTK auction management/snipe tool for eBay
bzip2	1.0.3-1	Block-sorting file compressor
bzip2-dev	1.0.3-1	Developer files for bzip2 package
bzip2-shlibs	1.0.3-1	Shared libraries for bzip2 package
c-scan-pm	0.74-3	Perl module to scan C declarations for h2xs
ca-roots	1:1.0-3	List of SSL CA root certificates
ccache	2.4-20	C/C++ compiler cache
ccache-default	2.4-20	C/C++ compiler cache—as default compiler
cctbx-10.5	71118-2	Computational Crystallography Toolbox
cmatrix	1.2a-1014	Scrolling random text effect like The Matrix
connect	1.96-1	SSH proxy command
contacts	1.1-1	Little command-line OS X address book viewer
context		[virtual package]
control-center	2.12.3-2	GNOME control center
control-center-dev	1.4.0.5-1021	GNOME control center
control-center-shlibs	1.4.0.5-1021	GNOME control center
control-center2-dev	2.12.3-2	GNOME control center
control-center2-shlibs	2.12.3-2	The GNOME control center

Table E-1: Fink Packages *(continued)*

Package	Version	Description
corkscrew	2.0-1	Tunnel TCP connections through HTTP proxies
crypt-blowfish-pm586	2.09-11	XS implementation of Blowfish cryptography
crypt-blowfish-pm586-man	2.09-11	Manual pages for crypt-blowfish-pm
crypt-cbc-pm	2.12-1	Perl-only Crypt::CBC cipher block chaining (CBC)
crypt-rc4-pm	2.02-1	Implements the RC4 encryption algorithm
curl-unified-dev	7.11.2-11	Lib. for transferring files with URL syntax
curl-unified-shlibs	7.11.2-11	Lib. for transferring files with URL syntax
curses-pm586	1.15-1101	Perl interface to the ncurses library
curses-pm588	1.15-1101	Perl interface to the ncurses library
curses-ui-pm586	0.95-1002	UI framework based on the curses library
curses-ui-pm588	0.95-1002	UI framework based on the curses library
cvs	1.12.13-12	Version control system
cvs-client		[virtual package]
cvs-proxy	1.11.22-2	Version control system
cvs-server		[virtual package]
cvs-stable	1.11.22-2	Version control system
cvs2cl	2.58-1	CVS-log-message-to-ChangeLog conversion
cvs2svn	1:1.5.1-11	CVS-to-Subversion repository converter
cvs2svn-py24	1.5.1-11	Python modules for cvs2svn (Python 2.4)
cvs2svn-py24-bin	1.5.1-11	Binaries for cvs2svn (Python 2.4)
cvs2svn-py25	1.5.1-11	Python modules for cvs2svn (Python 2.5)
cvs2svn-py25-bin	1.5.1-11	Binaries for cvs2svn (Python 2.5)
cvs2svn-ssl		[virtual package]

Continued

Table E-1: Fink Packages *(continued)*

Package	Version	Description
diffutils	2.8.1-1	Tools to compare files
emacs22	22.2-1002	Flexible real-time text editor
emacs22-carbon	22.1-3003	Flexible real-time text editor, Aqua native
emacs22-gtk	22.2-1002	Flexible real-time text editor
emacs22-nox	22.2-1002	Flexible real-time text editor
emacsen		[virtual package]
emacsen-common	1.4.15-5	Common facilities for all emacsen
fwipe	0.35-1	Deletes files irrecoverably
gawk	3.1.5-11	The Awk processing language, GNU edition
gc	7.0-1001	General-purpose, garbage-collecting storage allocator
gc-shlibs	7.0-1001	Shared libraries for gc package
gcalctool	5.8.25-1	GNOME calculator widget
gcc2	2.95.2-0	[virtual package representing the gcc 2.95.2 compiler]
gcc2.95	2.95.2-0	[virtual package representing the gcc 2.95.2 compiler]
gcc3.1	3.1-0	[virtual package representing the gcc 3.1 compiler]
gcc3.3	3.3-0	[virtual package representing the gcc 3.3 compiler]
gcc4.0	4.0.1-5484	[virtual package representing the gcc 4.0.1 compiler]
gcc4.2	4.2.1-5564	[virtual package representing the gcc 4.2.1 compiler]
gcc42	4.2.2-1000	GNU Compiler Collection Version 4.2
gcc42-shlibs	4.2.2-1000	Shared libraries for gcc4
gconf	1.0.9-1052	Configuration database system
gconf-dev	1.0.9-1052	Configuration database system

Table E-1: Fink Packages *(continued)*

Package	Version	Description
gconf-editor	2.6.2-1019	Editor for the GConf configuration system
gconf-shlibs	1.0.9-1052	Configuration database system
gconf2	2.14.0-1	GNOME configuration database system
gconf2-dev	2.14.0-1	GNOME configuration database system
gconf2-shlibs	2.14.0-1	GNOME configuration database system
gd-pm586	2.16-2	Perl interface to the GD graphics library
gd-svg-pm586	0.27-1	Perl module to create svg output from gd
gd2	2.0.33-3	Graphics generation library
gd2-bin	2.0.33-3	Executables for gd2 package
gd2-shlibs	2.0.33-3	Shared libraries for gd2 package
ghostscript	8.54-3	Interpreter for PostScript and PDF
ghostscript-esp	7.07.1-35	Enhanced GNU Ghostscript with better CJK and printer support
ghostscript-fonts	8.11-3	Standard fonts for Ghostscript
ghostscript-nox	7.04-3	Interpreter for PostScript and PDF
ghostscript6	6.01-4	Interpreter for PostScript and PDF, v6.01
ghostscript6-nox	6.01-5	Interpreter for PostScript/PDF, v6.01, no X11 support
gif2png	2.4.6-2	GIF-to-PNG graphics file conversion
giflib	4.1.4-2	GIF image format handling library (LZW)
giflib-bin	4.1.4-2	GIF image format handling library (LZW)
giflib-shlibs	4.1.4-2	GIF image format handling library (LZW)
gift-utils	1.0.0-1	Miscellaneous tools for giFT
gimp	1.2.5-1007	The GNU Image Manipulation Program
gimp-default	1.2.5-1007	The GNU Image Manipulation Program
gimp-dev	1.2.5-1007	The GNU Image Manipulation Program

Continued

Table E-1: Fink Packages *(continued)*

Package	Version	Description
gimp-print-shlibs	4.2.5-1	[virtual package representing Apple's install of Gimp Print]
gimp-print7-shlibs	5.0.0-beta2-1	[virtual package representing Apple's install of Gimp Print]
gimp-shlibs	1.2.5-1007	The GNU Image Manipulation Program
gmt	4.2.0-2	Generic Mapping Tools
gmt-coast	4.2-1	Generic Mapping Tools (Hi-res coastlines)
gmt-dev	4.2.0-2	Generic Mapping Tools
gmt-doc	4.2.0-2	Generic Mapping Tools (Documents)
gmt-shlibs	4.2.0-2	Generic Mapping Tools
gnet	1.1.9-1	Simple Network Library
gnet-shlibs	1.1.9-1	Shared Libraries for gnet
gnet2	2.0.7-2	Simple Network Library
gnet2-shlibs	2.0.7-2	Shared Libraries for gnet
gnopernicus	0.7.1-1009	Assistive Technologies (AT) for blind and visually impaired persons
gtk+	1.2.10-51	The Gimp Toolkit
gtk+-data	1.2.10-51	The Gimp Toolkit
gtk+-shlibs	1.2.10-51	The Gimp Toolkit
gtk+2	2.6.10-1003	The Gimp Toolkit
gtk+2-dev	2.6.10-1003	The Gimp Toolkit
gtk+2-shlibs	2.6.10-1003	The Gimp Toolkit
gtk-doc	1.3-1012	GTK+ (API documentation generator)
gtk-engines	0.12-3	Theme plugins for Gtk
gtk2-engines	2.6.10-2	Theme plugins for Gtk
gtkglarea	1.2.3-15	OpenGL widget for GTK+
gtkglarea2	1.99.0-1004	OpenGL widget for GTK+

Table E-1: Fink Packages *(continued)*

Package	Version	Description
gtkglarea2-shlibs	1.99.0-1004	OpenGL widget for GTK+
gtkglext1	1.0.6-1002	OpenGL extension to GTK
gtkglext1-shlibs	1.0.6-1002	OpenGL extension to GTK
gtkgraph	0.6.2-4	Graphing calculator using Gtk+
gtkhtml	1.0.2-1054	HTML rendering/printing/editing engine
gtkhtml-dev	1.0.2-1054	HTML rendering/printing/editing engine
gtkhtml-shlibs	1.0.2-1054	HTML rendering/printing/editing engine
gtkhtml1.1	1.1.7-1014	HTML rendering/printing/editing engine
gtkhtml1.1-dev	1.1.7-1014	HTML rendering/printing/editing engine
gtkhtml1.1-shlibs	1.1.7-1014	HTML rendering/printing/editing engine
gtkmm2	2.2.12-1002	C++ interface for the gtk+2 library
gtkmm2-dev	2.2.12-1002	C++ interface for the gtk+2 library
gtkmm2-shlibs	2.2.12-1002	C++ interface for the gtk+2 library
gtksourceview	1.0.1-1007	Source code viewing tool
gtksourceview-dev	1.0.1-1007	Headers and libraries for developing with gtksourceview
gtksourceview-shlibs	1.0.1-1007	Shared libraries for gtksourceview
gtkspell2	2.0.4-1005	Highlight misspelled words as you type
gtkspell2-dev	2.0.4-1005	Highlight misspelled words as you type
gtkspell2-shlibs	2.0.4-1005	Highlight misspelled words as you type
gtop		[virtual package]
gtypist	2.7-1002	GNU Touch Typing Tutor
gucharmap	1.4.1-1010	Unicode character map and font viewer
help2man	1.29-1	Generates man pages from program output
hermes	1.3.3-3	Optimized pixel format conversion library

Continued

Table E-1: Fink Packages *(continued)*

Package	Version	Description
hermes-shlibs	1.3.3-3	Optimized pixel format conversion library
hevea	1.08-1	LaTeX-to-HTML translator; uses Objective Caml
hexcurse	1.55-1012	Terminal-based hex editor
hfsutils	3.2.6-12	Read/Write Mac HFS media
hlfl	0.60.0-1	High-Level Firewall Language
host	991529-1	Enhanced DNS and ns/mx/rblookup utilities
hotbabe	0.2.2-1002	Displays system activity
html2text	1.3.2a-1022	Advanced HTML-to-text converter
hugs	1998.200102-1017	Haskell interpreter
hyperref		[virtual package]
i18n-langtags-pm586		[virtual package]
i18n-langtags-pm588		[virtual package]
imagemagick	6.2.8-1003	Image manipulation tools
imagemagick-dev	6.1.8-1007	Image manipulation tools
imagemagick-nox	6.2.8-1003	Image manipulation tools
imagemagick-nox-dev	6.1.8-1007	Image manipulation tools
imagemagick-nox-shlibs	6.1.8-1007	Image manipulation tools
imagemagick-nox10-dev	6.2.8-1003	Image manipulation tools
imagemagick-nox10-shlibs	6.2.8-1003	Image manipulation tools
imagemagick-shlibs	6.1.8-1007	Image manipulation tools
imagemagick10-dev	6.2.8-1003	Image manipulation tools
imagemagick10-shlibs	6.2.8-1003	Image manipulation tools
imap-client		[virtual package]

Table E-1: Fink Packages *(continued)*

Package	Version	Description
imlib	1.9.14-15	Image handling library for X11 and Gtk
imlib-shlibs	1.9.14-15	Image handling library for X11 and Gtk
imlib2	1.2.1-1022	Image handling library for X11
imlib2-rb18	0.5.2-2	Ruby wrapper for imlib2
imlib2-shlibs	1.2.1-1022	Image handling library for X11
less	394-1001	Feature-full text pager
lesspipe	1.53-11	Preprocessor for less
lesstif	1:0.93.18-1	Free implementation of OSF/Motif
lesstif-bin	1:0.93.18-1	Free implementation of OSF/Motif
lesstif-shlibs	1:0.93.18-1	Free implementation of OSF/Motif
lftp	3.1.0-1010	Sophisticated command-line-based FTP client
lha	1.14i-ac20050924p1-2	Utility for creating and opening lzh archives
libxml	1.8.17-14	XML parsing library
libxml-pm586	0.07-13	Perl modules for working with XML in Perl
libxml-shlibs	1.8.17-14	XML parsing library
libxml2	2.6.27-1001	XML parsing library, version 2
libxml2-bin	2.6.27-1001	XML parsing library, version 2
libxml2-py24	2.6.27-1002	Python bindings for libxml2 library
libxml2-py25	2.6.27-1002	Python bindings for libxml2 library
libxml2-shlibs	2.6.27-1001	XML parsing library, version 2
libxslt	1.1.15-3	XML stylesheet transformation library
libxslt-bin	1.1.15-3	XML stylesheet transformation utility (xsltproc)
libxslt-shlibs	1.1.15-3	XML stylesheet transformation shared libraries
libzvt2	2.0.1-1014	Zed's Virtual Terminal

Continued

Table E-1: Fink Packages *(continued)*

Package	Version	Description
libzvt2-dev	2.0.1-1014	Zed's Virtual Terminal
libzvt2-shlibs	2.0.1-1014	Zed's Virtual Terminal
lightlab	0.3-1014	Demo program to experiment with OpenGL lighting
lilypond	2.10.33-1004	GNU Music Typesetter
lv	4.51-1003	Powerful Multilingual File Viewer/Grep
lynx	2.8.5-3	Console-based web browser
lynx-ssl	2.8.5-3	Dummy upgrade package for lynx with system-openssl
lzo	1.08-1	Real-time data compression library
lzo-shlibs	1.08-1	Real-time data compression library
mtr	0.54-22	Combines traceroute and ping
mule-ucs	0.85+0.20061127-3	Mule universal encoding system
multi-c-rehash	1.1-2	Replacement for c_rehash included in OpenSSL
multitail	3.0.6-2	UNIX "tail" on many files at once
mutt	1.4.2.1-1004	Sophisticated text-based mail user agent
mysql	5.0.27-1001	Open-source SQL database
mysql-client	5.0.27-1001	Open-source SQL database (client)
mysql-dev	3.23.58-1023	Open-source SQL database (development headers and libraries)
mysql-shlibs	3.23.58-1023	Open-source SQL database (shared libraries)
mysql12-dev	4.0.22-1012	Open-source SQL database (development headers and libraries)
mysql12-shlibs	4.0.22-1012	Open-source SQL database (shared libraries)
mysql14-dev	4.1.10-1002	Open-source SQL database (development headers and libraries)
mysql14-shlibs	4.1.10-1002	Open-source SQL database (shared libraries)

Table E-1: Fink Packages *(continued)*

Package	Version	Description
mysql15-dev	5.0.27-1001	Open-source SQL database (development headers and libraries)
mysql15-shlibs	5.0.27-1001	Open-source SQL database (shared libraries)
naga10	1.1-4	Japanese 10dot font suitable for small screen
nano	1.2.2-1002	Improved clone of the Pico text editor
natbib		[virtual package]
netrexx	2.05-1	Rexx programming and scripting language
news-reader		[virtual package]
newspost	2.1.1-1	USENET Binary Autoposter
nfs-tuner	1.0.0-1	Tunes NFS default settings
ngraph	6.3.30-2	Tool for creating scientific 2D graphs
ngraph-doc	6.3.30-2	Tool for creating scientific 2D graphs
nmap	4.20-1001	Network exploration utility
nmap-nox	4.20-1001	Network exploration utility
noip	1.6-4	Client for the no-ip.com dynamic DNS service
normalize	0.7.4-1003	Audio file volume normalizer
num-utils	0.4-1	Command-line utils for dealing with numbers
openssh	4.2p1-3	Deprecated package! Security issues; please remove
openssl	0.9.6m-11	Secure Sockets Layer and general crypto library
openssl-dev	0.9.6m-11	Secure Sockets Layer and general crypto library
openssl-shlibs	0.9.6m-11	Secure Sockets Layer and general crypto library
openssl097	0.9.7l-1	Secure Sockets Layer and crypto library
openssl097-dev	0.9.7l-1	Secure Sockets Layer and crypto library

Continued

Table E-1: Fink Packages *(continued)*

Package	Version	Description
openssl097-shlibs	0.9.71-1	Secure Sockets Layer and crypto library
optipng	0.5.4-1	Optimizer for PNG files
orbit	0.5.17-16	The CORBA ORB used in GNOM
orbit-bin		[virtual package]
orbit-dev	0.5.17-16	The CORBA ORB used in GNOME
orbit-shlibs	0.5.17-16	The CORBA ORB used in GNOME
orbit2	2.14.7-1	High-performance CORBA Object Request Broker
orbit2-dev	2.14.7-1	High-performance CORBA Object Request Broker
orbit2-shlibs	2.14.7-1	High-performance CORBA Object Request Broker
otf-fontfiles	1.5.4-4	Virtual fonts and style files for otf in pTeX
passwd	20070812-21	User and group entries for daemons
pbzip2	0.9.6-1	SMP-capable bzip2
pcb	1.99.20060822-4	Printed Circuit Board design program
pccts	1.33.mr33-4	Purdue Compiler-Construction Tool Set (parser-generator)
pcre	7.2-1001	Perl Compatible Regular Expressions Library
pcre-bin	7.2-1001	Perl Compatible Regular Expressions Library
pcre-shlibs	7.2-1001	Perl Compatible Regular Expressions Library
pdfjam	1.20-1	Collection of PDF document-handling utilities
pdflib	5.0.1-2	Library for generating PDF (lite version)
pdflib-shlibs	5.0.1-2	Library for generating PDF (lite version)
pdfscreen	1.5-6	Resize LaTeX-produced pdf to fit on computer screen
pdfslide	0.50-4	Presentations with pdfTeX
pdftex		[virtual package]

Table E-1: Fink Packages *(continued)*

Package	Version	Description
perl586	5.8.6-6	The Perl programming language, v. 5.8.6
perl586-core	5.8.6-6	Core files for Perl, v. 5.8.6
perl588-core		[virtual package]
perlio-eol-pm588		[virtual package]
perlobjcbridge-pm588		[virtual package]
perltidy	20021130-1	Improves Perl script formatting and indenting
pforth	21-1	Portable ANS-like Forth written in ANSI C
pfqueue	0.4.2-1001	Interface for viewing postfix mail queues
pgf	1.01-1	TeX Portable Graphic Format
pgn-extract	15.0-1	Convert collections of Chess games into PGN notation
phpmyadmin	2.10.2-1	Web interface to MySQL
pine	4.64-1002	Text-based tool for managing e-mail
pine-ssl	4.64-1002	Text-based tool for managing e-mail
pkgconfig	0.21-1	Manager for library compile/link flags
ploticus2	2.20-12	Creates graphical data displays
ploticus2-dev	2.20-12	Ploticus C API
ploticus2-nox	2.20-22	Creates graphical data displays (no X11)
ploticus2-nox-dev	2.20-22	Ploticus C API (no X11)
ploticus2-nox-shlibs	2.20-22	Ploticus C API (no X11)
ploticus2-shlibs	2.20-12	Ploticus C API
plrpc-pm	0.2018-1022	Perl RPC client/server
png2ico	20021208-1	Utility for making Windows icons
pngcrush	1.5.10-1	Optimizer for PNG files
prime-el	1.5.1.3-6	Prime client for Emacs

Continued

Table E-1: Fink Packages (continued)

Package	Version	Description
procmail	3.22-1	Mail processing program
progressbar-rb	0.9-1	Text Progress Bar Library for Ruby
proj	4.5.0-4	Cartographic projections library
proj-shlibs	4.5.0-4	Cartographic projections library
prosper	1.5-1	LaTeX class for writing transparencies
ps2eps	1.58-1	Convert PostScript to EPS files
psmulti-dna	1.1.2-1	Multi-talented postscript filter
pstree	2.17-1	Show the ps listing as a tree
psutils	1.17-2	Useful tools to manipulate postscript files, "letter" size
psutils-a4	1.17-2	Useful tools to manipulate postscript files, A4 size paper
psync	0.69-2	Collection of Perl scripts to manipulate files on Mac OS X
ptex	3.1.10-1001	Bundle package for ASCII publishing TeX
ptex-babel	20060322-3	Correct hyphenation of Babel macros for pTeX
ptex-base	3.1.10-1001	ASCII publishing TeX
ptex-jisfonts		[virtual package]
ptex-nox	3.1.10-1001	Bundle package for ASCII publishing TeX
ptex-nox-base	3.1.10-1001	ASCII publishing TeX
ptex-texmf	2.4-57	Additional texmf tree for pTeX
ptex3-base		[virtual package]
ptexenc	0.96-1	Kanji code convert library for pTeX
ptexenc-shlibs	0.96-1	Shared libraries of Kanji code convert library for pTeX
pth	1.4.0-7	Portable library that provides scheduling
pth-shlibs	1.4.0-7	Portable library that provides scheduling

Table E-1: Fink Packages *(continued)*

Package	Version	Description
publib	0.34.0-1	C function library
pwgen	2.05-1	Simple password generator
pychecker-py24	0.8.14-4	Check Python programs for error (Modules)
pychecker-py24-bin	0.8.14-4	Check Python programs for error (Main binary)
pydns-py25	2.3.0-6	Python module for performing DNS queries
pyserial-py24	2.0-12	Python access to serial ports
pyserial-py25	2.0-12	Python access to serial ports
python	1:2.5.1-1	Interpreted, object-oriented language
python-mx-py24	2.0.6-1002	Python extensions from eGenix
python-mx-py25	2.0.6-1002	Python extensions from eGenix
python24	1:2.4.3-1002	Interpreted, object-oriented language
python24-shlibs	1:2.4.3-1002	Interpreted, object-oriented language
python24-socket	1:2.4.3-1002	Socket plugin for Python
python24-socket-ssl	2.4.2-1101	Socket plugin for Python (SSL version)
python25	1:2.5.1-1	Interpreted, object-oriented language
python25-shlibs	1:2.5.1-1	Interpreted, object-oriented language
python25-socket	1:2.5.1-1	Socket plugin for Python
pyvtk-py24	0.4.67-3	Tools for manipulating VTK files in Python
qca	1.0-1023	Qt Cryptographic Architecture
qca-shlibs	1.0-1023	Qt Cryptographic Architecture
qhull	2002.1-10	Calculate convex hulls and related structures
qt3	3.3.8-1026	Cross-platform GUI application framework
qt3-bin		[virtual package]
qt3-designer	3.3.8-1026	Cross-platform GUI application framework

Continued

Table E-1: Fink Packages *(continued)*

Package	Version	Description
qt3-designer-shlibs	3.3.8-1026	Cross-platform GUI application framework
qt3-doc	3.3.8-1026	Cross-platform GUI application framework
qt3-linguist	3.3.8-1026	Cross-platform GUI application framework
qt3-shlibs	3.3.8-1026	Cross-platform GUI application framework
qt3mac	3.3.8-12	Aqua version of QT3: Headers and dev tools
qt3mac-apps	3.3.8-12	Aqua version of QT3: Apps and plugins
qt3mac-doc	3.3.8-12	Aqua version of QT3: Documentation
qt3mac-shlibs	3.3.8-12	Aqua version of QT3: Shared libraries
quanta	3.5.8-1021	KDE—HTML Editor
qucs	0.0.13-1001	Qt-based integrated circuit simulator
quit	1.2a-1	Bicycle with trailers such as "sl"
ren	1.0-1	Rename multiple files
rep-gtk	0.15-1025	Gtk+ and GNOME bindings for librep
revtex		[virtual package]
riece	4.0.0-3	IRC client for Emacs
rlwrap	0.28-2	Allows editing keyboard input for any command
rman	3.1-1	Generalized filter for UNIX manual pages
robodoc	4.99.26-1	Documentation extraction tool
root-pythia	6.4-52	Interface libraries Pythia (ROOT)
root-pythia-shlibs	6.4-52	Interface libraries Pythia (ROOT)
rsync	2.6.9-1	Synchronize file systems between hosts
rtf2latex2e	1.0fc2-1	Translates RTF files into LaTeX files
ruby	1.8.1-2	Symlinks to Ruby1.8
ruby18	1.8.1-2	Interpreted, object-oriented script language
ruby18-dev	1.8.1-2	Ruby static library
ruby18-shlibs	1.8.1-2	Ruby shared libraries

Table E-1: Fink Packages *(continued)*

Package	Version	Description
rxvt	2.7.10-3	VT102 emulator for X11
rxvt-ml	2.7.10-2	Placeholder package to update to rxvt. (OBSOLETE)
sam	4.3-1002	Unorthodox but powerful X11 text editor
sed	4.1.5-11	Stream editor, GNU version
sitecopy	0.16.3-4	Website uploader
sitecopy-ssl	0.16.3-4	Placeholder package to update to unified sitecopy. (Obsolete)
sjeng	11.2-1	Engine for Chess Variants
sjeng-zhbook	11.0-1	Crazyhouse opening book for Sjeng
skk		[virtual package]
skk-dict	20060312-1	Dictionary file for SKK
skycal	5-1	Astronomer's almanac tools
sl	1.0.4-2	Corrects your mistyping
sqlite	2.8.5-1014	Embedded SQL database
sqlite-dev	2.8.5-1014	Embedded SQL database
sqlite-shlibs	2.8.5-1014	Embedded SQL database
sqlite3	3.2.8-1001	Embedded SQL database, version 3
sqlite3-dev	3.2.8-1001	Embedded SQL database (include files and linkable libraries)
sqlite3-doc	3.2.8-1001	Embedded SQL database (HTML documentation)
sqlite3-shlibs	3.2.8-1001	Embedded SQL database (shared libraries)
sqlite3-tcl	3.2.8-1001	Embedded SQL database (Tcl/Tk bindings)
squid	1:2.6.stable16-1	Proxy caching server
squid-ssl	1:2.6.stable16-1	Proxy caching server
squid-unified	1:2.6.stable16-1	Proxy caching server

Continued

Table E-1: Fink Packages *(continued)*

Package	Version	Description
svn	1.4.4-11	Subversion (svnserve, tools)
svn-client	1.4.4-11	Subversion (client)
svn-client-ssl	1.4.3-11	Obsolete; use svn-client instead
svn-dev	1.4.4-11	Subversion (development headers and libs)
svn-doc	1.4.4-11	Subversion (documentation)
svn-javahl	1.4.4-11	Subversion (Java bindings)
svn-pm588		[virtual package]
svn-shlibs	1.4.4-11	Subversion (shared libraries)
taglib	1.4-1023	Audio meta-data library
taglib-shlibs	1.4-1023	Shared libraries for the taglib meta-data library
tar	1.16.1-1	GNU tar (tape archiver)
tcltk	8.4.13-3	Tool Command Language and the Tk toolkit
tcltk-dev	8.4.13-3	Tool Command Language and the Tk toolkit
tcltk-shlibs	8.4.13-3	Tool Command Language and the Tk toolkit
tcsh	6.15.00-1001	TENEX C Shell, an enhanced Berkeley csh
unzip	5.52-12	Decompression compatible with pkunzip
vim	7.1.123-1000	Improved version of the vi editor
vim-nox	7.1.123-1000	Improved version of the vi editor
visual-py24	3.2.9-1003	VPython (3D Programming for Ordinary Mortals)
visual-py25	3.2.9-1003	VPython (3D Programming for Ordinary Mortals)
wcalc	1.7-1001	Command-line calculator
wdiff	0.5g-11	Word-based front end to GNU diff
web2png	2.4.6-2	Batch-converts entire web pages with gif2png
wget	1.10.2-15	Automatic website retriever (SSL)

Table E-1: Fink Packages *(continued)*

Package	Version	Description
wget-ssl	1.10.2-16	Placeholder package to update to unified wget. (Obsolete)
wmweather	1.31-2	Local weather dock app using METAR
wtf	1.7-3	Translates common Internet acronyms
wv2	0.2.2-1036	MSWord parsing library
wv2-shlibs	0.2.2-1036	Shared libraries for the MSWord parsing library
x-ghostscript-fonts	20020206-3	Enables Ghostscript fonts to be used within X-Window systems
x11		[virtual package]
x11-dev		[virtual package]
x11-shlibs		[virtual package]
yatex	1.73-4	Yet Another TeX mode for Emacs
yc	4.0.13-8	Yet another Canna client for Emacsen
yorick	1.6.02-2	Interpreted language and scientific graphics
yorick-doc	1.6-1	Yorick documentation
ytalk	3.1.1-1022	Enhanced talk program
ytalk-nox	3.1.1-1022	Enhanced talk program
yydecode	0.2.9-1	Decoder for yEnc encoded binaries on USENET
zenity	2.6.2-1010	Scriptable GTK+2 dialog
zip	2.31-11	Compression utility
zip-ssl	2.31-11	Compression utility, with encryption
zsh	4.2.6-1001	The Z Shell
ztools	981107-1	Set of Z-Machine tools
ztrack	1.0-1	Curses-based pseudo 3D driving game

F

Perl Primer

This appendix provides a brief and gentle primer to Perl. I'm using one of my Perl scripts as an exemplar and launching point to discuss the language.

IN THIS APPENDIX

An introduction to Perl

Introducing Perl

Perl was invented by Larry Wall in the late 1980s. He needed a language that would give him more power than shell scripting, but require less formality than more structured languages such as C.

Hence, Perl was born, a language that you either love or hate—I've rarely found anyone in the middle. Whatever your feelings about it, it's an incredibly useful glue language used by system administrators worldwide.

Your Mac OS X system should come with the latest version of Perl installed—it's fairly easy to verify, too, just by using the following command line:

```
perl -v
This is perl, v5.8.8 built for darwin-thread-multi-2level
(with 1 registered patch, see perl -V for more detail)

Copyright 1987-2006, Larry Wall

Perl may be copied only under the terms of either the Artistic
License or the
GNU General Public License, which may be found in the Perl 5 source
kit.

Complete documentation for Perl, including FAQ lists, should be found
on
this system using "man perl" or "perldoc perl".  If you have access
to the
Internet, point your browser at http://www.perl.org/, the Perl Home
Page.
```

If you don't get this response, or if you have a very old version of Perl (say, Perl 4), then use Fink to update your copy. Chances are good, though, that you'll have everything you need to get started.

One of the things that makes Perl so easy to use is precisely what makes it so frustrating for those new to the language. Perl has a bit of what I like to think of as "idiomatic elasticity." This is just fancy linguistic talk for being able to use different syntactical structures and commands to do the same thing.

Although many programmers find this infuriating, it makes perfect sense to me—I had a lot of training in linguistics, as did Larry Wall. For example, if I'm sitting in a restaurant and want to pay the bill and leave, I have many different ways to express this. I can wave the waiter over and nod when he asks if I want the check. I can just ask, "May I have the check?" I can pull out my wallet and place it on the table.

Each of these different approaches gives me the same result—the waiter's attention, and eventually, a hard-copy bill in my hand.

The same thing is true with Perl. In many cases, it supports a variety of different approaches to do any one job—or as Larry Wall has said, "There's more than one way to skin a cat." Yes, it's certainly a cliché, but Perl makes this cliché a real-world possibility—hence its power. That's why when you gather five or more Perl programmers in one room and then ask them to solve a certain problem, you'll often get at least three divergent solutions.

In this appendix, I'm going to present you with a common problem (checking the links on a website) and show you how I go about using Perl to automate the tedious, error-prone manual processes for solving that problem.

If you're already a Perl demon, you can skip this next part, secure in your knowledge and mastery. If you're a complete novice, it is hoped that the next section will get you started down the path to Perl mastery.

Checking Links on a Website

About six or seven years ago, a client asked me if I knew of a tool that would help quickly check the links on a web page. At the time, there were many link checkers (both free and not) available, but I took the opportunity to write a quick 20-line Perl script that would do the checking.

I needed a small and portable script, one that would accept a URL as a command-line argument, visit that URL, check all the links it found, and then follow all the in-site links to determine whether they were reachable or not. Then I needed a report.

I knew from experience that I would need some help to do this task. Perl comes with a number of handy libraries, each of them a specialized toolkit to do a specific job.

In my case, I needed a simple user agent that would visit a URL. For this, I'd use the LWP::Simple package. I also knew that I'd need a quick way to extract links from every HTML document I encountered. For that, I could use the HTML::LinkExtor package.

In the old days, I would have tried to construct my own user agent and my own link extractor, but fortunately with age comes wisdom (and a simple desire just to get the job done quickly and efficiently). You'll find the same thing in your own Perl coding—you'll want to do something more advanced, but you don't have time to figure it out yourself. Simple solution: See if someone has written a module or package.

For now, let's get going with the script.

The Entire Script

Let's look at the entire script first, so you know what we're getting into. As you can see, it's only 20 lines or so (not including comments), so it won't be that hard to get your head around. Before we leave this section and dive into the details, I'll show you some common things you'll find in just about any Perl script.

Here's the script:

```perl
#!/usr/bin/perl -w
# churl.pl - check urls

use HTML::LinkExtor;
use LWP::Simple qw(get head);

$base_url = shift or die "usage: $0 <start_url>\n";
$parser = HTML::LinkExtor->new(undef, $base_url);
$parser->parse(get($base_url));
@links = $parser->links;
print "$base_url: \n";
foreach $linkarray (@links) {
    my @element = @$linkarray;
    my $elt_type = shift @element;
    while (@element) {
        my ($attr_name , $attr_value) = splice(@element, 0, 2);
        if ($attr_value->scheme =~ /\b(ftp|https?|file)\b/) {
            print " $attr_value: ", head($attr_value) ? "OK" : "BAD", "\n";
        }
    }
}
```

The first thing you need to know is the first line—known colloquially as the shebang line. This line tells the script where to find the Perl interpreter. Note the use of the -w flag, which tells Perl to run with warnings enabled. With this flag up, Perl will complain a lot more, and you'll have to be a bit more careful, but it's a good idea to run in this mode.

Other common things you'll see in this script are as follows:

❑ Scalar variables (i.e., variables that store one value) begin with a dollar sign ($).

❑ Arrays (i.e., a list of scalar values) begin with an ampersand (@). Not used in this script are associative arrays, which begin with the percent symbol (%).

❑ The use command enables you to use another module or package, making it easy for you to get things done.

❑ The body of the script is a simple `foreach` loop that iterates over the links that have been extracted by HTML::LinkExtor. It is considered a very Perlish thing, that little `foreach` loop. Many C programmers don't use it, opting to use the `for` loop instead. Learn to love the `foreach`, as it gives you a lot of power.

❑ The `while` block gives you a different kind of power—a block of code that continues until some state changes. In our case, the `while` block inside the `foreach` loop keeps running until we get to the end of our link elements.

❑ In Perl 5, you can use the `my` operator to restrict a variable to a certain block. In the preceding code, the `@element` array and the `$elt_type` variable are both private to the `foreach` block.

Let's go through this script section by section to get a better understanding of what's going on.

Initializing the Script and Loading Packages

The first few lines of the script are very straightforward. We need to initialize the script with a she-bang line and then load up our two packages.

The she-bang line is fairly standard. Just tell the script where to find the Perl interpreter (you can double-check your installation by typing in the appropriate Perl version on the command line). Be sure to add the –w flag to throw warnings:

```
#!/usr/bin/perl -w
```

Once you've done that, load your two packages with the use command:

```
use HTML::LinkExtor;
use LWP::Simple qw(get head);
```

Notice that when you use the LWP::Simple package (a lightweight user agent that is useful in browsing URLs), you are only loading two functions (`get` and `head`)—that's all we really need to make our script work, as we're not planning on doing anything too advanced.

The nice thing about doing things this way is that you don't have to know anything about how these packages work, nor do you need to invent functionality. It would take several hundred lines (at the very least) to code up a link extractor and a lightweight user agent, but now we don't have to.

Targeting the URL and Extracting Links

Now it's time to actually go to a URL and extract the links. In Perl, as in most other command-line-oriented languages, you can pass arguments to the script very easily. All command-line arguments are stored in a special array called @ARGV. To get to the first argument, you would normally use the shift command, like this:

```
$argument = shift @ARGV;
```

However, the shift command, when given no argument, always defaults to the @ARGV array, so you can simplify things like this:

```
$argument = shift;
```

However, for our purposes, we need to determine whether the shift operation actually works. If it does, fine; set a variable called $base_url. If not, the script needs to die with a certain error message telling the user what the accepted usage is.

Here's the change:

```
$base_url = shift or die "usage: $0 <start_url>\n";
```

Notice the use of the shift or die syntax. That's where that idiomatic elasticity comes in. C and Java programmers might prefer to see the following instead:

```
$base_url = shift;
if (length($base_url) == 0){
    die "usage: $0 <start_url>\n";
}
```

Truth be told, you could do that if you like, but the original syntax is so much more concise!

Once you have a base URL to work with, you can invoke the HTML::LinkExtor package by passing in the $base_url variable, resulting in all the links being stored in an array called @links (thanks to $parser->links below).

You can then print out the base URL as a header for your output:

```
$parser = HTML::LinkExtor->new(undef, $base_url);
$parser->parse(get($base_url));
@links = $parser->links;
print "$base_url: \n";
```

In just four lines, we've captured every single link on the URL we're targeting. Instead of being out there on the HTML document, or living in some captured stream of text, they're safely encapsulated in an array that we can process with no fuss or muss.

Processing the @links Array

Now that we have a neat array of links, we can do something useful with them. The best way to do that is to use a `foreach` loop; that way, we can step through the entire array until we fall off the end of it (meaning no more links to process!).

Here's the code, which is followed by a line-by-line explanation:

```
foreach $linkarray (@links) {
    my @element  = @$linkarray;
    my $elt_type = shift @element;
    while (@element) {
        my ($attr_name , $attr_value) = splice(@element, 0, 2);
        if ($attr_value->scheme =~ /\b(ftp|https?|file)\b/) {
            print "  $attr_value: ", head($attr_value) ? "OK" : "BAD", "\n";
        }
    }
}
```

Notice that when we use the `foreach`, we use the following syntax:

```
foreach $linkarray (@links) {
```

This way, each time through the loop, the next value in the `@links` array is assigned to the `$linkarray` value. We could have used the following:

```
foreach (@links) {
```

This way, each time through the loop, the next value in the array would have been assigned to the special variable `$_`. There's nothing wrong with that approach at all—in fact, a lot of Perl scripts make use of this handy variable—but it can be a little confusing trying to figure out what `$_` is set to, especially as your scripts get more complex. Therefore, it's a good idea to explicitly set your variables.

Once we're in the loop, we can start doing some hard work. Notice how in the next two lines, we create two private variables using the `my` operator:

```
my @element  = @$linkarray;
my $elt_type = shift @element;
```

In the first case, we create a private array called `@element`. This array contains the value (forced into array context) of `$linkarray`. In other words, as we pass through the array `@links`, each value is then converted into array context. That's because each link is really a series of anonymous arrays (the link type, the link tag itself, followed by one or more attributes, and so on).

In the second case, we use the my operator again to create a private variable for what we shift out of the newly created @element. The first variable will always be the element type, which is why it is called $elt_type.

Why are we bothering to grab it? Simple. We need it out of the way, and shift will cut it from the array very nicely, leaving only the things that we care about.

Now that we have an @element array for this pass, we can use a while block to work on each anonymous array inside it. In the code that follows, we first use splice to cut out an attribute name and value from @element. Then, if the value we've captured has a scheme that matches ftp, http, https, or file, we run the head() function from LWP::Simple to try to reach the link address. If we can, we print out OK. If we can't, we print out BAD:

```
while (@element) {
        my ($attr_name , $attr_value) = splice(@element, 0, 2);
        if ($attr_value->scheme =~ /\b(ftp|https?|file)\b/) {
            print "  $attr_value: ", head($attr_value) ? "OK" : "BAD", "\n";
        }
}
```

As you can see, Perl's syntax compression enables you to get an astonishing amount of work done in just a few lines. Some folks appreciate that, but others don't care for it. I leave it up to you where you fall—it's just as easy to write this same script with 100 or more lines depending on your approach.

Running the Script

Once you have the script written, save it somewhere on your file system as chur1.pl (which stands for "check url") and then make it executable with chmod +x chur1.pl.

Next, run it from the command line, giving it a URL to start with:

```
./churl.pl http://www.apple.com
http://www.apple.com:
  http://www.apple.com/: OK
  http://images.apple.com/main/rss/hotnews/hotnews.rss: OK
  http://www.apple.com/sitemap/: OK
  http://images.apple.com/global/scripts/lib/prototype.js: OK
  http://images.apple.com/global/scripts/lib/scriptaculous.js: OK
  http://images.apple.com/global/scripts/browserdetect.js: OK
  http://images.apple.com/global/scripts/apple_core.js: OK
  http://images.apple.com/global/scripts/search_decorator.js: OK
  http://images.apple.com/home/scripts/ticker.js: OK
  http://www.apple.com/global/styles/base.css: OK
  http://www.apple.com/home/styles/home.css: OK
  http://images.apple.com/global/nav/scripts/shortcuts.js: OK
  ...
```

Extending the Script

As a fond farewell, I will pose two challenges for you to explore on your own. The first challenge isn't a true challenge at all, just a simple puzzle. The second is a bit harder.

In true Perl fashion, either of these challenges can be answered in any number of ways. There are no right or wrong answers, but the way you attack them will certainly give everyone a clue as to what kind of Perl coder you are:

❑ The first challenge is really simple. How would you redirect output of the preceding script to something other than the Terminal screen? For example, to a log file? I can think of at least two ways to do this. Can you figure them out or come up with other ways?

❑ The second challenge is a bit more complex, and will take you more time. Right now the script only processes the links on a single page. How would you rewrite the script to handle an entire site? Remember that you only want to process links that stay on the same site or domain where you started—no sense in writing a bot that jumps out to the Internet at large.

I've written an advanced script that spiders an entire site. If any of you want that script, simply send an email to tom@tripledogs.com.

Happy Perl coding, and thanks for reading this book!

Index

D

daemons, man pages, 8
Darwin, 3, 12
   kernel, folder for, 17
data, copying, 54
database, local, generating, 55
data files, types of, 43
date, system. *See* **date**
      command; time/date
date command
   time/date, changing, 138
   time/date, displaying,
      137–138
   warning, 138
dd command
   backup, compressed, 54
   boot image, copying, 54
   clone partition of IDE drive, 54
   data, copying, 54
   ISO image, copying, 55
   USB flash drive, installing
      from, 53
   warning, 54
deleting text, vi editor, 203
desktop, files/folders, home
      directory, 18
Desktop DB, folder for, 16
Developer Connection,
      resources of, 4
device(s)
   drivers. *See device files*
   listing, location for, 46
   man pages, 8
   types of, 46
device files
   examples of, 46
   folder for, 16
   functions of, 43, 46
df command
   disk space usage, checking, 92
   drive information, displaying,
      24
   file system type, display output,
      100
   inode utilization, checking,
      99–100
   limit output to local file system,
      100
   mounting file systems,
      utilization summary, 99
DHCP, configure setting for,
      143–144
DICT protocols, downloading
      files, 161–162
diff command
   files, comparing, 73
   merge file output, 74
   output, unified format, 74

dig command
   host IP address, viewing, 151
   hostname, search DNS servers
      for, 150
   record type query, 150
   reverse DNS lookup, 151
   specific name server query,
      150
   trace recursive query, 150
directories, 44–53
   adding/removing, 52
   compress all files in, 106
   creating, 45, 48
   execute bits, turning on, 45
   files, copying to, 53
   finding, 58
   functions of, 44
   home directory, 18–19
   permissions, 47–51
   root directory, 16–18
   sharing. *See remote directory*
      sharing
   symbolically linked directories,
      viewing, 52
dirs command, directories,
      changing order, 53
disk resizing/partitioning. *See*
      hard disk partitioning
diskutil command, hard disk
      partitioning, 95
DISPLAY, 209
DistroWatch, BSD distributions,
      4
DNS servers, configure setting
      for, 143–144
Dock
   Terminal, adding to, 12, 14
   Utilities folder, adding to,
      12, 14
documentation, subdirectory
      for, 6
documents, files/folders, home
      directory, 18
Domain Name System (DNS)
      servers, hostname
      queries, 150
dot files
   in home directory, 19, 211
   See also configuration files
double-spacing, text files, 69
downloading files, 159–161
   files/folders, home directory,
      18
   interrupted, continuing, 161
   mirror web site, 160–161
   from remote servers, 159–161
   single web page, 160
DragonFlyBSD, features of, 3
drive(s)

file system information,
      viewing, 24
   mounting/unmounting, 23–24
du command
   disk space usage, checking,
      100–101
   multiple directories, specifying,
      100
   permission issues, avoiding,
      100
   totals, obtaining with root user
      account, 100
   users directory, disk space
      use, 193
DVD(s)
   backup to, 110–111
   ISO image, copying, 55

E

echo command
   bash history, number of
      commands, 29
   environment variable
      completion, 30
   labels in scripts, adding, 79
editors. *See text editors*
else command, file name test,
      38
Emacs editor
   emacs-style commands, bash
      history, 30
   functions of, 65
e-mail, 173–174
   basic functions, commands
      for, 174
   configuration files, 212
   downloads, location of, 18
   exiting, warning, 174
   Fink packages for, 231
   mail command, 174
   MBOX format, 173, 174
   script based, sending, 174
   troubleshooting with **telnet,**
      178
Enter, info screen navigation, 9
env command, environment
      variables, listing, 36
environment variables
   concatenate string to, 36
   defined, 35
   displaying, 35
   inheritance, 35
   naming convention, 35
   setting/resetting, 35
   strings, concatenate to
      variable, 36

249

remote servers

with Network File System
(NFS), 165–167
with Samba, 167–171
remote servers
downloading files from,
159–161
types of, 159
**remote system administration,
177–197**
GUI tools for, 179
legacy communication tools,
178
screen **terminal multiplexer,
184–186**
Secure Shell (SSH) service,
177–184
Virtual Network Computing
(VNC), 188–189
Windows Remote Desktop,
186–187
X Window System (X), 187–188
renice command
nice value, changing, 126
running processes, adjusting
priority, 126
replace
characters, 73
text, 71–73
resident size, RAM, 134
rm command, backups, rotating,
110
root directory
accessing, 16
directories/subdirectories, 44
files/folders in, 16–18
go to, 51
**root file system, files, finding,
57**
root user
password for, 34
shell, enabling, 34
route command
default gateway, adding, 152
default route, changing, 155
delete route, 155
local routing table, displaying,
155
new route, adding, 155
permanent route, setting, 155
routing table
displaying, 156
See also **route command**
rshapshot command
snapshots of file system, 108
Web site/resources for, 108
rsync command
hard links, use of, 110
incremental backups, 110
mirror directory, 109

network backups, 108–110
running processes, 115–131
active, watching ongoing basis,
121–123
column output, 118–120
custom views, 121
hang-up signal, avoiding, 129
killing, 122, 125, 127–129
priority, adjusting, 125–126
ps command, 116–121
resident memory use order,
displaying, 134
running in foreground/
background, 126–127
run priority, adjusting, 122
scheduling runs, 129–131
searching for, 123–125
signaling, 127–128
**top command, 121–123,
134–135**
viewing, 116–123

S

Samba, 167–171
brief output, 169
configuration files, checking,
170–171
current connection, viewing,
169
existing user, adding, 168
file locks, viewing, 169
FTP-style file sharing, 168–169
hosts, lookup, 167, 170
mounting shares, 169
network neighborhood, text
representation of,
167–168
remote directory sharing,
167–171
services, listing, 168
user, adding, 168
scalar variables, Perl, 242
**scheduling, running processes,
129–131**
scp command
client ID, accessing, 182
recursive copies, 164
remote files, copying, 164–165
specific port, connecting to,
164
timestamp/permission,
preserving, 164
warning, 164
**SCP protocols, downloading
files, 161–162**

**screen(s), splitting, vi editor,
201**
screen command
naming sessions, 186
screen operation options,
184–185
session, reconnect to,
185–186
sharing screens, 186
screen terminal multiplexer,
184–186
control key functions, 185
functions of, 184
installing, 184
naming sessions, 186
reconnect to session, 185–186
sharing sessions, 186
**script(s). See AppleScripting;
Perl; shell scripts**
script command, 83–84
transcript, producing, 83–84
Script Editor, 84–85
scrolling
arrow keys for, 29, 68–69
less command, 68
sdiff command, files output,
merging, 74
search
bash history, 30
colorize search term, 70
files, commands for, 55–59
regular expressions, use of, 57
for running processes,
123–125
text strings, 69–70
**search engine, Spotlight,
19–21**
SECONDS, 210
**Secure Shell (SSH) service,
177–184**
configuration files, 212
different port, accessing on,
180
forceful exit, 179
functions of, 164, 179
OpenSSH, 108, 179
public key authentication,
181–183
remote commands, preventing,
181
remote files, copying, 164–165
remote log-in, 179–183
starting, 149, 180
stopping, 149
tools, functions of, 177
Virtual Network Computing
(VNC), 177
X11 port forwarding (tunneling),
179–181

256

Take a look inside the Linux® toolbox.

Check out other books available in the series.

978-0-470-08292-8   978-0-470-08293-5   978-0-470-08291-1

Available now at www.wiley.com

Now you know.

wiley.com